THE SQUASH WORKSHOP

The SQUASH WORKSHOP

A Complete Game Guide

Ian McKenzie

The Crowood Press

First published in 1992 by
The Crowood Press Ltd
Ramsbury, Marlborough
Wiltshire SN8 2HR

www.crowood.com

This Impression 2006

British Library Cataloguing in Publication Data

A catalogue record for this book
is available from the British Library.

ISBN 1 85223 728 7 (PB)
EAN 978 1 85223 728 8

Throughout this book the pronouns 'he', 'him' and 'his' have been used
inclusively and are intended to apply to both males and females. The
instructions assume that the player is right-handed.

Dedication
To my parents, Mamie and Stuart, for their patience and perseverance.

Picture credits
All colour and black and white photographs by Stephen Line.
Line-drawings by Taurus Graphics.

Cover photography by Stephen Line.
Cover line-drawings by Taurus Graphics.
Cover design by Visual Image.

Typeset by Keyboard Services, Luton
Printed in Malaysia

Acknowledgements

A large number of people had a part in this book. It could not have been as comprehensive but for their assistance, help and guidance.

My thanks go to Jansher Khan, Ross Norman, Del Harris and Lucy Soutter for participating in the photographic sessions and for contributing advice and comments throughout.

I am indebted to Ross for all those character-building defeats he inflicted on me in his early professional years and to Lucy for the opportunity to work comprehensively with her in that exciting run from unknown junior to World Junior Champion, and senior success as British Champion and World Masters Champion.

When Jansher Khan came to England he based himself at Stripes Squash and Health Club in Ealing, London where I worked as a professional for many years before moving to edit *Squash Player International* magazine. I came to know him well, as I did Del Harris from his occasional visits and by seeing him at his many tournament successes.

My thanks must also go to Hashim Khan, that legendary figure regarded as the father of modern squash for his undoubted wisdom, generously dispensed.

The demonstration, sequence and feature photographs for this book were all taken by Stephen Line. Squash photography is a difficult and specialist area in which Stephen is the world's acknowledged expert. It is his expertise and care that has allowed us to produce the graphic and authoritative pictures showing exactly how champions play. It was our purpose to use photographs that would be useful for instructional and not just pictorial purposes. The demonstration shots and sequences were shot at Stripes and the action sequences at the British National Championships at Bristol and the British Open at Wembley. Canon UK were kind enough to provide their high-speed F1 camera, which was used at fifteen frames per second. Ilford Photo supplied the XP1 400 film used for all the demonstration sequence photographs.

Dunlop-Slazenger International, the sponsors for Lucy, Ross and Del were particularly supportive in releasing their players for the photographic sessions.

Much of the book's content is within specialist areas and could not have been written without the assistance of experts. I would like to record my grateful thanks to Dr Frank Sanderson and Dr Craig Sharp.

Frank Sanderson is Head of the Department of Sport and Health Sciences at Liverpool Polytechnic and is an acknowledged expert in tactical analysis and sports psychology. I am indebted to him for the use of his popular sports psychology articles in *Squash Player International* magazine on which much of the temperament section was based and for the lengthy conversations with him.

Craig Sharp, Head of Physiology at the British Olympic Medical Centre assisted in providing references on which much of the fitness chapter is based although it must be stressed that any errors are mine alone. Parts of the fitness sections are based on his articles for the National Coaching Foundation (as are the two training programmes) and for *Squash Player International*.

Thanks also go to Vivian Grisogono for her advice and assistance; to the NCF for use of their resources throughout; and to my wonderful secretary Pam Butler, who saved my life many times.

Contents

Preface

Whenever a bout of silliness overcomes me and I am involved in some harmless but highspirited jinks, my mother usually brings me down to earth by pitching in with a shrill, 'Be careful Ian! Remember how many windows you broke as a child'.

It's true. When I was a boy, windows seemed to shatter whenever they looked at me. I stuck my head through one and my arm; ruined my leg on one, but most of all I put balls through them. Mainly tennis balls. Old tennis balls with casing hanging off; tennis balls discovered in gutters, on rooves and dug out of hedges.

And how did these tennis balls get through these windows? Well, I hit them there. Not on purpose of course, often not directly, and always accidentally.

I was driven by some compulsion to hit, throw and kick balls against walls and various bits of unsuitable concrete. Now good walls are rare things, flat walls that is, that give a good rebound. Good walls with a good piece of ground in front that will give a consistent bounce are more rare. The problem with the walls was that ill-advised people kept putting windows in them.

It was a trap. A trap that kept me penniless through boyhood and brought a little tension into the relationship between me and my parents.

Looking back, the day I stumbled upon the squash club Colin Brownlee had built in our home town was one of those events that change your life. Someone had invented walls. Walls without windows. Smooth white walls that gave a true rebound. Floors, level and sprung that gave a true bounce and that you could run, jump and grip on without sending shattering vibrations up your spine.

I found you could run to your heart's content and compete. Squash was a happy

discovery. I joined the club. My parents were very encouraging.

Since those days I have spent a large part of my life showing people how to ricochet balls off walls. From country towns in New Zealand to the fashionable clubs of London, from Tahiti to South America to Europe.

We have discovered and worked at the exercises in this book. *The Squash Workshop* is for people who want to hit balls against walls and work at getting better at it. It is for those who want to use this activity to compete and get fit. For them there is no better game in the world than squash.

Introduction

You can get better at squash. It's that sort of game. Of course it's marvellous exercise for the recreational player and the serious competitor. Of course it's compelling competition and there is sometimes the satisfaction of winning. But it's more than that. There is also the challenge to get better, to reach a new standard or goal. You can improve your squash by working at it – by working at the parts and at fitting these together. *The Squash Workshop* will show you how.

Squash is a ball sport. How good you are

Fig 2   Ross Norman: World Champion 1986.

Fig 1   Jansher Khan: World Champion 1987, 1989 and 1990.

at hitting that little black ball around determines your standard as a player. If you improve at hitting, your squash improves. This book will help you, by improving your *technique* and by developing your *shots*.

Squash is a tactical battle. It's a rallying sport where defensive, attacking, pressure and postional plays are used in constructing rallies, where opportunities are taken or lost and risks calculated. Improving your *tactics* can totally transform your game.

Squash is a mental battle. It's a battle with yourself to concentrate and be patient, disciplined and decisive, and with your

Fig 3 Del Harris: World Junior Champion 1988, British National Champion 1987 and 1989.

Fig 4 Lucy Soutter: World Junior Champion 1985, British National Champion 1985 and 1989.

opponent to be assertive and competitive. Improving your mental preparation, overcoming anxiety and improving concentration and decision making under competitive pressure will make you a stronger competitor. Improving mental performance is a question of *temperament*.

Squash is a physical battle. The fittest survive and often win. More than in nearly any other sport, fitness in squash is multidimensional. It includes endurance (aerobic and anaerobic), strength and muscular endurance, speed, flexibility and agility. The physical area also includes movement. Your success as a player depends on how well and efficiently you move. Assessing

strengths and weaknesses and working on fitness constitute an important element of *training*.

You get better at squash by working at it. This book is your workshop. It has the ideas, methods and exercises you can use to improve and it tells you how to fit them into your programme.

Beginners should turn to Chapter 2, Getting Started, and make plans to start mastering the basics. The experienced player wanting to progress should turn to Chapter 3, Improving Your Game, to assess where to start and where work could be most profitably put in.

1
Squash Today

Squash is said to have started at Harrow School where boys, waiting for a turn on the rackets court, hit around on outside walls. The ball they used was a soft hollow ball unlike the hard ball used in rackets.

From these humble beginnings in the nineteenth century squash evolved, but the rules and court dimensions were not formalized until 1911. In America the game evolved differently, with a different ball, a narrower court and a scoring system to 15 rather than 9. Today there are two branches to the game – the American game and the International or Softball game, as the North Americans call it.

In the United Kingdom squash grew rapidly in the 1960s and in the 1970s experienced a unique boom in the history of sport. International growth quickly followed. Coinciding with this growth of the game world-wide was the growth of the international competitive game. National championships that were once held in front of small audiences in private clubs were now held on transparent courts, in vast auditoriums in front of TV cameras.

People discovered squash and it boomed. It suited them. Now they could work out, play and compete at the same time. Those who were keen worked at it, and it rewarded work.

Squash is a simple game, easy to grasp. The most basic rule is that the ball must hit and rebound off the front wall above the tin (a line 48cm (19in) above the floor) and below the out-of-court line. It can be hit directly to the front or rebounded off the side or back walls.

The walls keep the ball in, allowing a player to take it off the side and back when passed, thus encouraging continuous action and allowing squash's development as both a fitness and a tactical sport. Walls also allow the addition of a roof, facilitating all-weather sport, and of course they introduce angles. With angles a whole new range of shots are available to be discovered and invented. An understanding of angles is required not just to play shots but in judging the rebound of balls off walls. Beginners need to become familiar with these and with how to anticipate and position for this rebounding ball.

As well as angles, the beginner has to become familiar with the court and its dimensions, for it is the understanding of length, width and height (discussed in Chapter 6 and in Part 3) that allows a player to place the ball accurately.

Squash is in a unique position among the major racket sports because players share the same territory. This can lead to traffic-flow problems but clear obligations are placed on players to avoid interference and players must become familiar with these rules.

The Court

The front wall on a squash court rises 4.57m (15ft) with a play area between the out-of-court line at this height and the tin at 48cm (19in). One of a beginner's first jobs in learning the game is to be able to use all of this wall, from soft drop shots just above the tin which make an opponent run right into the front corners to the high shots which will travel down the 9.75m (32ft) length of the court and into the back corners.

A court is 6.4m (21ft) wide. Width is an important but often overlooked concept in all shots. The longest you can run on a

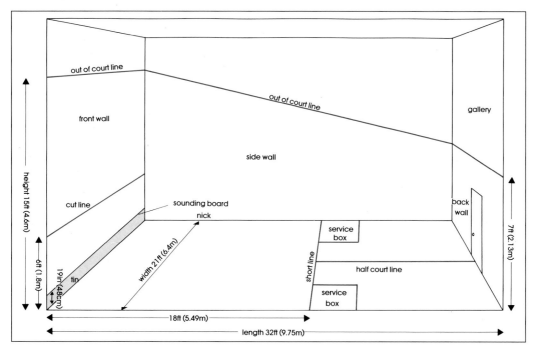

Labels on figure: out of court line, out of court line, gallery, front wall, side wall, height 15ft (4.6m), cut line, sounding board, nick, back wall, 7ft (2.13m), 6ft (1.8m), 19in (48cm), tin, width 21ft (6.4m), short line, service box, half court line, service box, 18ft (5.49m), length 32ft (9.75m)

Fig 5   The Court.

squash court is, of course, the diagonal – 11.7m (38ft 3in).

Court lines are useful reference points. The intersection of the short line and the half-court line is referred to as the T. The short line (the nearest edge is 4.27m (13ft 10in) from the back wall) is short of half-way.

The Score

You score points in squash only when you are serving. If the receiver wins a rally he wins the service and therefore the opportunity to score points.

The server's score is called first. A score of 7–5 means that the server has 7 points and the receiver 5. A game is to 9 points, except that if 8 all is reached the receiver may play to 9 (No set) or 10 (Set two).

A match is usually the best of 5 games (although it can also be the best of 3), and can be won 3–0, 3–1, or 3–2. In 1986 in the World Championships Ross Norman beat Jahangir Khan 9–5, 9–7, 7–9, 9–1 (that is, a 4

game match won 3–1 by Norman.)

The top men in the world often play point-per-rally scoring in which the receiver as well as the server can score points. Games are played to 15 and at 14 all the receiver can choose to play to either 15 or 17. This scoring system was used when Jansher Khan won the 1989 World Open, beating Chris Dittmar 10–15, 6–15, 15–4, 15–11, 15–10 in 1 hour 44 minutes.

Concise Rules

Warm-up

The rules allow 5 minutes hitting across to each other before a match starts. Change sides at 2½ minutes.

Service

Starting the Match
The right to start serving is decided by spinning a racket (rough or smooth).

Fig 6   The transparent glass court used in the 1988 World Open held at the Rai Exhibition Centre, Amsterdam.

Sides

On becoming the server at the start of, or during a match, the player decides from which service box (left or right) he wants to serve. Thereafter, while still winning points and therefore remaining server, he serves from alternate sides.

A 'Good' Serve

1   A 'good' serve must go above the cut (service) line and land in the opposite back quarter of the court. If on or below the cut line or outside the quarter, it is a fault.

2   The server must have at least one foot completely inside the service box. If not, it is a fault and is called a foot fault.

3   If a server serves a fault or foot fault he loses the service (this is called a 'hand out').

Interference

With two players sharing the same territory in a fast and competitive sport interference can and does occur. The rules are designed for safety as well as fair competition. If interference occurs a player must stop and request that the rally is replayed by asking for a let (by saying 'let please'). He is not entitled to a let if he plays or attempts a shot. The referee will make a decision on whether to award a let, no let or a stroke. In the absence of an official referee (in social and friendly matches) the players will decide by mutual agreement.

No Let

The referee will call no let in the following circumstances.

1   If the player would not have got the ball.

2   If the player did not make sufficient effort or show that he could have got the ball.

3   If the player attempts the shot. (The exception to this is if he hits his opponent on the backswing and appeals immediately saying 'let please – backswing'. A let is then allowed.)

Let

The rally is played again if the player would have got the ball, but there was interference. The referee will call 'let allowed'.

Stroke

The word 'stroke' refers to the winning or losing of a rally, since you only score points when you are serving. The rally is awarded (i.e. a point is given if serving) in the following circumstances.

1 If the striker is in a winning situation.
2 If the striker's opponent has not made enough effort to get out of the way.
3 The referee may award a stroke on appeal or by stopping play.

Appeals

1 A player may appeal at the end of a rally if he thought that during the rally a ball was 'down', 'not up' or 'out'.
2 He may also appeal on a marker's call. If the referee is doubtful in either of these situations he will play the point again – that is, play a let.

Hitting an Opponent with the Ball

1 If the ball would have hit the front wall first, and been up, the striker wins the rally.
2 If the ball would have hit the side wall first and then the front, it is a let.
3 If a player 'turns' in the back corner and hits his opponent, it is a let.

Times

Warm up – 5 minutes
Between games – 90 seconds
Referee calls 'fifteen seconds' to advise players to be ready to resume play.

Marking and Refereeing

There are two officiating positions in squash. For convenience, these two roles are often performed by the same person.

Fig 7   Jansher Khan under pressure against Ross Norman, but intent on getting the ball back. Note that even before he has fully arrived he has his racket down under the ball.

The Marker

The marker keeps and calls the score and calls the play (whether the ball was down, out, and so on).

The Referee

The referee keeps the times and decides on appeals and disputes. He will award a let, no let or stroke according to the rules, and he also has the power to award conduct warnings, strokes, games and matches.

Note

These concise rules are a summary of some of the key points in the rules of squash. They are not comprehensive. Readers are advised to learn the 'referee's line of thinking' and become familiar with the official rules and guidelines.

15

2
Getting Started

Build on Basics

Your first outing on a squash court is a big step. It will open up a new world of shots and angles as you start learning the skills of chasing and of rebounding the ball off the walls. A sympathetic friend or acquaintance could help you. Ease yourself in with plenty of gentle hitting onto the front wall, across to each other, and with a brief introduction to scoring and the rules. There's a lot to learn and you're not going to be an expert after one session.

If a friend is not available to help, the club coach is an expert at helping people learn and there is no better person to turn to.

One of the first things to try is hitting to yourself. Start softly and slowly, gradually building up the pace. This is an ideal way to develop control and learn the basics of technique. This process is outlined in Chapter 5, where the ten steps to basic control are described.

You can, of course, become familiar with these steps off court and then practise them with a partner. Plenty of hitting across to your partner, taking time to get control and be aware of what's happening with your technique, is important.

Coaching and Practice

Squash is a game of habits and part of a coach's job is to help you develop the right habits. An initial series of lessons on the fundamentals before you develop bad habits is an investment in your game.

Use *The Squash Workshop*. Run through the off-court exercises and on-court practices. You can learn by yourself but getting even a minimum amount of advice can provide a useful check that you're on the right track and can also help solve problems and order priorities.

As your skills develop with practice and play, a coach will be able to assist in helping you fit these skills together a little better in a game. Use lessons to expand what you are doing in your game and arrive for your lessons with questions at the ready.

Habits are formed through repetition. What you are shown by a friend or a coach or what you read in *The Squash Workshop* will not immediately become part of your game. It will need a lot of repetition. Use the ten steps to basic control, the technique practices in Part 2, the practice progressions in Part 3 and the solo and pairs practice sequences in Part 4.

Initially, practice is more important than play. You need to develop the skills that you will use in a game.

Getting on Court

Beginners introduced to squash and keen to get into the game often run into problems immediately after their initiation. They just don't have people to play. This is a problem you must work at to really get into the game. Collect telephone numbers, ask friends and seek referrals. Ask. Try to pick people of about your own standard. Don't be afraid. If people don't want to play they will say so.

Joining a club will provide the opportunity to meet partners and provide social rewards. Keep practising by yourself, get on court as much as possible and look for opportunities to get involved in activities at your level – leagues, ladders, club nights and competitions.

3
Improving Your Game

Before you rush out and embark on copious training you need to think about your game. What are the parts that need working on? Which can be improved? Next you need to select activities that will work on these areas. Then these activities must be fitted realistically in with the rest of your lifestyle. Let's look at these three questions briefly under the headings 'Assess', 'Select' and 'Programme' and see where *The Squash Workshop* can provide assistance.

Assess

What are the most important things for you to improve in your game? You may be one of those people who know their game well, or perhaps you are one who flexes scrawny biceps in the mirror and sees rippling muscle. The more realistically you can assess the areas you can improve on, the more successful you will be in the long term. The danger is that you will concentrate on what you like doing and not on what you're not good at and probably don't like doing (the unfit talented shot maker will practise shots rather than train for fitness.) Self-assessment is not easy so get advice.

I am constantly amazed when keen players in training who have had the good fortune to play a top player or have a session with a top coach fail to ask advice, ask what they could get better at. Don't waste these opportunities when they arise. Ask senior and experienced players for advice on your game. Ask experienced players to watch you play for a while. Get a coach's assessment, whether in an on-court session or from observation of your game.

Practise and training will provide feedback to help you assess your strengths and weaknesses. Work out the areas you want to improve on, then set out some goals (preferably on paper) to work towards.

Select

The Squash Workshop provides a large number of activities you can use in order to improve your game.

Select the activities that are going to work on the parts of your game you want to improve. Don't ignore the basics. Practise to overcome areas of weakness and to develop grooved strokes that will give you greater consistency and accuracy. Work on technique.

Work on your shots. Practise the weaker ones. Use the practice progressions in Part 3 to discover the best level to practise at. Work at developing and grooving your shots.

Improve your tactics. Develop a game plan and practise setting up rallies. Develop practice sessions that incorporate the above practices.

Programme

Your programme is about how you fit the activities you want to work at into a timetable. The more specific you are about this the more successful you will be. Your practice and training need not be a casual affair just squeezed in when you can. Take charge of it. Organize yourself.

At club level this may involve decisions such as changing from playing four matches a week to, say, one match; one solo session followed by one practice game; one pairs practice and practice game; one solo session;

three sessions of court sprints; good warm-ups before each session and stretching afterwards. This programme would still involve four sessions and would need a little more time and some organization.

Ross Norman was a comfortable No 8 in the world when in June 1983 during his first parachute jump he crash landed on the runway at Thruxton, Hampshire.

A crippling knee injury seemed to have ended his career but his resolve to return and eventual triumph is a story of sporting heroism. Weeks in traction, months on crutches and many more months painstakingly building up the strength and mobility to compete again, he returned with new dedication to become World No 2 and set out in pursuit of the great undefeated Jahangir Khan.

In Toulouse on 11 November 1986 his quest was rewarded when in one of the greatest upsets in sports history he defeated Jahangir for the first time in 5½ years to become World Champion.

A New Zealander, Ross won his first tournament at eleven and collected every junior age group title available. Today he is the senior professional on the world circuit and is still playing a tough game characterized by superb defence, aggressive exploitation of openings and a true professional discipline. He is part of the Dunlop Pro-team.

Del Harris has been the dominant British squash player since he thrust his way into the senior ranks, by winning the British National title in 1987 when aged just eighteen.

Del started playing at nine, and at eleven decided to concentrate on squash rather than football. Hours of solo practice after school helped establish him as the best British Junior. He won every British age group championship including four British Open Under-19 titles, the first when he was only fifteen.

In April 1988 he won the World Junior championship in Edinburgh, Scotland. Del was also British Champion in 1989. He is one of the most athletic and powerful of players and is part of the Slazenger Pro-team.

Advice

Jansher Khan, Ross Norman, Del Harris and Lucy Soutter give advice throughout this book as well as demonstrating shots and techniques. Their comments, and also those of the great Hashim Khan (seven times British Open Champion) suggest what you can do to improve your game.

It is no exaggeration to say that Jansher Khan burst onto the world scene. His first victory over Jahangir Khan came in Hong Kong, the next in Pakistan, followed by the dramatic semi-final of the World Open when Jahangir was beaten in four. It was a stunning run of eight successive victories that left the young Pakistani World No 1 and World Champion.

Jansher started squash in Peshwar in turbulent northern Pakistan. Older brothers Mohibullah (former world No 2) and Atlas (four times Singapore Open winner) were squash stars and heroes for the young Jansher to look up to.

Running before school, playing and practising when school was out Jansher quickly improved until he was Pakistani Junior Champion at thirteen, later Asian Junior Champion and at fifteen he won the World Junior Championship in Brisbane, Australia.

World Champion in 1987, 1989 and 1990 he is the fastest man in squash.

At fifteen Lucy Soutter won the Under-16 and Under-19 National Championships double. At sixteen she retained her National title without dropping a point in the final. In 1984 at seventeen she created a storm of publicity in a dramatic finals victory over World No 1 Susan Devoy in the World Masters at Warrington.

In the 1985 World Championships, she easily won the Junior title, came third in the senior event and clinched the team event for England. She was National Champion in 1985 and 1989, British Open Under-23's, Champion in 1986 and 1987 and runner-up in the British Open in 1987. Her game is characterized by consistency, accuracy and tactical astuteness. Lucy is part of the Dunlop Pro-team.

4
Equipment

'Off the wood' is now just a figure of speech. Rackets have entered the space age with an array of new materials and for anyone taking up the game now an old wooden racket will be a strange curiosity.

The wooden squash racket was initially developed from those in the older games of rackets and real tennis. Early frames were made from sticks of wood steam-bent into shape and glued or screwed. Strings were of natural gut made from the twisted intestines of cattle and sheep.

In the 1930s the plywood (Maxply) racket was developed, with six veneers of ash and beech glued together. Later, synthetic glues, carbon-fibre laminations and reinforcing glass fibre overlays improved the strength-to-weight performance.

In 1983 the International Squash Rackets Federation (ISRF) removed the restriction that racket heads must be made of wood, thus allowing the use of aluminium alloy tubes and of high-strength fibres of glass and carbon to reinforce plastics. The latter, commonly called graphite or composite rackets allow a larger head size, more strength and less weight. Another development has allowed head sizes to be extended. Since the early days a revolution has occurred in shapes, materials and performance.

The ball too has come a long way. As the standardization of court, rules and racket size was being established in the 1920s, the original type of ball – known as a 'holer', made from india rubber with a hole in the middle so that it collapsed when hit – was abandoned in favour of a more standard ball. The Silvertown ball, which was squashy and had different playing characteristics from the modern ball, was the most popular before the late 1940s. After 1949 the Dunlop Championship Black ball was adopted and every tournament in the United Kingdom was played with it. As playing standards improved this ball went through a number of developments and eventually the non-marking ball arrived. Later, white balls were designed for the all-glass court and balls with expensive reflective material were developed to reflect light into the TV cameras, making the ball visible.

A squash ball hit hard will travel at about 150mph but rebound from a solid wall hit head-on at about only a quarter of that speed. This rebound speed gives you the chance to intercept it before it bounces a second time. The court size, ball, racket and equipment that allow us to do this have evolved over time. Getting your equipment right may not make a dramatic improvement in your game but using poor, unsuitable, faulty or poorly maintained equipment can mean that you start at a disadvantage.

Rackets

A player's requirements of a racket include: lightness, which allows manoeuvrability; power, which is determined by the speed with which a ball leaves the strings; low vibration and jarring to avoid arm and shoulder injuries; and strength to accommodate severe impacts with the walls and floor. Generally, the stiffer the racket the more power and the more vibration. Often these are the graphite rackets which tend towards a 100 per cent graphite composition. They have a tendency to greater initial shock and hence a harsher feel. Vibration damping helps reduce this.

Fig 8   The Revelation compression-moulded graphite racket from Dunlop, the world's leading racket company.

Composite rackets produced by mixing fibres tend to greater flexibility and less vibration.

Wooden rackets and injection-moulded composites are better at absorbing vibration than compression-moulded composites, which in turn are better than metal. Players have different physical characteristics so the resonance frequency of the vibration affects them differently. If this is a problem, trial and error is the only way to find a suitable match.

Graphite rackets, although strong and light, still break. Seek a retailer's advice on which models have low returns for breakage, which are guaranteed and which present value for money. Metal rackets have a performance near to graphite at half the price but often have more vibration problems. Wood rackets don't give the same power as graphite and metal but are more sensitive to touch and more economical. They are a good choice for the beginner.

Try to test a racket on court before you buy. Often clubs and shops have test rackets, or you may be able to borrow one.

Strings

Natural gut has excellent playing properties but is expensive and prone to breakage. The first serious replacement for gut was monofilament nylon, which was cheaper and stronger than gut but had poorer playing qualities. Monofilament nylon has now been replaced by the improved multi-filament strings made by twisting, wrapping and braiding.

String tension affects the speed with which a ball leaves the strings. Lower string tensions give greater ball speed: extra deflection of the strings reduces the ball compression, energy loss is less and speed is therefore increased. Impacts on the edge of the strings produce less power.

Grips

A racket grip needs to be firm, secure and not slippery. Leather grips tended to slip when sweaty and traditionally towelling has been the standard grip. It is still used by many competitors and provides a good grip if replaced when worn or greasy and if brushed up (a small suede brush is good for this) when flat and matted.

A large number of synthetic grips are now available. Experimentation is needed to find one that gives control and is absorbent, so as not to provide a slippery surface.

Grip Size

Grip size can be changed easily to suit the individual, but try to avoid building it up so large that it will restrict the wrist action. Laying lengthways strips of tape or thin cardboard as well as wrapping tape round the handle will increase the circumference.

Grip Aids

Grip aids can provide a little more feel and security between your grip and the racket. A slipping grip can destroy your game and it is worth experimenting with the traditional material, resin, or the many synthetic products that can provide 'stickiness'.

Shoes

Think what your feet go through in a game of squash – the jumping as you take off, the swivelling, twisting, dragging, the shuddering tension as you suddenly brake. The era of the plimsoll is long gone. Squash shoes are now designed specially for this mistreatment and a wide choice is available. It is advisable to stick with established brands. The companies making these have some experience in testing their shoes, correcting faults and getting them just right. Seek advice from your sports retailer when choosing a pair. Take your sports socks into the shop with you and try a pair for fit. You'll need a firm fit but allow room at the toe so that your foot can move a little when stopping.

Specialist shoes should be well cushioned against jarring but still be low at the heels to allow a player to feel the floor. Shoes also need to be strong, light (composition rubber soles help lightness) and, supportive (synthetic uppers add support) and have breathing holes, a sole which allows swivel but minimum slide, and low heel tabs so as not to cause Achilles tendon problems.

Insoles

Shock-absorbing inners can help avoid or alleviate sore feet. Sorbothane insoles absorb shock and Spenco insoles help blisters.

Balls

Squash balls are made of a rubber compound. They don't bounce well at room temperature but bounce when the temperature is raised. This, of course, is achieved by striking the ball against the wall, imparting energy to it and raising the temperature until a balance is reached between energy imparted and that lost due to heat transfer. The temperature a ball reaches depends very much on the standard of play; international players will get a ball hotter and may require a different ball from the average player or beginner.

Another factor affecting ball temperature is the surrounding temperature. In colder conditions the ball will reach a lower temperature and therefore will not bounce as much, and a faster ball will be more satisfactory.

Players of a lower standard are less mobile and may need a more bouncy (faster) ball, which does not 'die' in the corners of the court. For this reason balls of different speeds are produced with different colour-coded dots:

extra super slow	yellow dot	16–17 in.
slow	white dot	20–22 in.
medium	red dot	22–24 in.
fast	blue dot	24–26 in.

(The figure in the last column is the rebound height of the ball when dropped at 23°C from a height of 100in onto a hard surface.)

Experiment to find the ball which will give you the best game. Generally, I have found that too many beginners play with a yellow dot ball, through some misguided sense that it is the proper ball to use, even if it is giving them a poor bounce and short rallies. Select a ball that will give you the best game and allow you to rally.

Squash balls aren't meant to last for ever and some have the annoying habit of dying at a crucial stage in a match. If yours does last and last, throw it away when it is old or shiny as it will have a tendency to skid and provide a poor bounce. Keep spare balls of different speeds in your squash bag. The faster ones will be useful for coaching, hitting with beginners and practising single shots such as the drop or the back-corner shots.

Clothing

Squash clothing must be neither so tight as to restrict movement nor so loose as to impede a swing. Stretch fabrics are now incorporated into squash clothing and if

Fig 9 Australian Chris Robertson with some inopportune equipment problems.

you are playing regularly it's worth getting the right kit. Some cotton content in shirts helps absorbency and gives the sweat time to evaporate (rather than dripping off on the floor), hence assisting heat loss and helping to prevent overheating.

Some clubs still have restrictions on the amount of colour players can wear, though the 'all white' or 'predominately white' rule has generally been relaxed considerably. However, colours should not be distracting and pastel is recommended. Sports socks with the cushion soles provide some protection from jarring.

Sweat must be kept off the face and racket handle. Headbands and wristbands, changed between games, are useful for this. Hairbands too are useful, particularly for ladies, to keep hair out of the way.

Bag

A squash bag is a necessity for any regular player. It allows you to keep all your squash equipment together and readily at hand. Ideally you will have a spare racket, balls, grips, sweatbands, shoe laces, a toilet bag with soap and shampoo, and a small first-aid kit. Plastic bags for wet clothing are also useful.

A squash ball, hit hard, can travel at over 150mph. On impact with the front wall and on rebounding off the side, the back and the floor it loses velocity, which allows us to intercept it before it bounces twice.

Connecting with this small ball as it travels in various flights, and at different speeds, angles and spins, involves a complex range of abilities and skills. Under pressure, running, lunging, jumping, twisting and diving, we attempt to get to it, connect with it with the racket and rebound it accurately off the walls. Control is difficult. Things can easily go wrong.

The experienced player may well anticipate an opponent's shot before it has hit the front wall or even before he has played it. He will use cues he has picked up on his opponent's positioning, swing, impact point, and stance as well as observation of the flight of the ball. Getting to the ball will involve his perception, reaction, and movement abilities; hitting it, his hand-to-eye co-ordination; and aiming, the mental 'lining up' of the ball, positioning, line of the shot and the imaginary target on the front wall.

The beginner may not know where the ball is going until it is too late, may struggle to get near it, and, if he connects, may spray it inaccurately onto the front wall. Controlling this connection of the moving player, moving racket and moving ball is the basis of technique. To achieve control a player must have control over his movement and racket, and he must also 'time' the connection with the ball. Timing ability involves both natural ability and learned skills. It is something that can be improved with practice. The incompetent beginner can often become very proficient with practice, experience, and good technique.

If you have never played before, start with Chapter 5. Learn and practice the ten steps to basic control. These are the basic habits you build your game on. For players who want to improve their game these are the principles they need to have mastered before moving on.

Squash is a rare game because you don't aim directly at your target – you rebound the ball into your target area. It's a game of angles. Chapter 6 explains the three main dimensions of a squash shot which determine its placement and flight – the vertical angle, the horizontal angle and pace. Understanding these principles will help you work out how you can alter shots for better placement.

Chapter 7 explains how we aim a ball when we are not looking at the target, how we co-ordinate a shot and how we develop pace. Half the game of squash is getting in the right place for your shot. How well you move is vital. Some players move better than others, but it is something we all can learn to do better. Chapter 8 explains the important principles involved: being ready, moving, stopping, the different stances you can use and, of course, the recovery, so you can do it all over again.

If half the game is getting to the ball, the other half is hitting it – but not just hitting it anywhere. Consistency and accuracy are the keys. Chapter 9 explains the different actions involved in hitting, how we put them together, the appropriate size of swing for each shot and how you can go about developing your swing.

It's worth getting the basics right. You build your game on them. It's worth working for a good technique – technique gives you control over the ball. The rewards may not be immediate but get the basics right, improve them, develop smooth movement, good balance and a grooved swing and you are on the way to lifting your game to a new level.

5
Basics of Technique

Squash is a game of habits. The basics are the habits that give you basic control. This is what you build your game on. It is important to get these right from the start.

There are ten steps to basic control. This chapter outlines each step and provides practices and checks for each.

1   The Pat

The simplest connection of the ball and racket is effected by rolling and then bouncing the ball on the racket face. The simplest connection of the racket, ball and wall is the pat. This is the most suitable place for a beginner or someone developing ball control to start. Stand several paces back from and facing the front wall. Throw the ball high and soft off the front and using an underarm action, with the racket face slanting slightly back, pat the ball softly up onto the front. (If it is cool use a faster red or blue dot ball, which will bounce more.) Let the ball bounce each time, and use a short swing to get under it and lift. You will find the easiest place to hit the ball is as it is falling a little from the top of the bounce. Try to have your racket ready with a short backswing before you hit. This is the beginnings of racket preparation. Move your feet, allow room for the shot and try to be in position early.

Gradually move back down the court, hitting the ball high and soft. Practise this exercise on both the forehand and the backhand.

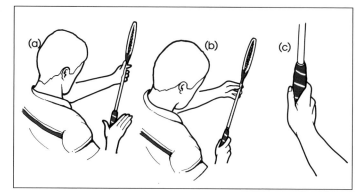

Fig 10   The Grip. (a) The palm approaches the handle from above, with the V shape over the inside edge; (b) The V grip; (c) The thumb is diagonally along the inside of the shaft, the V is on the inside edge and the knuckle sits up on the outside edge.

2   The Grip

The focus of any squash shot is the connection of the racket strings with the ball. The amount of control a player has over this is determined by the control he has over the racket head and racket face. These are controlled by the grip and wrist action. If this is a loose link the shot will lack precision.

The V grip (also called the continental grip) will give you control that you can feel over the racket head.

(a)   Hold the racket by the neck in your left hand with the racket face vertical. Spread the fingers of the gripping hand, forming a V between the thumb and forefinger, and sit this V down on top of the inside edge (the edge nearest your body) of the racket.
(b)   Sit the second joint of the index finger up on the outside top edge of the handle; let the finger sit around the handle – like pulling the trigger of a gun.
(c)   Sit the thumb diagonally along the inside of the handle.
(d)   Spread the remaining fingers, fitting them diagonally round the handle, and let the heel of the hand sit up just above the butt.

Check
V on inside edge; knuckle up; thumb diagonal; fingers diagonal and spread.

Hold the racket face vertical and the wrist up. You should be able to feel that you have control over the racket head. Give it a little shake and feel the racket head with the grip. This is the 'feel' check.

Grip the racket and, holding the shaft in your spare hand, move it around to check that the grip doesn't wobble but that it makes a firm link. This is the 'wobble' check.

25

Fig 11   For the forehand take the racket edge back towards the right shoulder. This cocks the wrist and opens the racket for the forehand.

Fig 12   Ready position.

Fig 13   For the backhand take the racket edge back towards the left shoulder.

There is an old saying in squash that 'the racket should feel like an extension of your arm'. It is the connecting grip that gives it that feeling.

3   The Racket Face

Hold your racket face parallel with the floor and bounce the ball up and down on the strings. You are hitting the ball vertically, straight up in the air. This is called a completely open racket face (90 degrees open). The racket head is impacting directly along the line of the shot so no spin is imparted. If you hold your racket at a different angle the ball will not travel vertically and you will lose control.

If you wanted to hit the ball on a 45-degree trajectory, then a racket face 45 degrees open would be the most appropriate. To hit on a higher trajectory you would open your racket more. A flat racket face (at 90 degrees to the floor or 0 degrees open) would be appropriate to hit the ball flat, parallel to the floor. With a closed face there is a tendency to hit down on the ball.

Generally in squash you will

use an open racket face. This is used to hit upwards on the ball, to provide cut (backspin), to provide feel on some shots and to help take the pace off the ball. The degree of openness should be the same as the trajectory of the shot, except where cut is used.

Hold the racket out in front of you with the wrist and racket head up. Take the racket edge directly back to the right shoulder by using the wrist. This will open the racket for the forehand. Again using the wrist, take the racket edge back to the left shoulder. This will

open the racket for the backhand.

The racket face is controlled by the grip and wrist action. When you hold the racket out in front in the V grip, the racket face will be vertical. Use the wrist to open the racket for the forehand and backhand. Do not alter the grip.

4   The Wrist

The wrist provides a firm link to the racket, controls the racket face and can provide extra power or be used to improvise a shot.

Hold your racket out in front

Fig 14   The Wrist. (a) A dropped wrist gives less control; (b) The cocked wrist for racket head control.

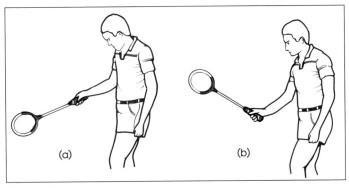

(a)   (b)

and lift the racket head by using your wrist. This is a cocked wrist. It provides control of the racket head and allows you to have a consistent technique. Dropping or breaking your wrist leads to less control and inconsistency in shots and technique.

5 The Stroke

The pat is a simple way to develop ball control but it is not a squash action. Pat as in step 1, but then turn side on to face the sidewall and hit across your body onto the front wall. Instead of the underarm action you used to pat, move to a side-on bent arm throwing action, with your racket approximately parallel to the floor, through the impact area. Check your grip, keep the wrist up and firm and open your racket face. Use a short swing that comes down, under and up through the ball. Lift the ball high and soft so that it will give you plenty of time to get ready for the next stroke. As the action you are now using is side on, you should try to find a position that is side on to the ball, with the ball between you and the side rather than behind it as on the pat.

Step back from the ball each time and move your feet to get in position at the side of the ball. Try to be ready in position and well balanced before you hit.

Practice stroking on both the forehand and backhand. Gradually build up your control over the ball and the number of strokes you can make by achieving better control over the various parts of your technique.

6 Footwork

Use your feet to get in the best position for each shot. Good squash movement is not the same thing as running fast. It

involves many different steps. Stand more on the balls of your feet and use sidesteps and adjusting steps where necessary. Do not just reach out for the ball. Use your feet to adjust your position for every shot. When practising, step back from each shot and allow room to approach the ball in the best way.

7 Positioning

One of the main problems in squash is that players run to the ball. Do not run to the ball. Move to the place you want to hit it from. This is positioning. Beginners see a ball and run to it. Often they end up awkwardly positioned, cramping their shots, and hit across court constantly or play loose shots because they have failed to position themselves to the side.

As the squash hitting action is a sidearm action we have to position side on to the direction we want to hit the ball. This very simple idea of being in the right place for your shot is one of the most important in squash.

While practising stroking the ball straight, try to anticipate where the ball will bounce and move early to a position facing the side wall at the side of and behind that point.

8 Stance

To obtain control over the ball you need control over your movement and racket.

Consider how a golfer carefully lines up a ball. He is

still and steady. Imagine the success he would have if he was twisting, falling, turning, moving or running to the ball. Squash pressures us into mistakes of these kinds. When our movement is uncontrolled, our shot is uncontrolled. To have control over your movement for a shot you need to be still and on balance. A basic stance allows you to do this.

Face the side wall. Step on to your front foot (the one nearest the front wall), pointing your toe to the side, and bend your knee. Lean forwards and let your weight move over the front foot. Move up and down and back and forth a little in this stance while maintaining balance. Can you swing, reach and adjust? Now, with a little footwork move around, stop on balance and swing.

Continue your stroking practice with the ball. Use different steps to change position for each shot and then stop on balance in a strong stance. As you practise, stop occasionally (just freeze on the spot) and check your balance. This is the freeze check.

9 Swing

The squash swing goes from a V to a V. It is a sidearm throwing action that hinges on the elbow. For the forehand, stand facing the side wall and point your racket directly at the back. Lift your wrist, open the racket face slightly and bend your elbow so that it sits over your hip. The racket head will now be about head high.

Bring the racket down (not round), under the back knee and up. At impact the racket will be pointing to the side, with the wrist up and the racket face open. Swing through so that the racket points at the front wall in line with the shoulders and with the wrist up. Use the feel check

Fig 15   Jansher at full stretch but still managing to keep his eye on the ball and take the utmost care in the stroke.

Sometimes check out control on the backswing, impact and follow-through. Use the 'feel' check.

(b)   *Practise your stance and swing without the ball.*
Practise co-ordinating your movement and swing without the ball. Step into the shot, stop in a strong stance and then swing through. As you practise this try to be aware of how it feels.

(c)   *Practise stroking with the ball.*
We started off with the simple pat and turned this side on into a simple stroke. As you get better at this, gradually move back down the court and firm up the stroke.

Stroke above the cut line. Stroke behind the short line. Stroke into the service box.

Summary

Ten Steps to Basic Control

1   Use a high soft *pat* to get started and to develop ball control.
2   Get control over the racket head with a *V Grip* – V on the inside edge, knuckle up, thumb diagonal and fingers spread.
3   *Open* your *racket face* to hit up on the ball.
4   Keep your *wrist up* for consistency on your shots.
5   Develop a side-on *stroke*.
6   Use *footwork* to adjust your position for every shot.
7   Move early to a *position* at the side of your shot.
8   Bend your knees and stop on balance in a strong *stance* for your shot.
9   *Swing* from a V to a V, hinging the throwing action on the elbow.
10   *Practise* with and without the ball to develop good basic habits.

to see if you still have control over the racket head.

On the backhand, turn your shoulder and point the racket at the backwall. Your elbow will be across your stomach and again you will swing from a V to a V.

Practise swinging without the ball. Take your racket back, stop it in the backswing and swing smoothly through to the follow-through position.

Now practise with the ball. Continue your stroking practice slowly. Take your racket back early so that it is waiting for the ball to fall to the impact point. This preparation gives time and helps achieve a more precise swing. One of the main reasons you practise is to develop your swing. Try to be aware of it and to develop flow and rhythm as well as control.

10   Practice
Practise the basics so that they become habits. When you first start you will be concerned mainly with controlling the ball. As you progress, try to become aware of the parts of your technique and the control you have over them. Try to feel it. Concentrate on one thing at a time. Stop and check it out, work on it and then try to get it into your practice.

When you are practising, try to pick up what goes wrong or what's not working well. Ask yourself questions and give yourself reminders (Am I moving my feet? I didn't get to the side of that one. Remember to stop for your shot. Racket ready. Your grip was loose that time. And so on.)

When basic control is achieved you will be on automatic pilot.

(a)   *Practise your swing without the ball.*
Take your racket to the backswing position, hold it and then swing smoothly through. Repeat this again and again, trying to improve rhythm and control.

6
The Geometry of a Squash Shot

Tactically squash is often likened to a physical game of chess. Technically it is a physical geometry lesson. The good technical player is constantly calculating how he should adjust the angles and paces at his disposal. These control the placement and flight of the ball and allow a player to direct it to his target area.

Placement and Flight

In looking at the placement of a squash ball we can use terms that specify exactly the events we are talking about. It is useful to talk and think in this vocabulary as the precise terms involved lead to a clarity about exactly what we want to achieve from a specific shot.

Length
A ball that bounces in the back corners is a length shot. If it bounces and forces an opponent to take it off the back we call it good length. A ball that is a little shorter and will not bounce out of the back is a dying length. This shot is often aimed at the back of the service box and played to die.

A full-length ball or one which is over-length will land near the back-wall nick or hit the back wall on the full and bounce out.

Width
The width of a shot is the angle it travels across the court. Generally, the angle is designed to beat an opponent's intercept (that is, get to the side before he can volley or drive it) but is not angled so much that it will bounce out into the court. The ideal shot will touch the side wall at the point an opponent would want to play it.

Fig 16   Mir Zaman Gul dominates the T with Ross Norman in the back recovering a length shot.

29

Fig 17   **Width**

(a)   Gawain Briars shapes for a drive with Neil Harvey ready on the T.

(b)   Briars crosscourts and Harvey looks for the opportunity to volley.

(c)   Harvey is forced right into the corner by a good width shot that gave him no chance to cut it off.

A dying width will die on the side on its second bounce.

Height
Height is the vital and most underestimated dimension in squash. Hitting higher will bring the ball back further so height has a vital interplay with length. Use the height and the flight of the ball to place it out of an opponent's reach, on the crosscourt and straight lob.

Tight
A ball very close to the side that gives little chance of an intercept is called tight.

Clinger
This is a ball that is angled in and then rolls along the side wall.

Nick
A nick is aimed to hit the joint between the wall and floor. This can be the target area in the front court for an attacking shot or in the back court for a crosscourt drive.

Dying
A ball is dying as it is about to bounce for the second time. If this part of the shot is placed in a restricted position for an opponent (for example on the side or back walls) it makes a return very difficult.

Loose
A loose ball is one that comes well out from the side, allowing easy access and no restriction to the shot.

Short
A short ball is one that has failed to travel to a length and does not get an opponent out of position. Often it will not give the striker time to get back in position on the T before his opponent strikes it.

Fig 18 **Dying Length**: (a) Jason Nicolle stretches for a drive from Stuart Hailstone, (b) which beats him (c) and dies at the back.

(a)

(b)

(c)

Target Areas

In Part 3 target areas are specified for each shot described. The precision, or accuracy and consistency, with which the ball can be directed to its target area is the result of how precisely the angles are adjusted for each shot.

The Dimensions of Shots

A squash shot has length, width, height and pace. These dimensions interplay to give it its flight.

A squash player has control over the vertical angle of the shot, the horizontal angle and the pace. It is by using, thinking in terms of, and adjusting these angles that a player controls his shot. A player will continually assess the results of his hitting and make adjustments. These may be automatic or very deliberate, even to the extent of a player talking to himself.

The Vertical Angle

The length of a shot is controlled by the height it is hit on the front wall (or, more precisely, its vertical angle) and by the pace of the shot. The higher you hit a ball the further back in the court it will travel. This is one of the fundamental principles of squash that we often tend to forget when we rush and hit hard.

Technically it is very simple. To hit upwards on the ball you need both an open racket face and an upward path to your swing. A squash swing goes in a U shape, swinging down, through and then up. If you get too close and cramp your shot you can tend to hit down or through on the ball. Keep back and allow room for your

31

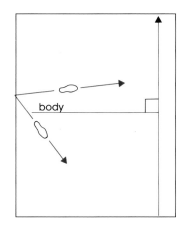

Fig 19   Positioning – the line of the shot is at right angles to the direction the body faces.

The Horizontal Angle

A squash hitting action is side on. Wherever you want the ball to go, you position yourself to the side of the line of the shot. That is, the ball will travel at ninety degrees to the direction the body faces at impact. This positioning to the side is one of the main ways we aim a squash ball.

Your ability to move from the T to the correct position in relation to the ball is one of the crucial attributes required in the game. Be clear as to what this position is exactly; try to anticipate and prepare for it.

Positions

There are three basic positions in squash.

The Straight Shot
'In squash you face the side walls.' This is an old squash saying (and a useful oversimplification) used to

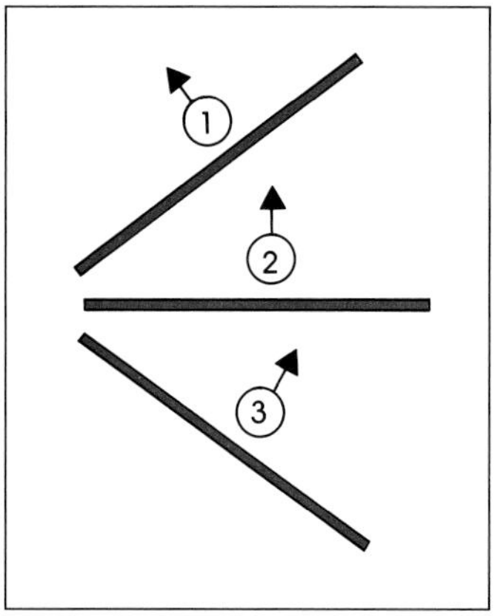

Fig 21   The three basic positions in squash – (1) crosscourt, (2) straight, (3) boast.

racket to go under and up on the ball.

Try to imagine bouncing the ball on your racket, to help you get under it and then hit upwards as well as through. This is the vertical angle of your stroke.

explain that for much of the game you should face the side and not the front. We do this to play straight.

If you are facing directly at the side and strike the ball at a right angle to the side it will travel parallel with the side wall. To angle it in to be tight

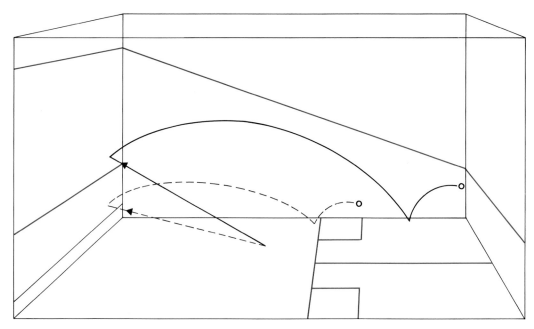

Fig 20   Length and height – the length a shot travels is controlled by its height rather than pace. Hit higher for length.

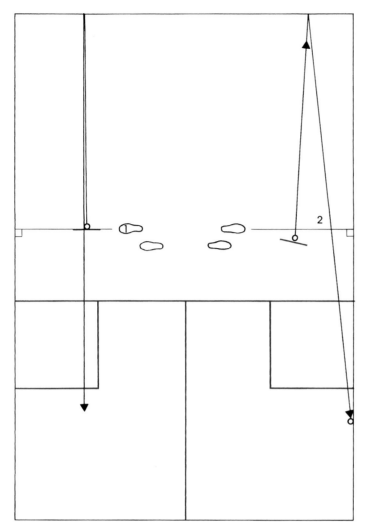

Fig 22   Tight and straight. (1) Striking the ball at a right angle with the side will send it parallel to the wall. (2) Let the ball come past the right angle, to angle it into the side.

or to cling you will take it slightly behind the right angle. This means changing your position to face back slightly, or let the ball come back to a later impact point – that is, take it later.

One of the basic rules of straight driving is, always hit the ball behind the right angle.

The Crosscourt Shot
Your general position when hitting across the court will be facing forwards towards the front corner.

The angle you calculate to put on the shot will depend on how wide you want it to go and from where you are hitting it (from the front or side you will need more angle than from the middle or back and will have to position accordingly). You vary this angle by altering your positioning to take the ball either further forward or back.

To angle the ball across the court more, take it further forward and position more behind it.

To angle it across less, take the ball further back and position more to the side.

The Boast
Theoretically, when positioning for the boast you will be facing backwards towards the back corner. In practice, however, when in the midcourt, we try not to make the shot so obvious and hence position or shape for the shot as for the straight drive, using a later impact point to direct it into the side wall. This may also involve twisting or swivelling on the knees to turn the trunk backwards and line the shoulders up with the line of the shot.

Taking or letting the ball come back further allows a sharper angle into the side wall and hence a sharper rebound across the court. Taking it farther forward means a shallower angle, rebounding the ball more towards the front.

The Front Wall Grid
Squash is unique in major racket sports in that the ball is rebounded into a target area. A player's aim is not directly at the final target. This entails a calculation as to where on the front wall to hit the ball.

In practice these calculations are made by trial and error, and adjustments made as to where the ball is to be hit. If the ball is not going wide enough, move it further across the front wall. Keep adjusting the angle back and forth until you get it right. If the ball is not going back enough aim higher. The exact point on the front wall you aim at will vary depending on your position in the court

Fig 24   Rodney Martin tangos with Chris Dittmar while trying to
retrieve a tight drive.

and the conditions (ball
temperature and so on).

It is often useful to use the
cut line and the imaginary
extension of the half-court line
running up the front wall as
reference points or boundaries
for general target areas.

1   Use the top part of front
wall for your defensive game.
2   Use the bottom part for the
attacking game. Remember to
leave an area for a margin for
error.

Fig 23 (*opposite*)   Ross
Norman prepares to
unleash a backhand drive
at full power. Notice how
the weight is about to
move forward, how the
trunk and shoulders are
turned and how the
backswing is poised and
ready – all perfectly
balanced and coordinated.

3   Use the middle part of the
wall for the pressure game.
4   To get length, hit above the
cut line.
5   From the back, lift drives
above the cut line.
6   When crosscourting from
the back, hit right across the
front wall.
7   When serving forehand
from the right box, aim 2 feet to
the right of the extended half-
court line.
8   When serving forehand
from the left box, aim 3 feet to
the right of the extended half-
court line.

Pace
The third ingredient a player
has control of in directing a
shot is pace. The harder a ball
is hit, the farther it will come
back down the court. A softer
shot will fall sooner and
rebound less.

Summary

The mix of the vertical angle,
horizontal angle and pace
affects all shots. A good
example is the serve, in which
the same angles can be used
and pace makes the difference
between whether the ball is
good, out, or easy.

Achieving length is the most
basic tactical idea in the game.
If it is lost, the height of the
shot is the most crucial factor
in recovering it. Do not hit
hard to get length; hit high.

A player is constantly
adjusting the angle of his shot
to place the ball – the
horizontal angle and the
vertical angle. To hit straight
face the side wall. To angle the
ball into the side, take it behind
the right angle.

7
The Mechanics of a Squash Shot

Aiming

A rifle is aimed by sighting. When aiming from the shoulder, you line the sights up with the target and shoot down the line of the shot. Shooting from the hip is less accurate and involves more feel. The sighting down the line of the shot becomes more imaginary.

Aiming a squash shot is more difficult to understand. Like a golfer, the player is not looking at the target while striking but maintains a mental picture of it from a sense of his position on court in relation to visual cues.

A squash ball is aimed by being struck in a particular place in relation to the body and the body's position on court. This involves positioning, selecting the impact point, directing the swing and improvising with the wrist and forearm.

Feedback, or 'knowledge of results', allows us to adapt positions, impact points and swing until we get it just right. One of the best ways to achieve feedback is practice, the systematic practice that is the theme of this book.

The Stroking Sequence

A squash shot involves the connection by a moving player, of a moving racket, with a moving ball. This complex connection involves an ordered sequence of events

Fig 25   Poised and ready to strike. The deadly eye of Rodney Martin lines the ball up. Note how the front foot is about to fall for a one-two action on the stroke.

performed to split-second timing. In the whole shot sequence a player reacts, moves, prepares, positions, stops, hits and recovers.

The hitting part of this sequence involves the co-ordination of the body and swing.

A player has the best control when he is stopped and steady before he swings. If he is still moving it is easy to lose control over movement and timing.

A squash shot is a one-two action. First the leading foot goes down and then the racket swings through. Accomplishing this action helps ensure the stability of the stance and facilitates transfer of weight.

Before, or as, the racket is drawn back to the backswing position, the upper body must turn in preparation for a full swing. This allows the body and the swing to unwind like a spring into a full and flowing action. After unwinding, the body and shoulder do not become part of the swing but must maintain balance throughout it.

As the foreward swing starts, the body's weight moves into the shot. This transfer of weight is accomplished mainly with the knees as the weight moves from the back leg to the front. As the swing moves down from the backswing position, the front knee bends until impact, after which it tends to straighten, pushing the player back towards recovery. This movement – the one-two action, the turning of the upper body for the backswing and then transfer of weight onto the front foot by bending the knees – is an integral part of the stroke sequence and must be controlled and co-ordinated.

A player's task is to develop control over each part of the sequence and to time their connection and the co-ordination. This will create a flow through the shot.

Time

Time is the crucial element in the connection of the moving racket, ball and player. The more time a player has, the easier the shot. Beginners are continually surprised that top players always seem to have time. One of the ways they do this is by preparing for each shot. Top players arrive in position early, have the racket ready and get a little 'stop' in before hitting. They perform this process quickly and precisely but still take time for the shot.

Racket Preparation

When under pressure beginners often get to a ball but, while they are getting their racket back ready to hit, the ball bounces twice. If only their racket were ready when they arrived they would be ready to swing.

Create time by preparing your racket early. Use this to take time for your shot. A good way to practise racket preparation is to drive solo into the service box or hit across to your partner and take your racket back as soon as the ball hits the front wall. Hold it in the backswing position until you are ready to swing.

Lining the Ball up

If you are in position, on balance, have your racket ready and are just 'stopped' for a split second, waiting for the ball to fall to exactly the right place, then you have the ball lined up. Everything is right and you know it is right before you hit the ball. You cannot get this feeling when you rush. It

Fig 26   Del Harris demonstrates perfect racket preparation for this backhand drive against Chris Robertson. Note the strength of the stance even at a stretch and the power about to unwind from the shoulder.

comes from good preparation, good control and taking time for your shot. Achieving this will increase your accuracy and allow easy adjustment.

The 'stop' before you hit may be a split second and does not need to be a laborious delay. It is a bit like a good squash photograph with the action stopped on the backswing just before the swing.

Summary

1   Step and steady yourself before swinging.
2   Use a one-two action.
3   Turn your shoulder and upper body before swinging.

Fig 27   Ross Norman braces himself for the swing and holds himself steady while the racket powers through the impact area. Note how he keeps focusing on the impact point.

4   Let your weight move into and through the shot. Develop 'flow'.
5   Establish control over each part of the stroke.
6   Create time for your shot.
7   Use a little stop before you hit.
8   Take your racket back when the ball hits the front wall.
9   Prepare so that you can adjust your position, select the impact point and, when necessary, improvise your swing.
10   Line the ball up by stopping on balance in position, preparing your racket and waiting for the ball to fall to exactly the right place.
11   Systematic practice provides the feedback that allows you to improve your aiming of the ball.

8
Movement and Balance

Squash has its own movement. It is a game of fast bursts and sudden stops. This pattern of moving and stopping is performed in seconds and at times, split seconds.

If you timed several squash rallies and worked out the average time available for each shot you would get a time between one and two seconds. This is all the time you have to react, move to position, stop and hit the ball. After hitting, you have the time in between finishing your shot and your opponent's shot to recover to your ready position.

A player uses a complex set of movements in attempting to get to the ball and recover position. He is anticipating, taking off, accelerating, turning, changing direction, jumping, skipping, lunging,

> If you're tired or you've had to run too much in a rally use some lobs and high straight shots until you feel strong and can put the pressure on again. Vary the pace like this throughout the match.
>
> **Jansher Khan**

decelerating, stopping, balancing, twisting, bending, adjusting, pushing back and recovering. These movements need to be controlled and co-ordinated in a simple sequence so that they can be performed quickly and efficiently.

The squash movement sequence involves being ready, moving to position, stopping to hit and then recovering to a ready position again. Your success at it depends on how well you perform each part. As there is little time to work out what to do in a rally, good

performance involves habits. This chapter explains these habits and shows how to develop them.

Being Ready

Being ready to move to the place you want to hit the ball from involves three things: being in the best position to move from (on the T), being ready to move off quickly (ready position), and watching.

On the T

There is one place on the court from which you can get to just about any ball and cover the four corners of the court equally well. This position, with one foot either side of the half-court line and about a racket length or so behind the short line, is called 'on the T'. It's not so far back that you can't get the short shots and not so far up that if the ball passes you you can't get back in time to hit it. It is also central, so you can cover both sides of the court equally well.

Where you stand exactly will vary depending on the conditions and the type of game. If it's cold or your opponent has a good short

Fig 28   In full flight. Del Harris intent on the ball leaves the ground as he lunges forward. Jahangir watches poised on the T.

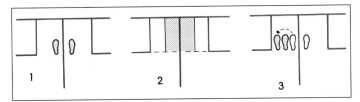

Fig 29 The T. (1) On the T in a ready position: toes to the front, one foot either side of the half court line; (2) recover to the central box area over the imaginary line joining the back of the service boxes and; (3) hang in to the side when your opponent can't crosscourt.

game you should stand up a little so that you can cover the short shots. If you are looking to volley and take the ball early you will stand up more. If the rallies are long and deep you may wish to stay back a little more but you must still be able to cover the short shots.

Sometimes, especially during straight rallies, the ball will pass your opponent but won't come off the back enough to allow a crosscourt. You don't, therefore, have to cover the crosscourt and so can 'hang in' more to the side, making interceptions easier.

Your position then can vary a little, but generally you should try to keep within the central box area. Imagine a line joining the back of the service boxes. You must at least get over (yes, completely over) this line when moving from the back, and at least behind the short line when recovering from the front.

Ready Position

Standing in a ready position is a little like being a sprinter ready to run. The difference in squash is that you have to be ready to move in every direction.

Stand on the T, a racket length behind the short line, feet astride the half-court line, toes to the front. If you have your feet to the side you can be caught out and have to waste valuable time turning before

you can move to the ball.

Crouch slightly or lean forward comfortably with your weight over the balls of your feet. Here you are on your toes. This is where you push off from. Try standing on your heels. You will see that you have to rock forward and hence waste time before you move.

Hold your racket up and forward so you are able to move it quickly for the forehand or backhand. Turn your head and shoulders to watch your opponent and the ball.

Now try out your ready position. Bend your knees slightly, feel your balance, bounce slightly on the balls of

your feet and practise taking off in different directions.

Watching

The vital ingredient in getting to the ball is not how fast you move but when you move. Move as soon as you know where the ball is going. Watch the ball and your opponent. Try to see it coming off the racket and then follow it with your eyes. Often, because of its speed, you will lose the ball on its way to the front wall. Watch your opponent's position, the impact point and swing to try and pick up cues to help you anticipate. Before he hits, ask yourself what shot is coming up. Study him as you move and anticipate, using your experience of the match.

Moving

The great players are the great movers. Hunt, who strode the court rhythmically and won eight British Open titles, was the athlete. Zaman was the dancer. Jahangir, the cat,

Fig 30 'On your toes.' Ross Norman on the T and up ready on his toes switches his attention to the front wall, in an endeavour to pick up Jansher Khan's shot.

39

Ross Norman

The most fundamental thing you can do to get better at squash is to spend a lot of time on court practising and playing games – you won't get better without doing this. Entering and playing competitions is also important and as you progress it's important to sort out your training programme.

Get used to practising on your own and in pairs. Getting length is the fundamental thing to get right. You have got to get a good basic game. If a ball's thrown at you in any part of the court it's important to be able to drive it straight and accurately down the wall – that's the most important fundamental in the game.

The number one practice is up and down the wall and in pairs the most important practice is boast and drive. Even if you have only ten minutes available use it to do some boasting and driving practice.

In your games try to win and try to be as ruthless as you can be. Develop this attitude. Use practice and condition games but in the end there is no substitute for hard matches.

At the end of the day you have to know what training is good for you and what's not, but I would suggest that you concentrate on on-court work – ghosting and court sprints. To lift my standard I spent a long period doing two sessions on court a day. Anyone seriously

Fig 31

thinking about a professional career in squash should do the same.

If you want to get better you can learn a lot from better players. Get out and watch top squash. Try to go to the British Open, to the county championships, and watch the better players in your club. This is part of your squash education. It'll give you new ideas.

---

sprung with a speed and unleashed a power that no other player could live with. Jansher fluctuates between unmatchable bursts of speed, a seemingly instantaneous recovery, and a languid relaxation that flashes into action.

As well as this ability to move well, top players seem to know exactly where and when to move. This is not chance or some innate ability but a matter of constant calculation. A good player judges where

the ball is going and then decides where he should move to and where he should wait for the ball. The place he travels to is his position; the way along which he travels is his path.

Paths and Positions

Remember: don't run to the ball, move to the place you want to hit it from. Half the game of squash is getting to the right place to hit the ball. If

you're in position, on balance, have your racket ready and are waiting for the ball, all you have to do is swing through.

The path to the final position from which the ball is hit is generally more up and down the middle than directly towards the ball. Room must be left between the final position and the ball. Moving up and down the middle allows you to play straight if required, leaves room between yourself and the ball, and allows you to cover both sides of the court if you are wrong when anticipating a shot.

Shadow Practice

Shadow practice is like learning the steps of a new dance. Place a ball on the court floor to act as the impact point of a shot. Practice moving from a ready position on the T to the position for this shot, and then recover. Use the simplest and most economical method to arrive there. Eliminate all unnecessary steps. Prepare for the shot as you move. Once you are happy with your footwork, gradually build up speed. Repeat this procedure to different points around the court.

Practising Movement

Squash movement involves patterns. These can be practised and worked out with shadow practice and also in pairs practice. Keep your movement as simple and efficient as possible. Use occasional sidesteps and

Fig 32 Jansher Khan, the fastest main in squash seems to float to the ball against the world's most attacking and deceptive player, Australian Brett Martin.

Fig 33 Anything to get the ball back. Del Harris, the most athletic of players, demonstrates a total commitment to getting the ball back against Jahangir Khan. Note the open face on the racket ready to slip under the ball, how one hand helps with balance and also cushions the impact of the dive.

sliding half-steps to adjust your footwork to arrive in exactly the right place.

In pairs practice, movement is one of the things you can concentrate on. Don't just hit the ball around; use the best movement you can. Force yourself to step back and approach the shot. When you have time, try to move from the T in simulation of the movement of a game. Try to make it smooth, rhythmic and economical. This book lists a great number of pairs exercises, which can be useful in practising movement. The three listed in Chapter 12 cover different parts of the court and include movement instructions.

Turning and Changing Direction

How good a player is at moving is seen in how well he takes off, turns and changes direction.

When turning, step and point your toes in the direction in which you want to move.

Turn your hips in this direction and swivel on the ball of the back foot. Don't turn in a wide arc, swinging your body and shoulders.

Ideally you will move on court in such a way that you can change direction. Try to move as if you are in a ready position and able to take off in any direction. Move so that you are balanced and your movement is controlled.

Stopping

To have control over a squash ball you need control over your movement while hitting. The crucial part of movement control is stopping for the shot. If you are still moving, twisting, falling or jumping you won't have control over your movement and you won't be accurate and consistent with the ball.

While stopped, you need to be balanced and the correct distance from the ball. There are a number of stances that give you this and they can be

41

Fig 34   Perfect balance at full stretch. Another classic backhand from Jahangir Khan.

adapted for each shot situation.

Balance

Being stopped and on balance for your shot allows your body to be steady so that you can aim the ball. Your lower body is a stable undercarriage for shot generation by the upper body. Without it, exaggerated upper-body movement would lead to less control.

Being stopped and balanced allows a transfer of weight into the shot, which helps provide power and flow. It also provides a bent knee position from which to push back and recover position.

Bend your knees for balance. Try out a stance. Rock back and forward in each direction, using your knees as your suspension system. Don't let your centre of gravity fall outside the area between your feet – you will overbalance. Allow movement of the knees to help you to brake and brace, to adjust your distance from the ball, and to allow a transfer of weight and a strong position from which to push back to the T.

Keep your feet wide for balance. If they are in line like a tightrope walker's you can easily overbalance. This wider stance also allows you reach over a greater impact area.

Distance

It's just as important to move away from the ball, to get the correct distance from it, as it is to move towards it. One of the common faults in squash is that players get too close to the ball. I know this seems strange but when we spend all that effort just getting to the ball we go too far.

Part of the problem, of course, is that we tend to run to the ball – something I have mentioned already. If you are too close to the ball when hitting you can cramp your swing, pull back when hitting, lose power, or look up and lose balance. If you are too far away you can overreach and overbalance.

Use your feet to adjust your final position so that you are an ideal distance from the ball. Plan your path so that you can arrive at the correct distance. It's better to leave a little more

room between you and the ball so that you can move into your shot rather than have to move away. Adjust the final step and where necessary use small adjusting steps when in position. Finally, use your knees; move back and forward on them to adjust your distance while maintaining balance.

When playing and practising, think of keeping outside the service-box sidelines. Of course you will have to go over them but use them as mental barriers, to help stop you running into the ball. Remember to allow room when the ball bounces out from the side (and side and back).

Often in the pressure of a game you will be pushed into poor positions but if you can stop and be balanced you will still be able to play a controlled shot.

Stances

Your choice of stance depends on your movement from the T, the body position required for the shot and the time available. The basic stance is often regarded as the formal or classic stance. It provides excellent balance but can take longer than the open stance as you have to step across your body and have further to push

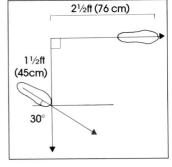

Fig 35   The basic stance

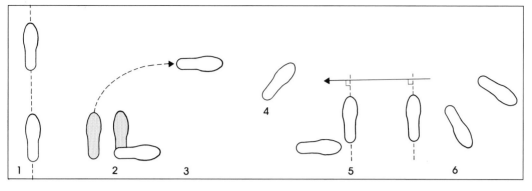

Fig 36   (1) Don't put your feet in line like a tightrope walker. Keep them wide for balance; (2) from a ready position move to a basic stance by swivelling on the right foot and stepping on the left; (3) for a basic stance step so your feet are about 2½ft (76cm) apart and 1½ft (45cm) wide; (4) in an open stance get some width between your feet and use your hips to bring your body and shoulders around; (5) the mid-stance, when braking is not needed – both feet are at right angles to the line of the shot; and (6) the back corner stance – keep your feet wide and evenly balanced to allow reach over a wide range of impact points.

back when recovering. In a game situation, moving from the T and attempting a basic stance can put the body in a poor position. Use the open, mid and back-corner stance where appropriate. (The best stance for each shot is described in Part 3.)

While reading this section try out the stances below and get a feeling for them. Try them out in different positions, not just those described.

Basic Stance

Forehand

1   From a ready position swivel on your right foot and step on the left to point your toes directly at the side wall.
2   Step so that your feet are about 76cm (2½ft) apart and 46cm (1½ft) wide.
3   Angle your right foot backwards about 30 degrees and take your weight on the ball of the foot. This gives you

more movement control than dragging your feet.
4   Bend your front knee so that when you are looking down it just hides your toes. Your front shoulder should be in a vertical line with your toes and knee.
5   Keep your shoulders parallel to the side.
6   Put your weight forward over the front foot (70 per cent weight forward, 30 per cent back.)
7   Practise moving on your knees and reaching for various impact points while keeping your upper body as steady as you can.

Backhand

Repeat the above steps on the backhand side.

Open Stance

This stance is used when going forward on the forehand, especially when under pressure, or when lobbing, crosscourting from a wide position and when stepping back. It's important to swivel on the hips and knees in order to alter the body position.

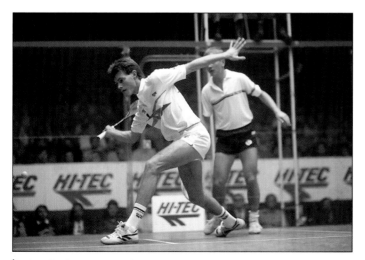

Fig 37   Perfect poise in a classic basic stance from Rodney Martin. Note the arms wide for balance.

43

Fig 38   Del Harris demonstrates power and precision as he lunges forward in an open stance. This stance allows the greatest speed and reach when frontcourt on the forehand.

Forehand

1   From a ready position swivel on the left foot, step back and across on the right and point your toes at the side (that is, step to the side).
2   Try to get some width between your feet.
3   Turn your hips to the side and bring your body and shoulders round too. This movement is important as the open stance does not automatically place the body in the best position for a shot.
4   Let your weight move over the right leg and again line up your foot, your knee and your shoulder.
5   When stroking, consciously turn your shoulders as these will not come round as easily as in the basic stance.

Backhand

It is difficult to maintain balance with an open stance on the backhand and hitting across the body is very restricting. This stance can, however, be used when stepping back to a ball if the shoulder and hips are well turned.

Mid-Stance

We use this comfortable stance around the midcourt when no strenuous braking is needed. Use a little turning jump and swivel to get into position.

Fig 39   World Champion Susan Devoy, poised with weight evenly balanced over both feet in mid-stance, starts her downswing on the backhand.

1   Stand with your toes pointing at the side, feet roughly parallel and just over a shoulder width apart.
2   Turn your hips for the backswing.
3   Start with your weight evenly balanced between both feet and let the weight rock from the back foot to the front.

Back-Corner Stance

With this stance you can get right down to the ball, allowing a wide range of impact points, and also swivel on the knees and hips to hit straight or boast.

1   Stand with feet apart and evenly balanced with your toes pointing into the back corner.
2   Bend your knees so that they move forward, over and obscuring your toes.
3   Squat down into a strong stance.

Recovery

In a squash rally you can only stop twice. Stop when you are hitting the ball and stop when you are back on the T. In between, keep moving.

Squash revolves round possession of the T. When in difficulty, top players give themselves time to recover it, rather than attempting a lucky shot which leaves them out of position. When on the T, they know they will be able to cover all shots. If you watch them in action you will see how hard they work to get back in position before their opponent hits the ball. You will also notice how they sense as soon as their opponent is off the T and exploit this with moving and pressure shots.

To get possession of the T, go there. Don't stop. Go there immediately you have finished your shot. Don't stop because

Fig 40 Jahangir Khan in a strong back corner stance turns his shoulder and gets down to the ball, preparing to power it out of the back.

but do allow room for your opponent to get to the ball if you play short. Run backwards, turning your head and shoulders, but move so you are ready to move forward again instantly.

Key Point
Only stop twice in a rally. Be back on the T before your opponent hits the ball.

Summary

1   Being ready to move means being on the T, in a ready position and watching.
2   For a ready position, stand a racket's length behind the short line, toes to the front, one foot either side of the half-court line, and crouch forward on the balls of your feet.
3   To position, don't run to the ball; move to the place you want to hit the ball from.
4   Move up and down the middle of the court.
5   Practise steps and develop smooth, efficient movement.
6   Stop on balance for your shot.
7   Bend your knees for balance.
8   Don't get too close to the ball: you will cramp your swing and could lose balance.
9   Think about keeping outside the service-box sidelines.
10   Practise using all the different stances. Use the basic, open, mid and back-corner stances.
11   In a squash rally you can only stop twice – stop when hitting and stop when you are back on the T.

you're relieved you've got the ball, relaxed at the end of your exertion or curious to see how the shot's gone.

As you finish your shot, pull your weight up and push off from the bent-knee position so that no time is lost. Move smoothly and comfortably, so that you can react and change direction if required. Take as direct a path to the T as possible, while allowing your opponent access to the ball. When recovering from right in the back after a straight drive, circle back via the half-court line. Walk briskly or trot. If your opponent's ball is short or has come right off the back, move directly to the T. From the front move directly to the T

9
Swing

The path of the racket head through the ball directs the shot. The more precise this path, the more precise the shot.

The basic squash drives use a U-shaped swing and it's the action required to produce this that we look at first. The type, path and size of swing you use, however, must be adapted to the particular shot and situation. We use many types of swing: a full, compact or short swing; an overhead smash action; the underarm pat; a half-volley; pushes, punches, flicks; swings that move horizontally, downward, upward, cut through the impact point and slice along the side of the ball.

With the basic control you have over the racket head, an understanding of the squash action and a well controlled basic swing, you will be able to adapt your swing for each of situations outlined in Part 3.

The control you develop over the basic swing is crucial to your control of the shot. Use the technique practices described in Chapter 10 and endeavour to be aware of your swing. Develop a smooth, flowing, rhythmic action that gives you power and control. Practise it so that you can reproduce it consistently again and again. This is called a grooved swing. A grooved swing will give you accuracy and consistency.

Squash Action

The squash action is a throwing action. When we pat we use an underarm throwing action. The overhead smash uses an overarm throw. For our main strokes we use a side-on throw. It's like a sidearm throw in cricket or the skimming of a stone on a lake.

The backhand action is used less commonly and this unfamiliarity can present a few problems in first learning a backhand stroke. It's like a backhand slap or like throwing a frisbee. Once learned it is the most comfortable stroke, because it's played with the front shoulder and is well clear of the body.

The squash action co-ordinates movements around three joints – the wrist, the elbow and the shoulder.

Wrist Action

The wrist action should be firm and controlled, allowing the player to feel control over the racket head right through the shot. The smoother the wrist action, the more grooved the stroke. This action can range between a locked wrist, in which the wrist becomes part of the forearm, and a 'wristy' action, which is used to compensate for position, to accelerate the racket head, or to provide deception.

Forearm Action

The basis of a squash swing is a forearm action hinging on the elbow. This incorporates both the 'turning' and 'hinging' actions of the forearm.

The turning action of the forearm involves pronation

Fig 41   Mir Zaman Gul prepares to drive against Ross Norman. Note how the elbow and butt lead the swing.

and supination. In the swing the elbow leads and the racket trails behind at about a right angle to the forearm. As the arm turns this accelerates the racket head through to the impact point, at which the racket and arm are in line.

If you hold your arm out palm up and turn it over, this movement is called pronation. It's used on the forehand. Turning it back the other way is supination. This is the backhand action that is rather like throwing a frisbee.

Arm Action

The action initiated in the trunk by the turning of the upper body moves like a whip through the shoulder, elbow and wrist to the racket. The upper arm action from the shoulders starts in line with the shoulders and swings right across the body. Point your arm out in line with your shoulder. Now swing it across your body to point in line with your shoulders. Reversing this movement gives the backhand arm action.

Relax the shoulders to allow maximum movement and to let the gentle body movement of the upper body translate into the arm.

The Co-Ordinated Action

From a V to a V
Point your arm out in line with your shoulders and bend your elbow to make a V. Staying in the line of your shoulders, bring your elbow and forearm down to waist height. This downstroke is the first part of the swing.

Next, come through, leading with the point of the elbow, forearm trailing, palm up and heel of the hand facing forward. Let the heel turn gradually to the vertical palm

Fig 42 Jansher under pressure tries everything to get the ball back but it's gone.

(pronate) at the point in front of your body where your arm is in line. This is the impact point. As your elbow travels right through across your body, bend your arm into a V and keep the wrist up.

On the backhand side, push your elbow across your stomach and make a V. For the downstroke, drop your hand behind your shoulder and take it down to your waist, with the palm down. Turn your forearm through to the impact point and bring your palm to the vertical. Let the elbow sit in just above your hip and swing up to a V, in line with your shoulders.

Down, Through and Up
The first part of the swing is back and down. The second, with the elbow leading, is through. The third is up into a V again.

Full Swing

Forehand

1 *Ready* Stand in a strong stance facing the side wall with the racket and wrist up in

front. Use the 'feel check' to feel control of the racket head.
2 *Backswing* Take the racket head straight back to a position in line with the shoulders and above head height. Lead with the racket edge as this will open the racket face and move the wrist back for the wrist action. Let the elbow sit in between the hip and shoulder.

More power is developed in the backswing if you take the shoulder back and round. Power is also generated with a fuller backswing by taking the arm and elbow higher.
3 *Downswing* Pull the elbow, butt and racket head down in line with the shoulders. The swing opens out here and doesn't come through tightly or round on the ball.
4 *Throughswing* Lead into the through part of the swing with the elbow and butt of the racket. In photographs of leading players you will notice that the racket is often obscured and just the butt of the handle is visible. This means that the racket is trailing at approximately a right angle. Turn your arm smoothly through to the impact point.

Fig 43 The Forehand Swing

(a) Perfect preparation. A high steady backswing, with the shoulder and trunk turned. Jansher Khan is in an excellent position for the stroke to flow comfortably across his body. Note his concentration on the ball throughout this sequence.

(b) The front foot goes down and braces the body, the racket is about to come down with the elbow leading and the trunk has opened to the ball. Note the V in the backswing.

(c) The front knee bends and the weight transfers. The elbow and the butt lead the racket as the forearm is about to accelerate the racket through the impact point. This turning action of the forearm is called pronation.

Fig 44 The Backhand Swing

(a) Perfect preparation and positioning. The racket is high overhead, the shoulder turned and the elbow right back behind the body. Jansher is about to stride into the shot, concentrating on the ball.

(b) Jansher's foot goes down and he braces himself to keep good balance throughout the swing. The racket starts to go down and around the body. Note how the knees provide balance.

(c) The weight continues to move into the shot and the shoulder turns. The butt comes through first and the forearm starts to accelerate the racket through to impact. This forearm action is called supination.

(d) The arm is straight at impact. Note the open racket face, the perfect balance, the concentration on the ball, the wrist up and the V grip.

(e) The swing comes through across the body. Note how Jansher holds himself steady as the racket swings through and how he is still concentrating on the impact zone.

(f) The racket swings through to a full follow-through with the wrist up and the racket head controlled. Note the swing has moved from a V to a V. His body is still balanced and not swinging with the shot. Jansher is already starting to push back.

(d) Jansher steady throughout the stroke concentrates on the impact area. The arm has straightened and the wrist is still up, giving good control over the racket head. Note the open racket face and the V grip.

(e) Note the perfect balance and control over the racket head as Jansher holds himself steady and swings right through across his body.

(f) The swing has come right through in a smooth curve. Note Jansher still has good control of the racket head and is already pushing back from the shot.

49

Fig 45 **The Forehand**: High

(a) Ross Norman brings his backswing down low to help come under the ball.

(b) Using an open racket, he bends, reaches down under the ball and swings up through it. Note the straight arm reach at impact, the grip, wrist and control of the racket head.

(c) The follow-through. Note how balance has been maintained and how the racket head is still well controlled.

Fig 46 **The Backhand**: High

(a) Ross Norman brings his backhand down to help get under the ball. Note how it is already open and he is well prepared and seems to be waiting for the ball.

(b) At impact note the open racket face, the control of the racket head by the wrist and grip and how the racket head is coming up through the ball.

(c) Ross swings through in a full smooth follow-through maintaining balance and racket head control throughout the shot.

5 *Impact* Impact is just behind the front knee, where the racket makes a right angle with the side wall and is parallel with the floor. If the ball is low, use your knees to get down to it and avoid dropping the wrist. The wrist must be up in relation to the forearm to obtain the best racket-head control. The angle of the racket face will depend on the path of the throughswing. If it's more open than the throughswing you will be applying cut.

6 *Follow-through* Continue to swing straight through the impact area so that your racket is still swinging down the line of the shot. Don't pull it up, turn it across the body, or roll over it. Let the elbow swing through and the forearm hinge and swing up into a V with the racket overhead, slightly closed and in line with the shoulders. Try to keep your wrist up here. Use the 'feel' check to see if you still have control over the racket head.

7 *Preparation* From this follow-through position, take the racket directly back to the backswing position. This is achieved very simply by hinging the movement on the elbow. Efficient preparation like this creates more time for your swing.

8 *Practice* Practise the swing off court as one smooth movement. Try to develop a rhythm. Stop occasionally and check your racket-head control at various points. Use a short pause on the backswing (point A) and follow-through (point B). Try to develop a grooved swing between points A and B.

Backhand

1 *Ready* Stand in a strong stance facing the side wall with the racket and wrist up in front. Use the 'feel check' to feel control of the racket head.

2 *Backswing* Turn your shoulder and, leading with the racket edge, take your hand round your shoulder. You can rest your hand up on the shoulder, or take your hand further up and round your neck. The racket here on the backswing is pointing behind the body. (On a very full follow-through some top players take the racket right round so it's pointing at the front wall but this is not something you should try to emulate.) Turn the trunk and shoulder to develop more power on the backhand when required.

3 *Downswing* Take the racket down and behind the body. Open the swing up, swinging right down under the ball.

4 *Throughswing* Lead into the through part of the swing with the elbow and butt of the racket. In the photographs you will see the racket trailing the forearm at a right angle, with the racket face completely open. Turn the forearm smoothly through to the impact point.

5 *Impact* Impact on the backhand is in front of the knee (because the shoulder is at the front of the body.) The racket here is in line with the arm; the wrist is up in relation to the forearm and if possible parallel to the floor.

6 *Follow-through* Continue to swing through the impact area but don't lock the elbow. That will lead to a straight-arm follow-through from the shoulder and a dropped wrist. Let the swing straighten at impact but tuck the elbow in slightly as it moves through so that the follow-through swings through to a V in line with the shoulders. Keep the wrist up so that you have control of the racket head and the follow-through is compact.

7 *Preparation* From the follow-through position, take the racket directly back to the backswing position. Open the racket face as you do so and take your hand round your shoulder. Good preparation creates time for your shot.

8 *Practice* Practise the swing off court as one smooth movement. Try to co-ordinate the turning of the shoulder with a smooth, flowing swing. Pause on the backswing and follow-through. Practise to groove your swing.

Swing Size

The size of the swing you use depends on the pace and control you want. A compact swing tends to be more controlled. A fuller swing with a shoulder turn and transfer of weight generates more pace.

It's very difficult to hit a ball softly with a full swing. Hitting softly means the racket must be moving slowly at impact and it's difficult to time a long, slow swing to connect exactly where you want. For touch shots, use a shorter swing.

Compact and short swings should also be used when time is short, when the path of the swing proves difficult when balance and positioning are awkward, when you are restricted by the walls and when precise control is needed.

Don't try to use a full swing all the time. You need to be well positioned and able to brace yourself against the turning of the upper body. If you can't, then the body loses balance and control.

If not well positioned, use a swing that will allow you to keep balance. If pressurized, use a swing that will allow you to time the ball more easily. Adjust the size of your swing for the pace and control you want.

51

Fig 47 **The Kill**

(a)   The high preparation for the kill as Ross Norman prepares to hit down on and through the ball.

(b)   Ross chooses to take the ball high and cuts down on the back of the ball as he comes through it. Note the wrist control.

(c)   The racket moves through on a lower arc before swinging up into the follow-through position. The kill swing follows a more diagonal path than the drive. Note the racket head control.

Compact Swing

A compact swing balances control and pace and should be used frequently in matches. Take your racket head straight back in line with your shoulder to ear height and swing through again to ear height.

Short Swing

Use the short swing for touch and control on drops, lobs and volleys. Start by pointing your racket at the back wall, use very little backswing and, with a firm wrist action, push through. This short swing has a shallower curve than the exaggerated downswing of the full U-shaped swing.

Developing your Swing

1   Develop an attitude towards your swing like that of a golfer, who practises swinging several times before each shot. Your swing is a crucial part of your game. It can be worked at and is worth improving in the long term.
2   Be aware of what your racket is doing. Try to keep control over your racket head at all times. Don't let it wave around. Use the feel and wobble checks. Check your grip regularly.
3   Practise swinging without the ball. Be precise with your movements. Study each part of the swing and use the feel check at the beginning and end of the swing. Most of all, develop a rhythm in your movement. Feel it.
4   Practise on court for technique and use the practices described in the next chapter.

Summary

1   Develop a smooth, flowing, rhythmic action that gives both power and control.
2   Develop a grooved swing that gives accuracy and consistency.
3   The squash action is a side-arm throwing action.
4   Keep your wrist firm and controlled.
5   Lead into the through part of the swing with the elbow and the racket butt.
6   Relax your shoulder.
7   Swing from a V to a V – down, through and up.
8   Use a compact or short swing when hitting softly, under pressure, and when precise control is needed.
9   Develop good racket-head control with the grip and wrist action.
10   Practise swinging off court without the ball and on court using the technique practices.

First get control over your racket and the ball, then develop rhythm and power.

10
Practising Technique

Improving Technique

Technique, as we have said before, is a habit. The object of this book is to help you develop better squash habits and thereby improve your game. The best way to develop habits is by repetition. Repetitive practice is not readily available in the game situation. In matches you should be thinking tactically; in practice you can think technically.

Make time to learn, practise and develop your technique. It is the basis of your game. Practise it off court, when warming up, and with solo, pairs and practice games on court. Develop an awareness of what you are doing technically. Don't rush around in matches. Try to implement the technique you have developed.

Mental Practice

Mental practice – or mental rehearsal, as it is often called – has been well researched and used in many sports. It involves the mind running through and organizing responses but stopping the body carrying them out. The player practising sees a mental image of himself completing a skill. This use of imagination assists concentration, attention to specific aspects of performance, and in building confidence.

Imagine preparing for a

> Practise grooving your strokes so you can get the ball really tight. Concentrate on hitting up and down the wall until you're seeing the ball like a football. Then when you get on in a game you know you've practised that shot over and over again and it's there.
>
> **Lucy Soutter**

particular shot – being in position, the stance, racket preparation, waiting for the ball, swinging through and the result. As well as the visual display, try to feel the sensations – the grip, swing, impact and body movements.

There are two types of mental rehearsal. First, you can visualize pictures of yourself as someone else would see you – as on a TV screen. This is external imagery. Second, you can imagine pictures as you would see them if you were really doing it. This is called internal imagery. Some people find it effective to be away in a quiet place with their eyes closed when practising mental rehearsal while others can do it in the physical practice situation.

Use mental practice as another tool to develop the best technique you can.

Movement Practice

Shadow Practices

Front Corners
From a ready position just behind the short line, run forward towards the front forehand corner. Turn your

body to the side as you run and prepare your racket. Play a forehand straight drive with the one-two action (one, foot down; two, swing through). Push back off the leading leg and run backwards to the ready position. Repeat on the backhand side and continue alternating corners.

Try to play a smooth grooved stroke.

Back Corners
From a ready position, step back on the foot nearest the corner and point your toes in the direction you wish to go. Swivel on the other foot. Run or lunge-jump into the corner to land in a squat position. To recover, step back towards the T on the outside foot and walk briskly. Repeat on the other side.

Four Corners
Repeat the above two exercises together, pausing briefly in a ready position after each movement.

Turning
1 *Ready position* Start in a ready position.
2 *Turning step* Step and point your right foot to the side.
3 *Step* Step across your

53

When I was at school I used to practise a regular practice sequence most days. I'd start on the backhand, hitting from the corner, and after fifteen minutes, timed on my stopwatch, I'd move over to the forehand for fifteen minutes. We were told that Hunt used to practise like that.

After the drives I'd spend ten minutes on straight drops each side and then I'd work through the other shots, concentrating on the attacking volleys.

Del Harris

body on the left and as you do so turn your body, prepare your racket, and swing, using the one-two action.

4 *Recover and turn* Push back off the left foot and swivel on the right. Stride, on the left to the T.

5 *Step* Stride through on the right, turning your body and preparing your racket as you do so. Swing through.

Sidestep and Lunge
Adapt the above exercise, using the full width of the court and several sidesteps.

Ghosting

Ghosting uses shadow practice routines as fitness as well as movement practice. For training times, see Chapter 44. An example may be between six and ten sets of one minute ghosting with one minute's rest.

Random Ghosting
Move to imaginary points around the court and return to the T after each shot.

Stations
Mark out (use old squash balls or half-balls) a number of stations on the court floor before the exercise. Run from a ready position each time. Try to keep up the quality of your movement with good racket preparation, a body turn and a one-two action.

See how many stations you can get to in a set time (say, one minute).

Numbers and Signs
When working with a partner, one can be ghosting and the other instructing. This can involve split-second changes in instructions so that you are always prepared to move in any direction and to change direction.

The player giving

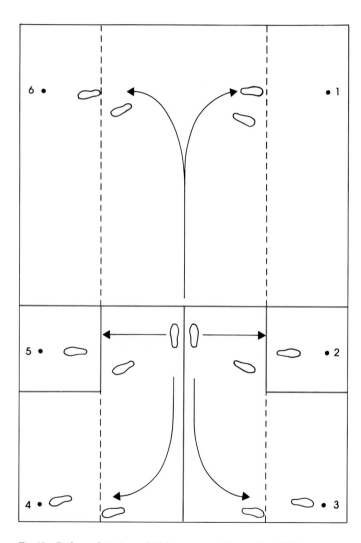

Fig 48 Paths and stations: (1) Move up and down the middle; (2) try to keep outside the 'sidelines'; (3) move directly to a spot one step away from your position; (4) don't run to the ball, move to the place you want to hit it from.

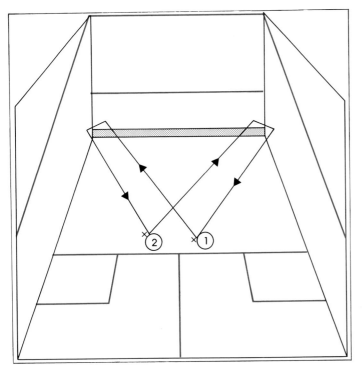

Fig 49   The corner exercise. (1) forehand crosscourt front/side, (2) backhand crosscourt front/side.

and practice turning the upper body and shoulder for each shot.

The Double-Corner Exercise
Forehand crosscourt front/side, backhand straight front/side, backhand crosscourt front/side, forehand straight front/side, and so on.

Concentrate on footwork, turning from a basic stance in the forehand crosscourt position, right round to the side for the backhand straight, and so on.

Boasting
Continuous boasting side to side, one forehand and one backhand.
Try to lunge in on the front foot, push back, sidestep, run and adjust your feet so that you can lunge in on the front foot on the other side.

This is an excellent fitness exercise. Start with 6 sets of 20 and build up either the sets or the numbers.

instructions can call the number of a station or point in the direction his partner must run.

Court Movement Practice

Pairs practice is ideally suited for practising movement. Squash movement, however, can also be practised in solo practice sessions, and incorporated into interval training.

Solo Movement Practice

The Corner Exercise
Forehand crosscourt to hit the front wall then the side wall (front–side), to screw out for a backhand to the opposite front corner.
Let the weight rock back and forth gently between the feet

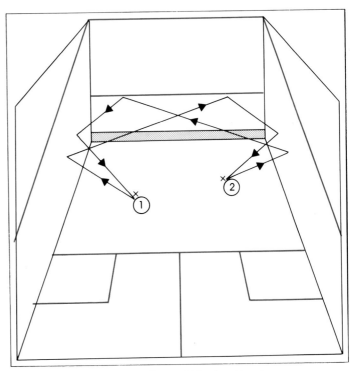

Fig 50   Boasting: (1) backhand boast, (2) forehand boast.

55

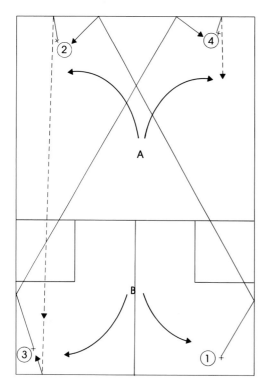

Fig 51 Boast and drive: A in the frontcourt straight driving; B in the backcourt boasting. (1) B forehand boast; (2) A backhand straight drive; (3) B backhand boast; (4) A forehand straight drive and so on.

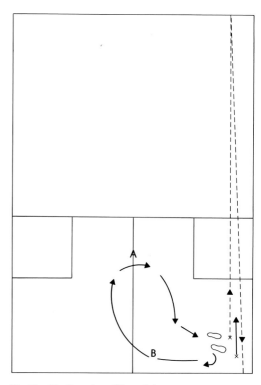

Fig 52 Circling: A and B straight driving and circling to recover the T via the half court line.

Pairs Movement Practice

Boast and Drive
Player A in the front court should lunge in, bending his knees in a strong stance, and push back from this stance towards the T after each straight drive. If B in the back court straight drives and then boasts this gives A time to recover to a ready position on the T and concentrate a little more on his movement.

If A drops and drives, this gives B time to recover the T and then practise the path to the ball from the T.

Circling
This is an ideal exercise to practise movement in and out of the back corners. From a ready position A moves into the back to the side of the ball and straight drives while B sidesteps towards the half-court line (creating room for A) and walks up to a ready position on the T. This is one of the game's basic patterns of movement and is well worth practising.

Diagonal Exercise
A crosscourts, B volleys, A boasts, B crosscourts, and so on. This is just one example of the many exercises allowing players to practise movement up and down the court.

After crosscourting, A will push off backwards and then have to turn and run to the back corner. B in a ready position steps across to volley and pushes back to a ready position on the T, again ready to move forward. A boasts and walks up to a ready position on the T ready to volley, while B moves forward to crosscourt, and so on throughout the practice.

> Pairs practice is important, because you are practising shots in a moving situation. It's easy to get bored, so go on court having worked out what practices you want to do.
>
> **Lucy Soutter**

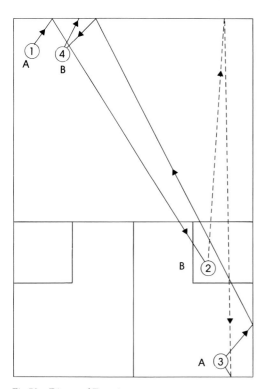

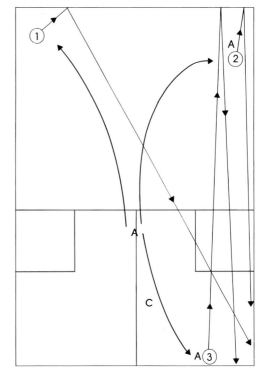

Fig 53 Diagonal Exercise:
(1) A crosscourts, (2) B straight volleys,
(3) A boasts (4), and B crosscourts.

Fig 54 Three Corner Exercise: Coach C
anchored in back corner feeds randomly
for A to move from the T and (1)
crosscourt (2) straight drive from the
front and (3) straight drive from the
back. More pressure is applied when C
volleys.

PRACTISING TECHNIQUE

Coaching Movement Exercises

Working with a coach will allow you to work on specific movement problems in various parts of the court. The coach should feed the ball easily at first, work in movement from the T, and gradually build up the pressure.

It may be useful to place a ball on the court floor and work out the path and positioning. Once well into the movement, the coach can then increase the pressure by pressure feeding – taking the ball early before a pupil has had time to recover the T.

The professional coach will design the exercises for a pupil's individual needs. Exercises easily developed for this are anchored practices, in which the coach stays in one corner, or exercises in which the pupil can only hit straight, whether to the front or to the back.

The Three-Corner Exercise
An anchored practice.
The coach C feeds for pupil A to crosscourt, straight drive from the front, or straight drive from the back (Fig 54).

Whole-Court Straight Driving
The coach C moves from side to side, feeding the ball anywhere in the court for A to straight drive.

Straight Drops
The coach C moves from side to side and feeds for A to make straight drops.

> If you have got a programme, then you can see how you are improving and with that improvement you will keep getting more and more motivated.
>
> **Lucy Soutter**

57

Three-Count Stroking Sequence

Practise your swing, your stance and co-ordinating the two, both on and off court, with the stroking sequence. Start slowly and 'feel' that you have control over each part of the sequence. Build up the pace at which you can perform the sequence, while maintaining control and rhythm. After mastering the basic sequence use different steps and stances.

Ready Position
Stand as if on court, feet astride the half-court line, weight forward on the balls of your feet, knees slightly bent, racket up in front, racket face vertical and wrist up.

Step
Count one. Step across your body to the side on the left foot to a basic stance, swivelling on the right foot. As you step turn your upper body, take your shoulder round and your racket back and overhead.
   Count 'pause'. Pause slightly after your foot goes down and before swinging.

Swing
Count two. Hold your racket steady on the backswing and then swing smoothly through to the follow-through position. As you swing, bend your knees and allow your body to turn so that you are co-ordinating swing and body movement.

Recover
Count three. When you have completely finished the swing, push back from the bent-knee position with one movement to the ready position.

Repeat
Repeat on the other side.

Fig 55   **The stroking sequence**

(a)   Ready position.

(d)   Recover. Push back to the T.

(b)　Step. Swivel step and prepare your racket for a forehand.

(c)　Swing. Swing through.

(e)　Ready position. Turn for a backhand.

(f)　Step. Swivel step and prepare your racket for a backhand etc.

Technique Practices

Technique breaks down under pressure. Don't practise technique at a level where it's breaking down and is erratic. There is also little point in practising repeatedly (once the initial learning has been acquired) at a level where it's very easy and comfortable. Progress your practice so that you are gradually performing what you are capable of doing in less time or with more accuracy. Give yourself targets and gradually increase the pace at which you can exercise. The progression below shows some of the stages you can go through.

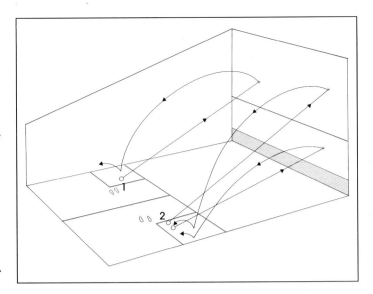

Fig 56   Technique Practice. (1) Service box drives all above the cut line. (2) Service box drives one above the cut line and one below.

Service-Box Drives

All Above the Cut Line

Practise driving to the service box. See how many shots you can land in it continuously out of ten. Take your racket back when the ball hits the front wall. Hold it steady. Step back and move your feet round between shots. Stop in a strong stance. Bend your knees when hitting and swing smoothly down and up.

One Above and One Below the Cut Line

Practice the technique as above, but every second ball is a full drive, hit below the line and into the box. The softer shot above the cut line gives you more time to get back in control.

All Below the Cut Line

At this level you will have little time to recover from mistakes. Create time with good preparation and try to build up the number of accurate shots you can play.

Reflex Drives in Front of the Short Line

Your technique may well break down at this level but if you practise it and work up to it you will improve the level at which you can get control. If you can hit the ball fast and hard here without your technique breaking down you have excellent control.

Length Drives

Practise length drives several feet out from the side wall so that you can get into a rhythm without scraping the balls off the side. Practising from the back like this allows you to use a full rhythmic swing and gives you time before the next shot. Use a bouncy ball that will sit up so that you can develop rhythm; if necessary, use a faster ball (blue, red or white dot) and occasionally let the ball bounce twice.

Feeding Practice

Feeding practice by a coach or partner provides a ball that you can hit full out and have retrieved for you so that the practice can be systematic and repetitive.

Summary

1   Technique is a habit. Practise to develop good habits.
2   Use mental practice. Imagine playing particular shots. It's another tool to help technique and skill learning.
3   Practise movement using shadow practice, ghosting, and solo and pairs court-movement practices.
4   Work on movement with your coach, gradually improving your ability to move well under pressure.
5   Practise your stance and swing with the three-count stroking sequence.
6   Gradually build up your ability to keep sound technique under increasing pressure by using the technique practices.

Shots are your weapons in the squash battle. Your victory or defeat depends on how accurate and consistent they are and how effectively they are used. Part 3 considers how, when and where to play and learn these shots. An entire chapter is given to each shot, and each is considered under the following three headings.

Tactics and Target Area

When looking at each shot, we consider its place and purpose in the structure of the game. When should it be used and why?

Combinations are the standard moves you should learn and use so that they become automatic responses in your game.

Many players play without knowing exactly where they want the ball to go when they play a particular shot. If you know exactly where you want the ball to go (rather than having a vague idea), then you can improve your accuracy by adjusting your position, the angles and the pace of the shot.

Use targets and a clearly defined target area in practice to improve accuracy. Place a small object on the floor or stick a target on the wall. Move these around to the exact place you want to aim for when practising.

Technique and Variations

Technique helps give you control over the shot. This section explains the basics of the shot using the ideas we have developed in Part 2.

Each shot has many variations and adaptions. This section in no way pretends to be comprehensive but points out the main variations in each shot, in placement, pace, technique and deception.

Practice Progression and Practices

The practice progression is an example for each shot of how to develop and extend your practices. It is designed to help you understand how to adapt practices to the level where you can most usefully practise and benefit.

The practice progression starts with the most basic practice ingredients of a shot. This is to help the player and particularly the coach understand the structure of the shot, as well as to give the beginner (and beginner pupil) a starting point. From this basic level it shows how practices can be progressed to a quite advanced level.

To find the best level to practise you move backwards or forwards along the progression until you reach a level where it is difficult but improves with practice. If it is too difficult, move backwards; if easy, move forwards.

Games and matches provide sporadic practice at squash shots. The best way to improve a skill is by repetition. Practise grooving your shots accurately and consistently into their target area.

Each practice section has been divided into four parts. *Solo* practices allow you to concentrate on technique and accuracy. *Pairs* practices allow you to practise technique, target areas and movement. *Condition games* allow you to practise the shot in a competitive situation. *Practice games* allow you to practise in the match situation.

11
The Straight Drive

One of the essential elements in squash is defence – placing the ball where it is safe and where it provides difficulties for your opponent.

The straight drive is the tightest shot in squash. It stays 'tight' or close to the side wall for its whole path. At its best, it will move in close and 'cling', or roll along the wall. This obviously makes it difficult for your opponent.

Both technically and tactically the straight drive is the most fundamental shot in the game. Technically it is the first to learn. The side-on action and learning to turn to face the side wall when playing it are two of the games fundamentals.

If the straight drive is hit at a right angle to the side wall it will travel parallel to the side. To get it 'tight' it must be angled in. This means that you must position, prepare and pause so as to allow the ball to come slightly past the right angle and to the ideal impact point. Experiment with and adjust this angle until you get it just right. Remember, the straight drive must be *hit past the right angle*.

Tactics

Tactically the straight drive sets the pattern of the game. It is the shot that gives the game order. All other shots can be seen as variations from the basic pattern of straight driving. This tactical pattern is not just for aesthetic appeal but because it works as a tactic. It is good advice to say, 'Keep your game mainly straight and vary it from there.'

Venturing to the forecourt or crosscourt involves risk and the decision to do this must be taken at the right time. If a game becomes loose, then 'go straight and get length'.

Target Area

Unless you are particularly fortunate and get the straight drive to roll or cling to the side wall, it will generally touch at one point only. It is ideally placed if this is the same area your opponent would wish to hit it from.

Endeavour to hit the side wall behind the back of the service box. Keep a count when practising or coaching. How many can you get out of ten? Aim to get the ball to bounce and come out off the back wall. This is good length. Dying length is hit a little shorter (often for the back of the service box) so the second bounce dies on the back wall. An ideal shot to practise is to get the ball to travel straight to the back, rebound and cling.

Vary the height of your shot

Fig 57   Rodney Martin in classic stance, faces the side wall and drives straight.

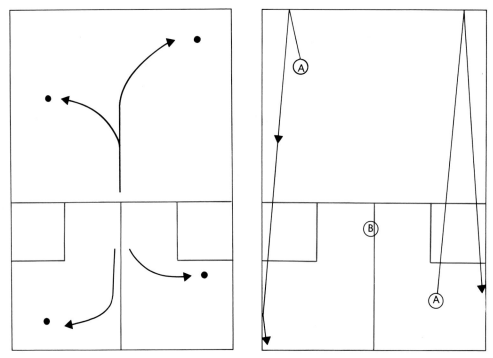

Fig 58   Path: Don't run to the ball. Move up and down the middle to a place at the side of the ball. Keep the ball between yourself and the wall. Tactics: Keep your game mainly straight. Angle straight drives to hit the side wall behind the service box or to beat a volley.

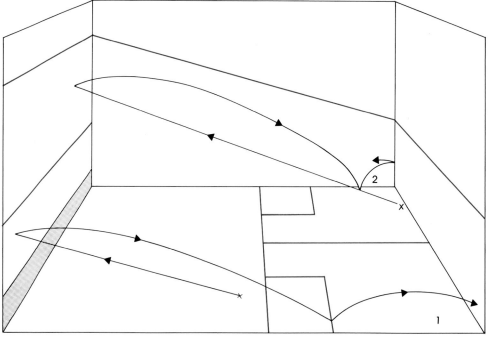

Fig 59   Target Areas: (1) The loose ball hit for dying length, so the second bounce dies at the back wall nick. (2) A good length that will force an opponent to take the ball off the back wall.

on the front wall to adjust length, and vary the angle behind the right angle to adjust width. It is often easier to concentrate on one of these at a time, get it grooved in and then move on. Practise and get used to using various heights and paces of shot.

Technique

Forehand

Path
'Don't run to the ball. Move to the place you want to hit the ball from.'

The most common fault on the straight drive is that players move directly to the ball. This often results in an impact point in front of the right angle, hence bringing the ball out from the wall and even crosscourt. For the straight drive, move to the side of the ball.

> Get your straight drives as tight as you can so that there is no danger of conceding a stroke or of your opponent volleying it.
>
> **Ross Norman**

Position
As you are moving, turn your body to the side, get your shoulder round and prepare your racket. Your movement should be more up and down the centre of the court, leaving room to step in towards the side wall. Position yourself so that at impact you are facing the side and the ball is between you and the side wall.

Stance
Basic Stance   Practise a basic stance and use it when you have time. It puts your body in

Fig 60   **The Straight Drive**

(a)   Neil Harvey positions to the side of a tight ball.

(b)   He lets it come between himself and the side and comes under and up on it.

(c)   The ball travels high down the wall giving him time to recover the T.

Fig 61   The Forehand Straight Drive

(a)   Ross Norman moves off from the T and starts to take his racket back on the forehand.

(b)   Eye on the ball, he turns to the side-on position, takes his racket up and waits for the ball to come in between himself and the side.

the best position for the shot. At impact, your shoulders will be nearly parallel to the side but a little more open. Allow your weight to transfer from the back foot to the front through the shot and allow your body and shoulders to turn with the shot, but do not swing your body. Your body must be balanced and controlled through the whole sequence.

Open Stance   The open stance allows quicker movement to the ball than the basic stance and is often employed on the forehand from the front. Although regarded as unorthodox (and by many as incorrect), it is the stance used by the top players most of the time. Make sure that you manage to turn your upper body to the side and twist your hips, otherwise you will be continually hitting crosscourt or will pull the ball out from the side and give away strokes.

Swing
Generally on the straight drive you will endeavour to use a full swing. Adapt this to a compact or short swing when varying the pace or relieving pressure – with, for example, a straight lob.

Backswing   From the line of the shoulders extend the backswing back and round from the shoulder until you feel it is restricted (up to 45 degrees). Keep the racket clear of the body and overhead. Cock the wrist at about 45 degrees to the forearm.

Impact   The impact point for the forehand straight drive is behind the right angle and generally just behind the knee. A strong basic stance will give you a wide range of impact points and hence allow adaptations in the stroke to get the correct angle.

Follow-through   Relax the shoulder and let it come through in front of the body. Let the elbow come right across the body for full movement from the shoulders (from a V to a V). The wrist should be at approximately 45 degrees to the forearm, the racket slightly past the line of the shoulders (say 20 degrees) and the racket head about 60 degrees from the floor, with the racket face closed about 20 degrees.

(c)   Leaving plenty of room he faces the side and strides in pointing his toe at the wall.

(d)   The ball comes in between Ross and the side. This is a fine study of the distance a player should leave between himself and the ball. Note how the swing is in line with the shoulders.

(e)   At impact Norman holds himself in a strong stance and releases the power in his shoulders. To be hit straight a ball must be struck just behind a right angle with the wall.

(f)   On the follow-through the body is still balanced and the racket controlled.

Backhand

Path

As you move to position, take a path that will allow the last step to be on your front foot. Vary the length of your steps and where necessary use an adjusting step (as soldiers do when marching and out of step) to facilitate this.

Some top players can hit the backhand beautifully off either foot you may find it difficult, so take the path that will put you in the best position.

Position

As you move, prepare your body and racket. Turn your body round past the point where it faces the side wall and twist your shoulder across your body. When you arrive you should have everything ready for the shot. Position to the side and allow room and time for the ball to come back between you and the wall.

Don't go up too far. It is difficult on the backhand to compensate for a ball that has gone past you.

Stance

It is more difficult on the backhand to play a stroke with an open stance, as this often restricts the swing. The difficulty of turning the body and shoulder to gain power while maintaining balance in an open stance makes the basic stance preferable.

Basic Stance Attempt to move into this stance with the body turned and hold yourself steady through the stroke. It is important to use the basic stance in the front court.

Open Stance In the front court use this only in emergencies. Adopt your swing size to maintain balance and control where necessary.

In the backcourt you may use an open stance (although the basic stance or mid-stance

Fig 62   **The Backhand Straight Drive**

(a)   As he moves off for a backhand straight drive Ross Norman takes his racket straight back and starts turning to the side.

(d)   The weight moves forward just before impact, the butt comes through and the forearm starts to turn.

is still preferred), but try not to overstretch. Keep your feet close enough together to maintain a relatively even distribution of weight.

Mid-Stance Endeavour to get both feet down to the side of the ball with your weight evenly on both feet. This will give the best balance and still facilitate a transfer of weight.

Swing

Backswing Use the full

68

(b)   Ross now positioned to the side predicts the impact point and waits for the ball to come in between himself and the wall. Note how the racket has gone up and the shoulder has started to go around.

(c)   A side-on position, shoulder round, eye on the ball and a long stride Ross waits for the ball to fall to just the right spot.

(e)   For a straight drive the body faces the side at impact. Note how the toe points at the side and the shoulders are parallel with the wall. An impact point marginally behind the right angle will angle the ball into the side.

(f)   On the follow-through Ross is still in a strong stance and well balanced, showing that he has held himself steady throughout the swing. Note that the racket has swung through in the line of the shot.

swing where possible and tactically sensible. Turn your shoulder and endeavour to place your right hand round the left shoulder (you may touch it here for practice). The cocked wrist will take your racket behind and over your head.

Impact   Swing back and down (think of swinging under your back knee and up and through the ball). As the shoulder on the backhand is in front of the body, the impact is in front of the leading foot.

Follow-through   Remember to hinge the swing on the elbow as well as the shoulder. Let the elbow sit in a little for a smooth flowing swing.

Fig 63   Ross Norman positioned to the side in a basic stance, straight drives on the backhand. Note how Jansher Khan is already airborne at the moment of impact.

Practice Progression

Develop your drives with solo practice. When you can reach your target consistently you are ready for the next stage.

Pat
Stand close to the front wall and, using a pat underarm action, pat the ball onto the front wall continuously.
Target – 20

High Pat
Practise hitting this higher and softer to lift it above the cut line. Come under the ball more and lift it with an action similar to bouncing the ball on your racket. Prepare your racket, attempting to get it into position early, and pause so

that you are waiting for the ball. If you can create this time in your practice you will become aware of what you are doing and be able to work out the problems involved.
Target – 20

Stroke
From the high pat, turn side on, open the racket face and endeavour to use a side-on stroke. Use your feet to move up and down, keeping to the side of the ball as well as adjusting back and forth. Wait until it comes between you and the side wall. At this point it will go straight.
Target – 20

Above the Cut Line
Hit high and soft, endeavouring to position and

pause before each shot. You will notice that hitting a little in front of the right angle will tend to make the ball move crosscourt, and a little behind will push it towards the side. Experiment with this angle. Move your feet and aim the ball by positioning and stroking it, rather than flicking it.
Target – 20

Behind the Short Line
Lift and firm your stroke to land continuously behind the short line.
Target – 20

Into the Service Box
Aim to land the ball consistently in the service box area.
Target – 20

Behind the Service Box
Lift the ball and endeavour to land it consistently behind the service box.
Target – 20

Off the Back Wall
Hit the ball continuously to bounce and rebound off the back wall.
Target – 20

Practices

Solo

11.1 Drives: Service Box
1 *Above*: Aim to land the ball consistently in the service box, aiming above the cut line.
2 *Above and below*: Service box drives aiming one ball above the cut line and the next below.
3 *Below*: Service box drives; aim all below the cut line.

11.2 Drives: Moving
Drives up and down the side, varying length and pace. Practise moving to the side of the ball.

11.3 Length
1 *Rhythm* Practise driving out from the side walls about the service box width, playing the ball to bounce and come out of the back, to be driven again. Practising out from the side like this can allow you to get into a rhythm. Move your feet and line up every shot.
2 *Tight* Practise taking the ball off the back and endeavour to get it to hit the side behind the back of the service box.

> On the straight drive you must get the ball to the back wall. It's better overhit than underhit.
> **Ross Norman**

11.4 Length: Before and After
1 Take three balls off the back and one before the back.
2 Take one ball off the back and one before the back.

11.5 Length: Varying Pace
1 High: Straight drive aiming the ball just under the out-of-court line – a straight lob.
2 Play one medium pace, one soft, one hard.
3 Play all drives as hard as possible while keeping control. Get into a rhythm.

Pairs

11.6 Feeding (Dropping) and Driving
From behind A feeds a drop for B to straight drive for length and width. If A allows the ball to bounce twice this will give B time to practise moving back to the T.

11.7 Boast and Drive
A straight drives; B boasts.

11.8 Drive and Boast or Drop
A straight drives; B boasts or drops.

11.9 Circling
Both A and B straight drive, taking the ball off the back. Lift the ball above the cut line and circle via the back wall to the half-court line and then to the T. This allows the striker to move directly to the ball.

See also chapter 19, 'The Back Corners'.

Condition Games

Rules
Hit off a straight drive for the service; a difficult service can be refused; American scoring (every point) to, say 9. No volleys.

11.10 Circling: Straight Condition Games Down One Side (Within the Sideline)
1 To the area behind the short line (half).
2 To the area behind the service box (corners).
3 Any shot within the side lines, down one side (side).

11.11 Boast and Drive
A drives to the area behind the service box (back corner). B boasts above the tin and below the cut line.

Practice Games

11.12 A plays a normal game while B concentrates mainly on straight drives. This is excellent practice at straight driving. It is a useful practice if A is the weaker player. This could become a condition game by making a formal rule or condition. (It is an option to allow B a boast from the back.)

12
The Crosscourt Drive

If the straight drive is the basic shot in squash the crosscourt is the natural one. It may be dangerous to call it natural in a learned game, but it is so in the sense that our positioning, when moving and facing forward, tends to put us in position for a crosscourt shot.

Along with the boast, the crosscourt is one of the loosest shots in the game. This is not, however, a fault in the shot but is because it is overplayed (being natural and easy to play), played badly or played at the wrong time.

The crosscourt has advantages and disadvantages, benefits and risks.

One of its advantages is that the full direction of its impact off the back wall (after hitting the side and floor) is not just back down the court but also to the side. This makes it more difficult to get out of the back and get behind to hit straight.

The crosscourt is designed to force a weak boast or a mistake – by dying in the nick, before the side, between the side and back, or on the back. Various degrees of pressures and width allow the crosscourt to become a passing shot (that is, it does not rebound off the back). Another advantage is that because of its longer path it can give a player time to get back into position.

The main disadvantage of the crosscourt is that it spends a long time out from the side wall, away from cover and safety, and so is vulnerable to attack.

Tactics

How do you decide whether to play straight or crosscourt? It is important to keep squash tactical ideas simple and perhaps the simplest answer to this problem is to 'keep your game straight' and crosscourt only when you feel you have an opening. Do not crosscourt just because you want to, or because it is easier.

As well as forcing mistakes and loose boasts, the crosscourt has a key role in the positional game. The good tactical player is continually looking for opportunities to move his opponent. He will move him from side to side as well as up and down the court.

Crosscourt when you have an opening or when your opponent is back off the T. If an opponent has been forced slightly off the T, or is slow in recovering, or if you can take the ball early before he has recovered, the opening is there to play the ball away from him. This will force him back in the court, keeping the pressure on as he is deprived of time to recover and of time to line the ball up and play his best shots.

The further back your opponent is in the court the

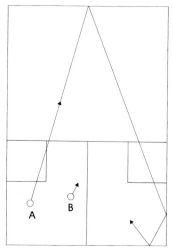

Fig 64   Tactics: use the crosscourt to hit the ball away from an opponent (B) who is out of position.

less danger there is of him playing a volley, and the more opportunity to crosscourt and provide him with a shot which will come angled off the back and cause him problems.

The further up the court your opponent stands the more risky the crosscourt, since it can be cut off on the volley. You will know if you have been stuck behind a volleyer and continued crosscourting. In this situation, tend to go straight. Do not

When you're forced to crosscourt try to be aware if your opponent is threatening a volley. If it is likely you've got to be alert and ready to cover all his options. Sometimes you'll put extra width on it but this can open up the court on the rebound and you can be blocked on one side.

Ross Norman

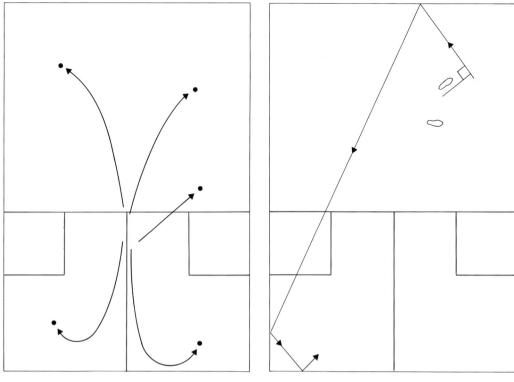

Fig 65 Paths: move to the crosscourt so as to keep the ball slightly in front of your position. Hit smoothly across your body for good width. Position and placement: target crosscourts to hit the side, floor and back.

crosscourt against a volleyer! Top Australian Rodney Martin is a great interceptor and one of the things he likes about the game is to read a crosscourt early and get on to it.

Use the crosscourt to apply pressure as well as for positional play. It is easy to hit hard, to take early, and you can inject pace into a rally as well as twisting, turning, wrong-footing and keeping an opponent on the move. Vary the pace on your crosscourts to create time and apply pressure as needed. Remember, you have the whole front wall to play with.

Use enough variety between the straight and crosscourt shots to keep your opponent guessing. Do not become predictable and prey to the volleyer. Try at times to shape the same way for the straight drive as for the crosscourt, thus providing disguise. Occasionally use deception in your shots. Set up a predictable pattern of play and then suddenly break it to provide tactical deception.

For example, set up a rally down the side wall and wait until your opponent hangs in, then use crosscourt drive.

> Give yourself reminders. For example with a guy like Rodney Martin who hunts that ball and may chip in a nice little volley off your crosscourt, remind yourself that unless it's going to be a perfect shot then don't bother crosscourting again.
>
> **Ross Norman**

Target Area

Crosscourts are about width. Angle them to beat a volley. The ideal width is to place the ball on the side wall at the point where your opponent would want to hit it. On the basic drive this is behind the service box, giving a target area of side, floor and back. Ideally, the ball will just drop off the back and force a weak return.

A harder, lower and slightly narrower ball aimed for the nick or the floor behind the box will tend to die in the corner. A hard low crosscourt can use speed and angle to pass an opponent.

If a volley is threatening, extra width may be added to beat the volley, but be cautious – the more you angle the ball into the side, the more it will bounce out.

Fig 66   The Forehand Crosscourt Drive

(a)   Jansher Khan,
shoulder turned, racket
ready, faces forward
towards the corner and
leaves the ball a little to the
front. Note how his weight
is about to move into the shot.

(b)   At impact the body
braces, the weight comes
through, the shoulder
turns into the line of the
shot and the forearm
turns.

(c)   The follow-through
swings right across the
body in a smooth curve
and comes up into a V.

Technique

Path and Position

The crosscourt is not propelled
across the court by flicking or
twisting but by stroking the
ball smoothly across the body.
To do this the body will face
into the front corners and the
ball will be taken out in front of
the body. Positioning will vary
depending on the angle
required onto the front wall.

Front Court
Here the path is almost directly
to the ball and slightly to the
side.

Back Court
As the ball must be in front of
the player at impact, the path
to a ball in the back court must
allow you to take up a position
further behind the ball. Failure
to do this can result in a ball
becoming too narrow and
hence presenting volleying
opportunities for your
opponent. From the T, you will
have to move down to the side
and a little behind the ball.

The knock-up is an excellent
time to practise crosscourts.
Move back from the ball each
time, leave room and practise
lining it up. (See the first of the
practice progressions on page
76.)

Back Wall
One of the weaker shots in the
game is the crosscourt off the
back wall. Often an
inappropriate ball is picked
and flicked across court, which
results in a weak stroke of poor
width. The ball needs to come
off the back enough to allow
you to get behind it and hit it

Fig 67   The Backhand Crosscourt Drive

(a)   Jansher Khan steps toward the corner for a crosscourt drive. Note how his weight is about to move forward, his shoulder has turned, the racket is up and his eye is on the ball.

(b)   At impact the weight has moved forward into a strong stance over a bent knee, the racket head is up and is well controlled. Impact is in front of the body.

(c)   Jansher maintains balance as he pulls out of the crosscourt. He uses a low follow-through on the backhand but note the control in the wrist.

across to the opposite half of the front wall.

Stance

Although both open and closed stances can be used on the forehand, the open stance is often preferred, especially when under pressure in the front court.

Supposedly 'correct' footwork can lead to problems if the closed stance is used and positioning is very square for a mid-court or back-court ball, resulting in cramping, flicking and swinging the body with the shot, to get the ball across. The closed stance is not always advantageous.

Swing

The swing size on the crosscourt depends on the time you have to line the ball up and the pace and control required. Often you will use a full swing on the crosscourt and adapt this to a compact or short swing when pressured or when requiring control or touch. The swing should move smoothly across the body and not result in any uncomfortable twisting.

Impact

The impact point for a crosscourt must be in front of the body. The further forward and to the side in the court you are, the sharper the angle needed onto the front wall. To get this angle the impact point needs to be further forward and the stance more open.

> It's very important to get your technique right at the beginning. It can take a lot of practice to get rid of bad habits later on.
> **Ross Norman**

75

Fig 68   Ross Norman takes the ball out in front for a crosscourt.

Practice Progression

While crosscourts can be practised off self-feeds, this is generally far too static an exercise for regular practice. It could, however, be used occasionally to clarify target areas. Hitting crosscourts is naturally how we warm up, and there is much that you can do here to develop your crosscourt.

Crosscourt Technique Exercises

Use the intersection of the service-box line with the short line as your target. Allow plenty of room, step back after each stroke, move your feet, get in the best position for your shot and groove your swing. (This is not a shot but an exercise to develop a rhythm in stroking.)

Pairs Crosscourts to Hit Side

A crosscourts to hit the side wall at the service box, B feeds/drives straight and returns to the opposite side. (Obviously this is not deep enough as a shot but it is a useful exercise to explore width.)

Pairs Crosscourts for Length

From the Service Box
A self-feeds straight to the service box and crosscourts for the side, floor, back. B repeats. (The ball may have to bounce twice in the back.) Each player should try 10–20 shots each and see who can get the best score (score one point if you hit the side, floor, back).

Off the Back   A drives several balls for length and over-length and picks an over-length ball that sits out a little more to crosscourt. B repeats.

Practices

Solo

12.1   Solo Crosscourts   Self-feed and crosscourt.

12.2   Length and Crosscourts   Drive for length or over-length, then pick a ball to crosscourt for side/floor/back. Straight drive on the opposite side, and repeat.

Fig 69   Hiddy Jahan, British Open finalist in 1982 demonstrates perfect poise and balance on this backhand crosscourt follow-through. Bracing the body and holding it steady while the swing whips through the impact point helps maintain control and accuracy.

Pairs

12.3   Pairs Crosscourt Exercises   See the practice progression.
1   Crosscourt technique exercise.
2   Pairs crosscourts to hit side.
3   Pairs crosscourts for length: from the service box.
4   Pairs crosscourts for length: off the back.

12.4   Crosscourt and Boast   A boasts; B crosscourts.

12.5   Drop and Crosscourt; Straight and Boast
(Two-Shot Exercise)   A in the back court drives straight and boasts; B drops and crosscourts.

12.6   Boast and Alternate Drives   A boasts; B alternates straight and crosscourt drives.

12.7   Crosscourt, Volley, Boast (Diagonal Movement Exercise)   A crosscourts (from the front), B volleys, A boasts, B crosscourts, and so on.

12.8   Crosscourt, Drive, Boast (Diagonal Movement, Exercise)   A crosscourts (from the front), B straight drives, A boasts, B crosscourts, and so on.

12.9   Crosscourt and Drops   A (in the back court) drops straight; B crosscourts.

12.10   Crosscourt and Alternate Boasts and Drops   A alternates boasts and straight drops; B crosscourts.

Condition Games

12.11   Normal Game with Crosscourt Rule
Crosscourts must hit the side wall on the full.

12.12   Back-Court Game   All shots into the back court only. If the ball goes short the rally is lost.

12.13   Back-Court Game Plus Crosscourt Rule

12.14   Back-Corner Game
Straight and crosscourt shots allowed to the area behind the service box. (It is an option to allow boasts, and extend the area to behind the short line – back-half game.)

Practice Games

12.15   Play a normal game but look for the crosscourt drive and emphasize this shot. Extend the rallies so that you get opportunities to play it. Pick one shot and emphasize this, for example a high wide crosscourt or hard low shots.

13
The Lob

The lob is the most under used and underrated shot in squash.

So often as a coach I have silently cried out 'Lob, lob!' as a player or pupil fails to use the one weapon that could get him out of trouble.

Its advantages are the time it creates for a player and the problems it gives an opponent in the air and in digging a soft, vertically falling ball out of the back corners. The masters of the lob are the veterans. Squash takes time to learn but it is amazing when you are forced to learn by necessity how easy it can be.

Jansher Khan, World Champion, uses a complete range of paces in his game. The great Australian competitor Chris Dittmar throws the ball into the air whenever under pressure in the front of the court and the legendary Jahangir Khan has a lob as smooth and efficient as any of his shots. At the top level the great players play a pressure (rather than touch) game but the lob is still an essential part of their weaponry. How many times have I played Ross Norman, prised a rare opening, struck for the nick and ended up banging my racket helplessly on the back wall endeavouring to dig out a perfect lob!

If the best players in the world use the lob to such effect why is it so underused? Part of the answer is explained by the psychology of the game. In squash we use the speed of the ball (and placement) to beat an opponent. Taking the ball early

Fig 70   Ross Norman gets down to the ball and improvises with his wrist to get under it and flick it up for a forehand crosscourt lob. His British Open opponent Brian Besson on the T will be looking for the opportunity to volley.

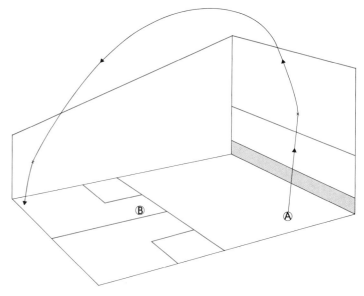

Fig 71   Tactics: hit high to give yourself time to recover the T. Target the lob for the side wall behind the service box.

Fig 72 **The Forehand Crosscourt Lob**

(a) Jansher Khan lunges and prepares to lob a low ball. Note the low backswing and the open racket face.

(b) Jansher crouches, the racket comes under and up through the ball. Note his head is down and he has steadied himself momentarily.

(c) Jansher holds steady through the shot, collects his feet under him as he stops, and prepares to push back.

and hitting hard requires, induces and reinforces an aroused and aggressive state which makes it difficult to slow shots and calculate pace. When we rush and hit hard constantly, it becomes difficult to lob.

Ladies will take immaculate care and concentration on a lob serve but fail to use the lob elsewhere in a rally. Technically it's as simple as bouncing the ball on a racket.

Use the lob in your game. Practise it. The clever tactical player realizes its importance and develops it as a weapon he has at his disposal. How much he uses it depends on the tactical requirements of the particular rally and match he is playing.

Tactics

The lob creates time. It can give you five times as long before your opponent hits it as a hard low drive.

Use the lob to defend. Lob when you are under pressure to give yourself time to recover the T.

Use the lob to attack. Attack an opponent's weaknesses in the air and in the back corners.

Use the lob to slow the game. A superior tactical player controls the pace of the game. Put up enough lobs to allow you to work at the pace you are best at.

Use the lob to vary the pace of the game – changes of pace can break up an opponent's rhythm and concentration.

Target Area

The lob is a high, soft shot that drops into the back corners. Height is crucial. It is designed to go over an opponent's head or to present him with a high ball that is difficult to control and attack.

Crosscourt Lob

This is played for length and width. The aim is to hit the side, bounce and then hit the back (side–floor–back). Ideally it will die or force a boast or recovery back-wall lob (also called a back-wall boast).

Cling Lob

This is a good safe shot under extreme pressure. Aim very high over your opponent's head and narrow the angle so that there is little danger of the ball going over the out-of-court line on the side. Because of the height of the shot the ball will often hit the back wall on the full. Angle it so that on its rebound it will move into the side wall and cling. This shot is often played with a flick.

England's Neil Harvey used this shot to great effect in his defeat of World Champion Ross Norman in the 1987 World Championships.

Straight Lob

It is easy to play quite a good straight lob and still hit out, so endeavour to keep the ball below the out-of-court line for its entire journey. Aim to have it move in and cling behind the service box, but if a volley is threatening, angle it into the side near the point where your opponent would wish to volley it.

Technique

To hit the ball high you must get under it and hit upwards. To hit softly your racket must move slowly; you must use a short swing or break your swing while moving through the ball.

Path and Position

For the crosscourt lob, take a path almost directly to the ball so that the ball is between you and the front wall. If the ball is

Fig 73 **The Lob**

(a)   Harvey under pressure lunges forward, racket open and outstretched, endeavouring to get under the ball.

(b)   Just getting under it he flicks it up.

(c)   Briars moves in looking for the volley while Harvey starts to recover.

Fig 74 **The Backhand Crosscourt Lob**

(a) Jansher Khan lunges forward for the low ball. Note how he has already prepared so that he can swing immediately he arrives. The low backswing will help him get under the ball.

(b) Crouching low to help get under the ball, racket well open, Jansher studies the ball. Note the low path of the swing as the racket prepares to come under the ball.

(c) Balanced, steady and concentrating on the impact point, Jansher swings up through the ball and lifts it high crosscourt.

wide at the side you will have to move in behind it more so that you can get an appropriate angle for good width.

Stance
On the forehand the open stance gives you the quickest movement and the biggest stretch to the ball. It also provides a position which allows you to hit across your body without losing balance or swinging your trunk.

A closed or mid stance can be used if you have more time or are near the middle of the court. On the backhand use the closed stance for balance.

Swing
Use a short backswing and prepare it as you are moving. Preparation is crucial. It will allow your racket to be moving through before your foot hits the floor. Take the racket head back to between shoulder and waist height. Do not get too

close to the ball. Allow room for your racket to get down under the ball and come up through it. The wrist should be firm or locked and the follow-through short.

Variations

Flick Lob
In emergencies when the ball is very low and you do not have time to swing, start with a very

Fig 75 Jansher opens his racket, crouches low and manages to get under a shot from Brett Martin, to play the lob that will put him back in the rally.

low racket and an open racket face. Flick upwards. Often this shot is played for a cling lob but if there is enough time it can be used as a deceptive alternative to a drop shot.

Straight Lob
Use the same positioning as for the straight drive. If you are under pressure the ball may not come back to you and you will have to reach for it. Make sure you push yourself right up to the side, so that the ball

does not come back into the middle of the court after being hit and bring about a stroke. When using the open stance, hold the wrist back and make sure that the impact point is behind the right angle.

Recovery Shots
When under pressure it is so easy to go for an outright winner when the percentages are against it. The reward is often a mistake or a shot that leaves you badly out of

position. Recovery shots give you time to recover the T and are the astute tactical player's answer to a pressure situation.

High Drop
Jansher Khan can get to and get his racket under almost any shot. At times all he can do is push it as he hasn't enough room to stroke or flick. These high drops are played to move into the side and cling. They serve as little lobs as they give him time to recover the T.

Practice Progression

Bounce the Ball on Racket
This is how your swing should move – under the ball and up through it.

High Pat
Stand close to the front wall and pat as high as you can, up above the cut line.

High Stroke
Make this a high stroke; turn side on, open your racket and come under the ball.

Feed and Lob
Feed the ball high off the front wall (to yourself by hand or a single racket feed). Allow room so that you can move in, get under the ball and lob to land in the back corner. Repeat. Warm the ball by driving or with a continuous front-court exercise where necessary.

Boast, Self-Feed, Lob
Have a partner boast, feed an easy ball that sits up (repeat feed until you have the right shot) and lob. Continuous.

Boast and Lob
Your partner boasts and you lob. Move back towards the T after each shot and gradually increase this movement.

Practice
Solo

13.1   Feed and Crosscourt Lob

13.2   Feed and Straight Lob
Drive straight continuously (either off the back or to the service box). Feed one ball short, run and lob straight.

13.3   Length and Backcourt Lob
Drive straight for length several times and pick the ball to lob crosscourt. Lift the ball high onto the top of the front wall, to hit the side wall behind the service box, bounce and hit the back. Repeat either side.

Pairs

13.4   Boast and Crosscourt Lob
A in the back court boasts, B in the front court, lobs.

13.5   Drop and Straight Lob
(a) A in the back court drops (start with feeding initially); B in the front court straight lobs. As they progress, B will be gradually able to increase the movement back towards the T. (b) A volley drops.

13.6   Alternate Lobs and Boast
A boasts; B alternates straight and crosscourt lobs.

13.7   Lobs and Alternate Straight Drops and Boasts
A alternates straight drops and boasts. B lobs.

13.8   Lob, Volley, Boast
A lobs crosscourt; B volleys straight (for length initially and then dying length); A boasts; B lobs; and so on.

There are two exercises here – one for the straight shot on the forehand and one on the backhand.

Condition Games

13.9   High Game
A game with all shots above the cut line.

13.10   Lob Short Ball Rule
A normal game with lob rule. If the ball is played short it must be lobbed. (A variation on this may be to lob a boast only, or a drop only.)

13.11   Front and Back Lobs
A can hit any shot to the front court. B must lob from the front – straight or crosscourt.

13.12   Soft Game
A and B can play only soft shots.

13.13   Hard and Soft
A can play hard and soft (or all hard). B can play soft only.

14
The Service

The service is the one shot in squash you can hit exactly how you want. Every other ball you play will have been placed by your opponent. How often is this dramatic advantage lost with a poor or indifferent stroke!

The server starts with a psychological and tactical advantage. He can win points, cannot lose them and can therefore be more attacking. Positionally he takes command of the T and therefore controls the territory of the court, while his opponent is out of position. He serves in his own time (the receiver must be constantly alert), at a pace he chooses, and attempts to place the ball where he wants.

These advantages can be lost when the service is rushed, or seen as just a way to get the ball into play. Think of the service as an offensive situation. Try to dominate from the start of a rally. Work out exactly what you want to achieve and where you want the ball to go, and take the time you need to get it there.

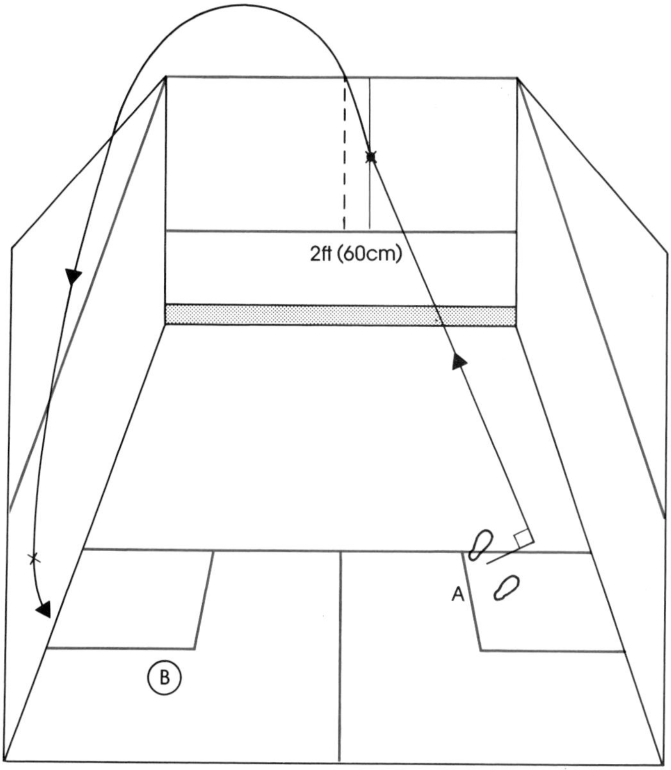

Fig 76   Service: stand facing the front corner. Aim 2ft (60cm) to the right of the imaginary centre line. Lift the ball high to hit the side, floor and back.

Tactics

The first cut and thrust, the first exchange of shots in a squash battle is the serve and return of serve. The server will use this opportunity best if he keeps in mind his aims and assesses his results in terms of these aims. These aims are:

1   Safety – he must not present an attacking opportunity to his opponent or risk hitting out.
2   To beat his opponent's attempted return on the volley.
3   To push his opponent into the back.
4   To force a mistake or weak return. This may be attempting to force a boast rather than a straight return.
5   To take control of the T.
6   To anticipate returns and have prepared countermoves.

If you've left the serve open – you should know immediately its left your racket that it's not going to hit the side wall – then get yourself ready immediately in case your opponent attacks it on the volley.

Ross Norman

Fig 77   **Service: Right Box**

(a)   Jansher Khan prepares his racket and drops the ball out in front of the short line. He lets his weight rock rhythmically from the right to the left as this helps facilitate his movement to the T.

(b)   Jansher comes under the ball and lifts it up into the front wall. Note that at impact his body is facing towards the front corner. Club players can start in this position.

(c)   As he comes out of the swing Jansher steps toward the T.

To achieve these aims a good player should develop a variety of weapons and adopt these to probe an opponent for weaknesses. He may mix his various services as a fast bowler at cricket would vary his deliveries. If you ever get the opportunity to watch Jahangir Khan play you will see him varying his serves from a lob to a smash and then also throw in the odd 'bouncer' when going for the back-wall nick.

The service presents one other tactical opportunity to the server. The server decides when to serve and as he prepares he has a moment of brief respite in which to assess his tactics. I would suggest a regular service routine that could act as a mental knot in your handkerchief. Use a check list:

1   *Length*   When did I last get him to take the ball off the back wall?

2   *Width*   Where is he volleying from?
3   *T*   Am I getting on the T?

Target Area

To beat an opponent's volley you will want to angle the ball into the side wall just before your opponent would choose to volley it. This is good width and it will be high on the side wall just behind the service box. If you do not hit the side you could present an easy opportunity for a volley, and if you hit it too early the ball will bounce well out from the side and present an easy target.

Give your opponent the problem of deciding whether

> You must have a clear idea of exactly what you are trying to do in a game, of how you are going to keep the ball away from your opponent. The first step is to get the ball straight and in the back.
>
> **Lucy Soutter**

(d) Jansher is transferring his weight right throughout the service so that at the end of his stroke he is already half way to the T.

(e) There is no stop after the serve. Jansher keeps moving. The serve is one long rhythmic movement that ends on the T.

(f) Astride the T, ready for any return, Jansher studies his opponent.

For me a good serve is one that puts the ball into play and limits my opponent's choice of return. One that doesn't give him an opportunity to attack.

Ross Norman

to volley before or after the side. Forcing him to volley just off the side makes it difficult and will usually result in a defensive shot.

To push your opponent into the back you will ideally have the ball bounce, hit the back and come off the back only just enough to allow a weak boast. Put simply, the target area is the side, floor and back.

Technique

The Basic Service – Right Side

Position
Stand facing the front right corner with your left foot on or just forward of the short line and with the toe pointing into the front corner. Put your right foot completely in the service box.

Stance
Stand in an open stance, evenly balanced on both feet. Prepare your hand to throw the ball upwards about 15cm (6in) and check that you are lined up with your target area on the front wall. Let your

weight move onto the back foot and as you swing let it come forward rhythmically onto the front foot. Often a small step forward helps this process.

Swing
Start your swing in line with the shoulders, have a firm wrist and an open racket face. Swing down under the ball, bending your knees a little as you do and swing up through it.

As you complete the serve you will start moving towards the T with the front foot stepping to the side, followed by a quick sidestep into the ready position.

85

The Basic Service – Left Side

Position

Stand at the front of the service box facing the opposite wall and step forward on the front foot along the short line.

Stance

As you serve let your weight move forward and step along the line on your way to the T.

Swing

Use the same compact swing as from the right box. Usually from the left we serve a little lower and firmer, as it's easy with the narrower angle to serve out. Aim about 1m (3ft) to the right of the extended half-court line.

Changing the Angles

Develop a consistent routine and a grooved action for your serve. When you have achieved this it will be easy to

Fig 78 **Service: Left Box**

(a) Jansher Khan facing the side wall steps into his serve. Note that he is moving along the line, his racket is prepared and the ball is about to leave his fingers in a little upwards throw.

(b) His body faces the side at impact, the racket is open and Jansher has stepped through into the shot.

Jansher Khan

There's only one way to improve your game and that's hard work.

When you're starting you must practise by yourself for control. I see some players starting off squash going for long runs. This has no meaning. You must go on court and practise control. After a year or two, when your control is good, then you can go running.

On your deep shots it's important that you get the ball into the wall. If it's loose your opponent can kill it. A tight shot will force him to just return.

I don't use my shots until I'm a hundred per cent sure the ball is going in the nick. If I'm not sure, I hit it to the back and wait until I've got a really easy ball and my opponent is in the back.

Try not to make mistakes. As soon as I hit the tin I just stop playing that shot and concentrate on hitting back. Then I might try another shot and I pick the one that's working well.

Fig 79

(c) A short controlled follow-through. Jansher has finished his shot with his weight still moving through towards the T.

into the side wall (more width), turn your position slightly towards the front, keeping the same impact point in relation to your body. Vary this angle back and forth until you get the width you want.

If the ball is not travelling back enough, lift it higher on the front.

Margin for Error

When you start serving, allow a good margin for error below the out-of-court line on the side wall. When you have your serve grooved in you can gradually decrease this.

Pace

The high, softer serve involves more risk (of going out or being volleyed) but it has rewards in that it will not bounce out of the back as much. A harder, lower serve is safer and may unsettle an opponent. The pace and height of the serve is a judgement that depends on your opponent's competence, your touch or feel on the day and the limits of safety you set yourself.

Variations

Semi-Lob

This is the standard serve hit with a side-on action. The height and angle are varied to

Fig 81   A still moment of perfect symmetry as Gawain Briars prepares to serve. Note his concentration on the ball.

provide different problems for the receiver – for example, whether to volley before or after the side.

Lob

This is the main attacking service. Come under the ball and lift it as high as possible on the front wall. It is often best to build up gradually to this position and allow room for error on the front and side walls.

Cling Lob

A very high service used to go over the receiver's head, rebound off the back and move in towards the side wall to cling or at least restrict the return to a straight shot.

Hard

A low, safe service, difficult to volley and one that is aimed low on the side wall. It will force the receiver to take it off the back, where it can sometimes die.

Smash

A hard service with the overarm smash action, often

adjust the angles for greater accuracy.

For a standard service from the right, aim approximately 60cm (2ft) to the right of the imaginary half-court line running up the centre of the front wall. Adjust the horizontal angle of the service by a small change in your position. To get the ball more

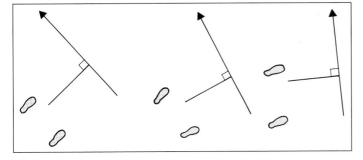

Fig 80   Changing the angles: adjust the horizontal angle of the service by small changes in position.

Fig 82   **The Backhand Service**

(a)   Lucy Soutter faces the opposite wall, takes her shoulder around, racket up and steps forward throwing the ball up as she moves.

(b)   At impact her weight is forward, racket open and her eye is on the ball.

(c)   Lucy swings right through aiming for the opposite side of the front wall.

aimed for the side-wall nick behind the service box, occasionally for the back-wall nick, or for the floor so that it hits the back and comes in to cling.

Backhand
For the right-hander this should be used from the right box only. Serving backhand from the left box places your back to the receiver, making it difficult to pick up cues on the receiver's return, and obstructs smooth movement to the T.

From the right box this serve provides a good view of the receiver and his position plus easy access to the T. A narrow angle keeps the ball closer to the side wall.

Bodyline
A surprise shot that's played so close to an opponent's body that he often cannot change position quickly enough to create room for the swing and may be tempted to push a

weak return. It can be played soft, to die, or hard, to 'rattle' an opponent. The dangers are that if played too wide it can present an easy opportunity to the receiver and if played too narrow the receiver may turn and trap the server against the

side wall. This serve can be played directly for the back-wall nick. This is a variation Jahangir Khan uses frequently.

Corkscrew
A serve played high and hard onto the front wall as close to

Fig 83   Rodney Martin with a backhand serve to Chris Robertson. This serve allows quick and easy movement to the T and early visibility of an opponent.

the side wall (on the server's side) as possible. The ball will screw out and travel down the court diagonally until it hits the opposite side wall. Here the spin imparted from the front corner will cause the ball to rebound straight out from the

side at a right angle. This serve is most successful if it hits the side just before the back and rebounds parallel (and occasionally clings) to the back wall. In this situation it is best returned with a back-wall lob.

This is a difficult serve that

involves considerable risk and should only be used in the right conditions – with a hot court and ball. When serving, step out into the court to get a wide angle into the top front corner and swing down under the ball and hit as hard as possible.

Practice Progression

Pre-Service Practice
Bounce the ball up and down on your racket. Now take the ball in your hand and, with a short, gentle throw, throw it up to drop on the strings of the open-faced racket and catch it again. This little co-ordination exercise is useful if a beginner has trouble connecting up with the serve.

Short Service
After the above exercise, move close to the side or front wall and from the hand pat the ball up onto the wall and catch it again. Gradually move back from the wall.

Service
Remember to practise both sides. Often a right-handed beginner will find it easier initially from the left box.

Fig 84   Rodney Martin serves from the left box.

Practices

Solo

14.1   Serving
The service is obviously an easy shot to practise solo, the only problem being that the ball gets cold quickly. Alternate 10 serves of one type with another continuous solo practice that will warm the ball.

Pairs

14.2   Serving and Receiving
A serves and B receives, 10 shots each. This could be scored: for example, B gets a point if he returns the serve to the area behind the service box; A gets one if B doesn't.

14.3   Three-Shot Rally
As above, but with the receiver allowed to intercept the return.

Practice Games

To get extensive practice at either serving or returning, try a practice game with A serving all the time and B receiving. You could even do this from just one side. (Scoring would be American, of course.)

15
The Return of Service

Matches are often won on the service. A better way to put this might be to say that matches are often lost on the service. If you do not return the service well you will lose.

The server has the advantage of being able to place the ball exactly where he wants and of having time to take control of the T.

The receiver has the disadvantage of being out of position and not knowing what shot to select. He has to pick up myriad cues on the problems and opportunities posed by a particular ball and act in advance of impact by positioning and preparing to stroke. He is also faced with a multitude of decisions not just on what shot to play but where to hit it from. *The server is trying to force the receiver to boast. The receiver is attempting to avoid boasting by considering all the earlier options.*

These problems of *shot selection* are covered under 'Tactics' below. The tactics section also covers the key ideas of defence, losing points and lapses. Success at return of serve depends particularly on your ability to volley, as well as to drive and boast from the back corners. These are examined under 'Technique'.

Tactics

Your ability to return service well depends on your

Fig 85 Jahangir Khan is not going to miss this ball. Turning to the side from the receiving position he prepares to volley.

Fig 86 Danielle Drady studies the server as she prepares to receive service.

concentration and decision-making ability as well as your skill.

Except for the first point in a match, to be the receiver means that you have just lost a rally. This can be disappointing and sometimes depressing. It is a danger area. It is very easy to lapse – to go for a lucky shot (i.e. play a tactical error), to try to win a point too quickly, to make a mistake, or to play an indifferent shot. When you are the receiver, keep concentrating and try not to make a mistake.

The receiver is faced with a multitude of decisions – 'Should I volley? Will I mess it up? Should I leave it? If I do, will it bounce out from the back or die? Should I volley it before the side? Where should I hit it? Will I be able to get it out of the back?'

These options fit into four categories:

1 To volley before the serve hits the side.
2 To volley after the serve hits the side.
3 To take the ball (off the bounce) before it hits the back.
4 To take the ball off the back.

Making the best decision from the various options is not easy. A large number of factors will affect it – your assessment of your skill, the difficulty of the shot, what has gone before, the stage of the match, your opponent's ability to cover the T and volley crosscourts, and, of course, your level of concentration.

It is crucial to view the return of serve as a defensive situation. You can lose points but you can't win them. Minimize the risk. Your natural inclination here should be defence. Volley or drive straight for good length, putting the server out of

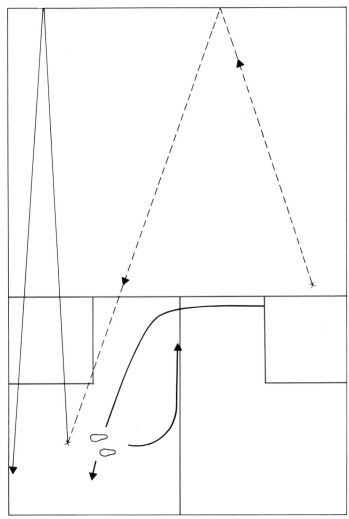

Fig 87 The receiver intercepts the serve, volleying straight for good length. This forces the server into the back corner and allows the receiver to take control of the T.

On the return of serve when you're dealing with a good serve, you are in a defensive situation and as a rule of thumb you should play it down the wall. However look for opportunities and if it's a bad serve take advantage of it.

Ross Norman

position in the back corner and therefore allowing you to win the T. Take the earliest, best opportunity to return service. Move out of defence to apply pressure and attack when opportunities present themselves.

The line of thinking a receiver should take and the main shot options open to him are outlined in the diagram overleaf.

Receiver's Line of Thinking   ## Preferred Options

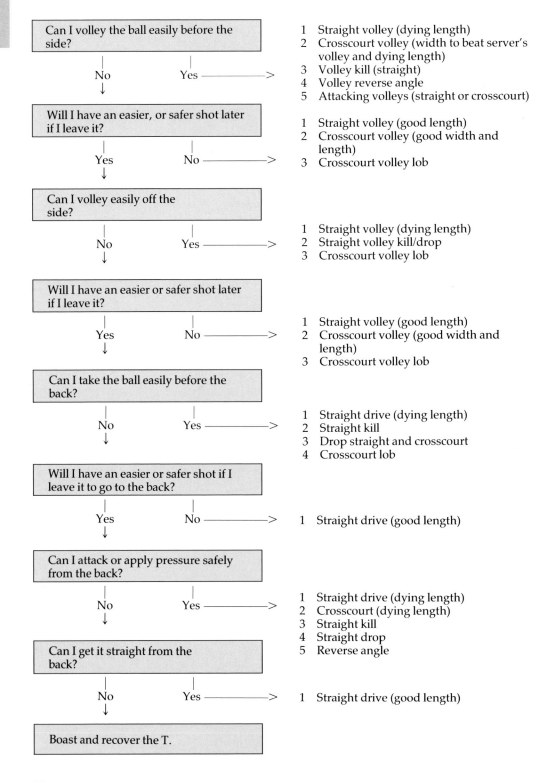

Can I volley the ball easily before the side?

No → (down)   Yes ————→

1 Straight volley (dying length)
2 Crosscourt volley (width to beat server's volley and dying length)
3 Volley kill (straight)
4 Volley reverse angle
5 Attacking volleys (straight or crosscourt)

Will I have an easier, or safer shot later if I leave it?

Yes (down)   No ————→

1 Straight volley (good length)
2 Crosscourt volley (good width and length)
3 Crosscourt volley lob

Can I volley easily off the side?

No (down)   Yes ————→

1 Straight volley (dying length)
2 Straight volley kill/drop
3 Crosscourt volley lob

Will I have an easier or safer shot later if I leave it?

Yes (down)   No ————→

1 Straight volley (good length)
2 Crosscourt volley (good width and length)
3 Crosscourt volley lob

Can I take the ball easily before the back?

No (down)   Yes ————→

1 Straight drive (dying length)
2 Straight kill
3 Drop straight and crosscourt
4 Crosscourt lob

Will I have an easier or safer shot if I leave it to go to the back?

Yes (down)   No ————→

1 Straight drive (good length)

Can I attack or apply pressure safely from the back?

No (down)   Yes ————→

1 Straight drive (dying length)
2 Crosscourt (dying length)
3 Straight kill
4 Straight drop
5 Reverse angle

Can I get it straight from the back?

No (down)   Yes ————→

1 Straight drive (good length)

Boast and recover the T.

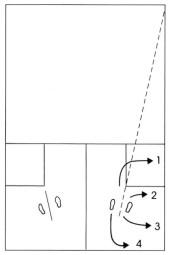

Fig 88 Receiving position: stand a racket length behind the corner of the service box, facing the front corner. Look for the receiving options in order of preference.

Target Area

The standard return of serve is a straight volley to good length (or, if an easy ball, to dying length) or a straight drive to good length and width. The server should have taken the T and the receiver will win this if he can get the ball past the server and into the back.

If the ball is easy the receiver may consider attacking. He would do this especially if the receiver was slow to the T, or too far back in the box.

Generally, if the ball is loose it will be more advisable to attempt a pressure passing shot – so that the ball passes the server but dies before he can get back for it. These volleys (and occasionally drives) should be aimed hard into the back of the service box. The straight shot should fade into the wall and not bounce out. The crosscourt must be wide enough to beat a volley and not so short as to provide an opening for the server to straight drop.

Technique

Receiving Position

The receiving position is a place you move from. It is a compromise between going forward to volley and back to take the ball out of the back corners. Stand a racket length behind and just outside the back corner of the service box with your toes pointing at the front corner. The imaginary line joining the front corner and box corner will pass between your feet (close to the heel of the right foot).

You stand in a receiving position as you would in the ready position – weight forward, ready to move. Turn your head and study the server for clues to the type of service.

Path

The shot you should be capable of playing on the

Fig 89 Serving and Receiving: Ross Norman about to serve with Rodney Eyles on his toes in the receiving position, studying him carefully.

93

Fig 90   **The Return of Serve**

(a)   Del Harris stands in a receiving position about a racket length behind the corner of the service box and watches the server.

(b)   Assessing the serve he decides to volley, starts preparing his racket and begins turning to the side.

(c)   From the receiving position he has now moved to be side on and in a strong stance for a backhand straight volley return. Note the balance, preparation and eye on the ball as he waits for it to fall.

(d)   The ball falls down to the impact point and Del starts the swing.

return of serve is a straight volley or drive. This means that you must take a path so that the ball is between you and the side wall at impact. From your receiving position you will twist sideways (whether moving forward, back or away) and use footwork that will allow you a strong and stable position.

Shots

The quality of your return of serve depends on how skilful you are at the elements involved – volleying, volleying a crosscourt straight, driving straight from the back and boasting from the back. Refer to the relevant chapters for more comprehensive lists of methods and practices.

Volley

This is covered in Chapter 16.

Problems can exist on the volley return of serve (especially timing the ball as it bounces off the side). Where the ball is difficult, use a short swing. Try it. The ball will easily travel to the front with a little push. Problems often persist because the swing used is far too large to time a very difficult connection.

Back Corners

Practise so that you have the option of driving or boasting. On the most difficult shot it may be necessary to use an exaggerated wrist flick to get behind and under the ball.

On the boast, allow a margin for error above the tin. The floating boast will give you more time to recover to the T.

Movement

Your whole purpose on the return of serve is to *recover the T*. Take up a strong stance you can pull out of towards the T as you are finishing your shot.

Practice Progression

Volley

Volley Pat,
Volley and Drive
Stand halfway between the short line and the front. Drive the ball softly above the cut line and occasionally volley.

Volley Behind the Short Line
Continue to drive and volley continuously, gradually moving down the court to behind the short line.

Volley Behind the Service Box
Continue this backwards, single-feed and volley.

Drive

Hand-Feeding
Stand on the sideline of the service box, throw the ball high off the side and let it bounce, come under it and lift it high on the front wall to return to the area behind the service box.
Skill test   How many can you get out of 10?

Behind the Service Box
Gradually move back until you are as close to the back as possible.

Off the Back
Throw the ball high off the back and lift it onto the front wall to rebound into the area behind the service box.

Skill test   How many can you get out of 10?

Continuous Drives
Throw off the back and drive continuously (initially you may do better with a faster ball e.g. a red spot, and with letting some balls bounce twice).
Skill test   How many can you drive continuously off the back on the first bounce?

Boast

Throw off the Back and Boast.
Skill test   How many good boasts can you make out of 10?

Practices

Pairs

15.1   Serving and Receiving
A serves easily for B to practice a straight return. 10 each and change sides.

15.2   Serving Game
A attempts his best serve for B to return. B gets a point if on the return he gets the ball behind the service box into the back corner. A gets a point if he misses.

15.3   Pairs Practices
These general pairs practices are particularly useful to develop the elements involved in return of serve.

1   Crosscourt and boast (and lob and boast).
2   A crosscourts, B drives straight, B boasts, A crosscourts, and so on (two-shot exercise).
3   A drops, A crosscourts, B volleys straight, B boasts, A drops, and so on (two-shot exercise).
4   Circling.
5   Circling and volleying.
6   Crosscourt volley game.
7   A crosscourts, B straight volleys, A boasts, B crosscourts, and so on (called a diagonal movement exercise).

15.4   Three-Shot Rally
A serves, B returns, A attempts to intercept.

16
The Volley

Squash is a pressure game. It is about time – time to execute the shot you want, time to line the ball up, time to recover position and time to think. How you create this time for yourself and deprive your opponent of it is one of the main tactical considerations of the game.

You will apply pressure by hitting hard, taking the ball early and volleying. Volley to apply pressure. Deprive your opponent of the time he would have had to recover position had you let the ball go by and bounce. Volley to keep control of the T and volley to stop the ball going into the back corners.

Tactics

As well as being used to apply pressure, the volley can be used as a defensive, positional, or attacking shot. There are a full range of alternatives – from the defensive volley lob to the pressure volley drive for dying length and the attacking volley nick or drop. Be clear as to what you want to achieve and do not attempt to smash every volley through the front wall or blast it into the nick.

Generally, you should look for and try to create opportunities to volley. Volley to keep in front. The person in front usually wins. Volley as much as possible without putting yourself at a disadvantage or attempting a difficult shot that could result in a mistake or weak reply.

When your opponent is caught behind and you have an easy ball you have the opportunity to go short. These are potential winning situations – don't just hit the ball back. When your opponent has been sent under pressure to the front, look for the opportunity to step in and intercept the return with a volley to the back.

Often when watching a game of squash you will see a large gap or opening that the striker ignores when hitting the ball straight back to his opponent. Volley away from your opponent. If he is out of position on the left, move him to the right, and vice versa.

Fig 91 Rodney Martin takes the opportunity to volley against Rodney Eyles. Note how the ball has come down the middle and how he has improvised a shot close to his body but is still intent on watching the ball onto his racket.

Look for these combinations and opportunities:

1 Volley to the side away from your opponent. Try to position yourself so that you are placing the ball away from your opponent as well as applying pressure. Endeavour to get the ball to die before the back or side so that your opponent won't have a second opportunity to recover it.

2 Volley deep when your opponent is in the forecourt. Follow up your short shots by looking for opportunities to step in and volley deep for dying length.

3 Volley boast off a loose straight ball. When your opponent has played a weak, straight ball and has been caught behind, volley boast and move him on the diagonal.

4 Volley drop straight off a weak crosscourt from the back. This is one of the standard combinations you will look for in your game. Pin your opponent in the back and wait for the loose crosscourt you can cut down for a winner.

5 Volley the return of service. When the ball has come round onto the back too far, allowing a return to be angled in to die, and when it is going to bounce off or well out of the back, it may be advantageous to let the ball go past – but generally you should look to volley the return of service.

Unless it is a weak serve giving an opportunity to attack, volley deep and straight or deep and wide crosscourt.

Target Area

A good-length shot will force your opponent to take the ball off the back and hence give you time to recover the T. When you are in position on the T you do not need the time that a good-length shot gives

Fig 92   **The Straight Volley Drop of a Crosscourt**

(a)   Del Harris anticipating the crosscourt, starts turning to the side and gets his racket up. A volley drop will allow him to hit away from his opponent.

(b)   Moving into position early he waits for the ball to fall to the impact point.

(c)   His swing cuts down on the ball as he carefully holds himself on balance in a side-on position.

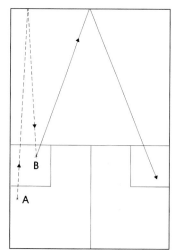

Fig 93   Volley to the side
away from your opponent.

you and you can often afford to
pull the ball a little shorter to
die – a dying length.

Target these straight
pressure volleys for the back of
the service box and crosscourt
for the side-wall nick behind
the service box, or angle them
to hit the floor and keep fading
in towards the side.

Technique

The Basic Volley

Position and Stance
For the basic straight volley,
move and face the side wall as
for the straight drive. Adjust
your feet so that you are the
right distance from the ball to
give you balance throughout
the shot. If you are reaching
up, your feet must be closer
together. Attempt to keep
the trunk reasonably steady
throughout the shot.

Swing
Early racket preparation is
crucial with the volley. Use a
short or compact swing with a
firm wrist, watch the ball right
through the impact point and
push the racket head down the
line of the shot.

Fig 94   **The Forehand Volley Swing**

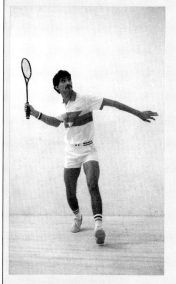

(a)   The racket goes up
early and Jansher Khan
watches the ball closely.
(Early racket preparation is
vital on the volley.)

(b)   Using a more upright
stance for the volley
Jansher Khan's foot goes
down and the racket starts
to come through.

Fig 95   **The Backhand Volley Swing**

(a)   Good preparation
with the racket up and the
shoulder around early.

(b)   Jansher Khan waits
for the ball to fall to just the
right spot.

(c) The forearm pronates. The full volley swing is similar to the drive but a little more compact and at a 'second story'.

(d) Impact, with good balance, a slightly open racket and good wrist control. Note the swing is a comfortable distance from the body.

(e) The short follow-through punching down the line of the shot.

(c) Starting to unwind the swing as the racket comes around the body.

(d) Jansher braces for impact. Note the wrist and racket head control and that the body is side-on to the shot.

(e) Still balanced Jansher follows through in the line of the shot.

This swing will often be at a higher level than for the drive – that is, at a second storey. Above head height, it will move from a sidearm action to an overhead or smash action.

Adapting the Volley

While the basic position and stance are similar to the drive, the speed with which the ball comes means that the volley is more often an adaptation of the ideal. Often this means a more front-on, or open, stance and the danger is that there is a tendency to over use the crosscourt volley.

Even when using an open stance, you should attempt to turn your body to the side to allow the straight shots that will move the ball away from your opponent. Adapt your swing size and pace of shot to maintain accuracy when under pressure.

Variations

Smash

This is an overhead shot, using an overarm throwing action rather than a sidearm action, and is similar to a tennis serve. Take the racket up high behind the head and wait for the ball to get to the impact point. This will be overhead and slightly to the right. The path of the swing will be from behind the head, up overhead, behind and over the ball, and down diagonally across the body.

Practise by standing on the short line, just to the right of the T, and feeding the ball up high and soft off the front wall (or front and side) and smashing down for the nick in the front left corner. Develop a smooth, grooved path to the swing. Do not hit too hard for a start.

Balls to the right of the body may be hit with sidespin to

Fig 97 Zarak Jahan Khan shows classic poise and preparation for a forehand volley smash.

allow an easy action and to impart feel.

After some practice this action can be adapted with a turn of the wrist to bring the ball down to the right front

Fig 96 **The Forehand Volley Smash**

(a) Jansher Khan reaches up overhead arching his back for a forehand volley smash. Note he has prepared even before the ball has appeared.

(b) Impact, with the racket imparting a little side spin to allow a comfortable stroke of the wide ball.

(c) Good balance and the use of some wrist to help bring the ball down into the corner.

nick. The smash action can also be used to play length and defensive shots, particularly off the service and lob. Often this will be a high, wide crosscourt. It is wrong to think that every high ball that can be smashed should be aimed at the nick.

> The volley is a pressure shot. There are stages in a match where you can dominate with the volley. Keep your opponent behind you and under pressure and then cut it short with a variety of different volleys – volley drops, volley crosscourts, volley nicks and volley boasts.
>
> **Lucy Soutter**

Volley Nick

These are the ultimate finishing shots and need practice to perfect and good judgement to select.

As well as the smash action above, use the high backhand overhead and forehand and backhand side-on actions. The high backhand is easiest hit crosscourt with sidespin. The forehand and backhand from shoulder height are best hit with cut and with the racket moving diagonally down through the ball and across the body.

Stand on the T and use the corner volley exercise (forehand front–side, backhand front–side) to feed the ball up and practise nicks.

Volley Drop

The volley drop is best hit heavily cut and with touch.

This may be achieved by using a short swing or by breaking the swing through the impact point. The cut helps apply touch, feel and control for the shot and helps pull the ball down on the front wall.

For the straight volley drop, the player must turn to the side and the impact point must be between the player and the side wall. The swing must come down through the ball and when the ball is overhead this means high racket

Fig 98   Welshman Adrian Davies demonstrates perfect balance, preparation and concentration as he prepares for a backhand volley, that he will probably cut down on for a volley drop.

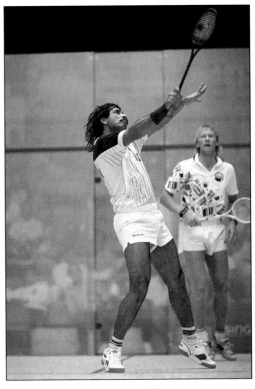

Fig 99   Jahangir Khan attacks a loose ball from Del Harris with a backhand crosscourt volley nick.

Fig 100 **The Forehand Volley Straight Drop**

(a) Jansher Khan reaches overhead in the same high preparation he uses to smash.

(b) Adjusting position slightly to the side, he cuts down on the ball in the line of the shot, imparting backspin.

(c) The follow-through swings comfortably down and across the body.

preparation, with an open face, a cutting action and a firm wrist. This can be practised by standing just outside the intersection of the short line and service box, feeding the ball high and softly cutting it down just above the tin. Allow 10–15cm (4–6in) for error (or whatever you need) and see how many you can get out of 10. Drive once or twice to keep the ball warm between shots.

Volley Kill

The technique for this is similar to the volley nick and drop. Allow a full, smooth action to generate pace. The idea is to beat an opponent with pace and get the ball to die (bounce twice) as early as possible. The

> Don't try to do anything too ambitious in the first game. Concentrate on keeping it back. I concentrate on my length, on hitting good crosscourts and then on moving in to volley a little more.
>
> **Lucy Soutter**

decision to play the kill will depend on your position in relation to the ball and your opponent's position. It may be safer or more advantageous to go for a kill than attempt a nick or drop. Play the ball so that it will die and not rebound off the side.

Volley Boast

The object of your volley boast should be to get the ball to die before the side wall. This will need a little experimentation

> One of the opportunities to look for in your game is to volley the crosscourt. I like to hit it straight, hard and low, so it dies.
>
> **Del Harris**

with the angles and a feel for the pace of the shot. The volley boast is a marvellous shot to move your opponent the whole diagonal and should be placed with care and sufficient margin for error. Too often it is blasted round the front corners or unnecessarily hit into the tin.

Use a compact swing, let the ball come in between you and the side and pull your shot when necessary. The forehand is the more difficult shot and may involve holding the wrist back so that the ball can be struck into the side wall. This is particularly necessary when an open stance is used.

The volley boast is easily practised in a pairs exercise

Fig 101   **The Backhand Volley Drop**

Fig 102   **The Backhand Volley Boast**

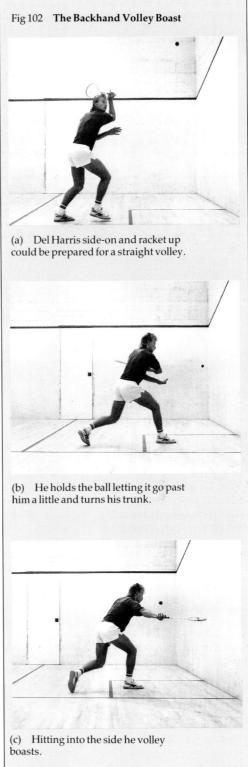

(a)   Del Harris has already turned side-on and taken his racket up in preparation for a straight volley.

(a)   Del Harris side-on and racket up could be prepared for a straight volley.

(b)   Stepping through he stops in a strong stance and waits for the ball to fall. Notice how the shoulders are parallel to the side.

(b)   He holds the ball letting it go past him a little and turns his trunk.

(c)   The racket has cut down through the ball on a diagonal path imparting cut.

(c)   Hitting into the side he volley boasts.

103

with the player in the front court feeding high, straight and a little loose with the player behind volley boasting on alternate sides.

Volley Reverse Angle

This is a very useful variation, especially on the backhand return of service. Use a very open stance, almost facing the front wall, a fullish swing hit hard and low enough into the opposite side wall so that the ball will move away from the server and die on the receiver's side of the court.

Volley Lob

This is used to win the T and break up an opponent's rhythm with a variation of pace. Use a very short swing with an open racket face. Extra touch may be obtained by pulling your shot through the impact point. Use plenty of width to beat an opponent's counter-volley. Lisa Opie uses the volley lob beautifully to win the T and break up an opponent's rhythm.

Practice Progression

Pat
Start with a simple underarm pat action close to the front wall.

Pat and Volley Pat
Continue with the above exercise and volley pat the returns when you feel that they are appropriate.

Volley Pat
Continuously volley pat, using an underarm action, hitting softly, while standing close to the front. How many can you do?

Volley and Pat
Turn this volley pat into a volley by turning side on. If a ball proves a little difficult to volley, let it bounce and feed it up (with a pat or drive) to volley with your next stroke.

Volley
Gradually move back down the court when you have achieved competence at a certain distance. The measure of this is when you can volley approximately 20 shots continuously.

Volley behind the Short Line
Stand behind the short line and without going over it see how many shots you can volley continuously on the forehand (and then the backhand). 20 would be a good target.

Volley behind the Service Box
A more difficult exercise, but excellent practice for the return of service.

Practices

Solo

16.1   Short Volley
Stand halfway between the short line and the front wall, facing the side, and volley continuously. Practise using your feet to position for each shot. Use a firm wrist, a short swing and fast racket preparation. Start slowly and smoothly.

16.2   Straight Volley
Stand behind the short line or the back of the service box and volley straight. Set yourself targets. How many can you do without a mistake? This is best practised out from the side wall so that it is easy to get into a rhythm, and then later moving in to play the ball as tight as possible.

16.3   Moving Volleys
A good practice on the volley is to place the ball so that you have to move to get it, so you are practising footwork, positioning and anticipation as well as stroking. This can be practised:

1   *Up and down*   Start close to the front wall and move back gradually till you are behind the service box. Move forward again and repeat.
2   *Side to side*   Play three or four forehand volleys straight and then feed a crosscourt, run and volley straight several times on the other side and repeat.

16.4   Volley Corners
This is the basic figure-of-eight volley exercise. Stand just in front of the T and hit forehand crosscourt front–side to rebound out to the middle. Follow with a backhand crosscourt front–side, then forehand, and so on.

   Start high and soft and let some balls bounce when necessary. Practise to develop a rhythm and gradually build up the speed of the exercise. At an advanced level this can be performed below the cut line.

16.5   Double Corner Volleys
An advanced exercise for

control. Forehand crosscourt front–side, backhand straight front–side, backhand crosscourt front–side and forehand straight front side, and so on.

16.6 Alternating Volleys
Stand halfway between the T and the front wall. Alternate a forehand and then a backhand hit to the front and to return directly. Increase the difficulty of the exercise by moving back behind the short line.

16.7 Reflex Volleys
Straight Stand close to the front and hit straight volleys as hard and fast as possible while keeping control. This is an excellent exercise to build up speed on volley intercepts, and to develop quick racket preparation, a firm wrist action and a short swing.

Alternating Reflex Volleys Stand close to the front and hit alternating volleys as hard and fast as possible while keeping control.

Pairs

16.8 Volleying Across
On the short line, volley across to each other and see how many you can do.

16.9 Volley Boast
A in the frontcourt straight drives for B behind to volley boast.

Fast A drives fast but well out from the side for B to develop a rhythm.

Tight A drives high, soft and tight for B to practise picking volley boasts off the wall. If the ball is too tight to volley boast, B moves back for a boast and up again for the next drive.

16.10 Crosscourt, Volley, Boast
1 From the front A crosscourts for B to volley straight for A to boast. B then crosscourts and so on.
2 As above, alternating straight and crosscourt drives from the front.

16.11 Circling and Volley
A and B practise straight driving and volleying. Loose balls are volleyed for straight length and tighter shots left and driven off the back.

Condition Games

16.12 Crosscourt Volley Game
A volleys across to the opposite back quarter and B replies. If the ball misses the area the striker loses a point; if it beats an opponent and lands in the area a point is won. American scoring to 9 and then change sides.

16.13 Volley Games
1 *Circling: Corner* Drive and volley straight to the area

behind the service box.
2 *Circling: Length Corner, Volley Half* Drive straight to the area behind the service box and volley to the area behind the short line. This allows good-length drives and dying length volleys.
3 Either drive straight to the area behind the service box and volley straight or crosscourt to the area behind the short line.
4 Drive straight to the area behind the short line and volley anywhere down the side. This allows volley drops and kills in a game up and down the side wall.
5 *Back-Wall Rule* Play a normal game except that the ball cannot hit the back wall. This can result in some overhitting but forces players to volley to stop the ball hitting the back.

Practice Games

16.14
In your practice games, work to a pattern. Go out with the idea that you will volley everything possible, sit yourself on the T and try not to move off it. Look for particular combinations of shots to practise, perhaps purposely extending the rally to set up these opportunities. For example, use the boast and then try to follow it up with a volley, or set up a straight backhand rally and look for opportunities to move in and volley.

17
The Drop

The drop shot has an impact and significance in squash which vastly outweighs the percentage of times it is played.

A sprinkling of good drops carefully selected when the opening is given can turn a closely contested match into a one-sided victory. When used to move and stretch, they can kill off a tiring opponent. Used for outright attack against a well matched opponent, they can lead to victory but often result in suicide.

This chapter looks at when to play a drop, something that is more important than with any other shot. It explains the shot combinations that should become reflex reactions in your game.

Because the drop is the *coup de grâce* in a rally – sometimes audacious, occasionally spectacular – it is easy to overdo. Do not try to do too much tactically or technically. Work at and use the principles of touch and cut. Define your target area exactly. Endeavour to achieve accuracy and consistency. You may not play many drops in a match so it is not a good place to practise them.

Learn the solo and pairs exercises so that you can work at your drops and make them a telling part of your game.

Tactics

The drop is an opportunist shot. The skill is as much in recognizing the opportunity as in playing the shot. Look to use all the variations and opportunities that arise but keep in mind the basic principles below.

There are six key points to remember, including the two key principles governing the attacking game, deciding when and where to drop.

Fig 103   Jahangir Khan crouching low, reaches forward and takes careful aim for his backhand straight drop.

Fig 104 **The Drop**

(a) Briars gets quickly onto a front court shot before Harvey recovers the T.

(b) With long reach and short swing he uses touch to lift it.

(c) Over stretching he pushes off the side but Harvey is still back out of position and it's a winner.

1 Drop When You Have an Easy Ball

Pick the balls to drop that you feel in control of from the point of view of both time and position. So often points are thrown away when a player tries to drop a ball that is rolling along the wall or when he is under pressure. As with all shots, you should feel before you hit it that everything is ready and that you are focused for the shot.

2 Drop When Your Opponent is out of Position

Drop when your opponent is behind and back off the T. If he is behind the line joining the back of the service boxes this is a good guide. As a general rule do not drop when your opponent is on the T or in front of you. Of course, there will be times when you can surprise an opponent and situations when an opponent is slow to react or tired, when dropping from behind will be successful. If, however, you lapse into playing your drops at any old time your opponent may easily get to them and smash them away for winners. Discipline yourself to keep to the general rules of positional play and treat attacking play outside these rules as exceptions.

3 Keep Your Game Fairly Simple

Keep your decision making simple. Do not let considerations such as wrong-footing or deceiving an

> On the drop I try for the nick but if I can't get the nick I try to get the ball near to the wall so my opponent can't play a good shot.
>
> **Jansher Khan**

107

Fig 105   **The Forehand Straight Drop**

(a)   Jansher Khan positioning to the side of the ball shows good preparation. Note that the swing is still sufficiently well prepared to change to another shot and that the position will allow a straight or crosscourt shot.

(b)   Jansher lets the ball come back slightly so he can angle the shot into the side. The swing moves through on a diagonal path.

Fig 106   **The Backhand Straight Drop**

(a)   Jansher Khan positions to the side of the ball and prepares his racket.

(b)   Jansher uses a slightly more compact preparation than the drive and less shoulder movement as pace is not required.

(c) Jansher cuts down on the ball. Note the balance, concentration on the ball and the wrist control.

(d) A short follow-through helps provide touch to the shot.

(c) The racket swings diagonally down cutting through the ball. No big downswing is needed but good balance and a firm wrist give precision. The impact point is behind the right angle so Jansher can angle the ball to cling or for the nick.

(d) Jansher still poised on balance. Note from the racket path that the racket has cut through the ball.

109

opponent spoil simple positional play. Hit the ball away from an opponent. Make him run. This advice must be balanced by saying that if you feel you are in a position to play another and better winner, then play it.

4 Do Not Be Afraid to Go for Winning Drops

Openings must be prised out, calculated and then used. This is the instinct you want to bring out in your squash. Do not, however, go for all-or-nothing shots.

5 Margin for Error

Squash matches are won and lost on mistakes. A major area of mistakes is when the ball hits the tin. The solution to this problem is simple. Aim high enough above the tin so that you do not make mistakes. Allow yourself a margin for error. If you aim 2cm (1in) above the tin and go for the ultimate shot, of course you will make mistakes. Vary the

> Try to pick the right time to drop. If you are looking for cheap winners, the chances are they will not come off and it's a signal to your opponent that you are getting tired or desperate.
>
> **Ross Norman**

margin for error depending on how difficult the ball is and how far from the front you are.

Only you can make the decision which balances the risks between aiming low and aiming higher. If you aim too high an opponent may get to the ball easily to hit it away for a winner.

The risk you take will also depend on the match situation. At game ball or match ball down you cannot afford to risk mistakes, but with a good lead, playing confidently and serving, perhaps you can.

6 Covering and Clearing Your Drops

When you drop, your opponent will have a range of alternatives to choose from.

You must be confident that you are able to cover each of these shots when you drop. For example, it is no good playing a crosscourt drop that will leave you out of position and allow a fast opponent to beat you with a straight kill or drive. If you drop from the back can you cover a counter-drop or angle?

Some players have developed the habit of standing in the position from which they have played their drop, thus blocking their opponents. This can lead to penalties – strokes – being awarded.

Do not play a drop if you cannot clear it when your opponent is likely to get there.

Fig 107   **The Backhand Crosscourt Drop**

(a)   For the crosscourt Lucy Soutter steps towards the corner and lets the ball sit out in front of her. The high backswing is ready to come down on the ball.

(b)   Croucing down with an open racket face she prepares to cut down through the ball.

(c)   Facing forward at right angles to the shot she sends the ball crosscourt to the nick with both cut and touch.

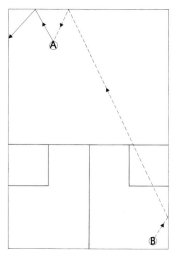

Fig 108 Straight drop of a
boast from the back.

Combinations

Combinations are standard
opportunities that occur. If you
can programme yourself to
respond automatically to these
you will give your game a
stable structure and learn to
play the right shot at the right
time.

1 Straight Drop off a Boast from the Back

This is a basic combination that
sums up the tactics of squash.
Force or wait for your
opponent to boast from the
back court and then straight
drop. This will move your
opponent over the diagonal,
the furthest you can make him
run on a squash court.

Do not drop off a front- or
mid-court boast (as your
opponent will not be out of
position) and do not drop if
you are under pressure.
Relieve pressure by creating
time. Use a lob.

Drop from a boast. This is one of your main attacking
opportunities – use the boast, drop, drive exercise to
practise this.

Ross Norman

An ideal opportunity for the drop is off the boast. It's not
necessary to make it complicated.

Lucy Soutter

2 Straight Drop off a Short Crosscourt

When this opportunity arises
and your opponent is behind,
a straight drop will again move
your opponent over the
diagonal.

3 Crosscourt Drop off a Short, Straight Ball

Any loose ball in the middle
can be dispatched crosscourt to
the front nick. Dropping of the
short, straight ball will move
your opponent over the
furthest distance. If you are
poorly positioned for this shot
it can be safer to play a straight
tight drop, even if your
opponent does not have as far
to move.

4 Counterdrop; Drop off Drop from the Back

If you can recover to cover
your drop, dropping from an
opponent's short ball when he
is back can be a good
opportunist move. When an
opponent has dropped from
the front, and is retreating
quickly with his momentum
backward making it difficult to
change direction, a quick
counterdrop can be effective.
Stop this practice immediately
if your opponent gets onto the
shot.

Target Area

There are two main targets on
the drop – the nick and the side
wall. It is necessary to have an
angle when aiming for the
nick, so this is our target on the
crosscourt drop. If at the point
your opponent wants to hit the
ball it is stuck to the side wall
and clinging, this is the most
difficult situation for him, so
this is our target on the straight
drop. The crosscourt drop is
for the nick and the straight
drop is to cling.

Occasionally a faded drop is
used. This is where an
opponent is wrong-footed in
the front court, when you are
not in position for an accurate
shot at the nick and so fade the
ball across the court. This shot
will not bounce off the side and
be retrievable and is always
moving away from an
opponent.

Technique

There are two special
techniques we use on the drop.
They are touch and cut.

Touch

Touch is the ability to hit the
ball softly. It is not as easy as it
sounds. Some players are
particularly good at it and we
may say things such as 'They
have got great touch' or have a
'feel for the ball'. A tense,
rushed, hard-hitting player
may find it difficult to judge
the speed of the racket head
through the ball to provide the
right degree of touch.

Developing touch, of course,
is so much easier with the right
technique. Bounce the ball up
and down on your racket.
When you use a bigger swing
the ball will go higher and
harder. You are starting to get
a feel for the pace of the swing
and the result. It is easier to hit

Fig 109   Jansher comes under the ball, on this backhand crosscourt drop and lifts it with touch towards the sidewall nick.

the ball softly, that is to get touch by using a short swing. We use this touch on the drop.

Cut

From moving the racket up and down vertically, while bouncing the ball on your racket start to push it through horizontally, spinning the ball on your racket. The ball may go the same height or lower but you are hitting it much harder and faster.

Being able to backspin or cut the ball means that the shot can be played more quickly and firmly but the ball still travels rather slowly. This is useful when you find that the squash ball is not hanging around for you to caress slowly.

Spin allows the ball to stay on the strings longer and this 'feel' can aid control. Spin is also used to allow a natural rhythm on a swing, and sometimes sidespin is used for this purpose, though it has no other particular advantages on the shot.

Cut or backspin will pull the ball down on impact with the front wall. This enables a player to aim higher, thus providing a margin for error, while still having the ball land short in the court.

Position

The positions for the drop shot are as for the straight and crosscourt drives. Often positions will need to be improvised by swivelling on the balls of the feet or turning on the knees.

Stance

A closed stance is necessary on the backhand straight drop, especially from the front court, as this gives the strongest stance from which to push back and clear the ball as well as putting the body in the best position for the stroke. An open stance can be used on the forehand but, although quicker to accomplish than the closed stance, it is less stable and there can be a tendency to pull the ball out into the court. Open stances with the weight evenly balanced on both feet are often used on crosscourt drops from the mid-court area.

Bend for the drop to give balance and to get down to the level of the ball so that you can hit through it and down the line of the shot. Take the ball out in front.

Swing

Use a short, firm swing. The backswing for a touch shot will be quite short, between the waist and shoulder. The wrist is firmer than in the drive, where the wrist action helps accelerate the racket head to the impact point. The drop is a shallower, steadier shot. The follow-through should be firm, controlled and with the wrist up. Often the follow-through is shortened – 'braked' or 'pulled' – so that the impact is softer and hence more touch is applied.

When cut is applied the swing will move down diagonally across the back of the ball, and be a little faster.

Variations

The drop can come in many variations. They will range from touch, cut and topspin to straight, crosscourt, fading, wristy and deceptive varieties. The criterion is what is effective rather than what is stylish.

> On the drops I go for the nick – the straight ones seem to sit in. I use the straight drop more because it doesn't leave the court wide open. Crosscourt drops can bounce out and straight drops tend to sit in close to the side wall.
>
> **Ross Norman**

Fig 110   Lucy Soutter prepares to cut a backhand straight drop down into the sidewall nick.

Fig 111   Left-hander Chris Dittmar lunging straight forward in an open stance uses his wrist to maneouvre his racket for a forehand straight drop with touch.

Practice Progression

Straight drop practices for forehand and backhand.

Pat
Start a few feet from the front wall and with a simple underarm pat action.

Touch Exercise
Turn this pat into a side-on stroke. Hit the ball just above the tin (but high enough so that it bounces appropriately) and quite softly. You will find that you need a short swing to acquire the appropriate degree of touch.

Feed and Drop
Stand halfway between the short line and the front wall, face the side and feed the ball high and soft to land between you and the corner. Drop straight, aiming high enough above the tin to allow a margin for error, and endeavour to get the ball to bounce and cling. For this shot you will find that you have to position round to the side even further than for a straight drive.
Repeat.
The ball can get quite cold with this exercise so after a few shots warm it with a continuous driving or corner exercise.

Drive and Drops
Stand outside the service box and drive the ball softly several times then straight drop. The ball will roll back to you. Try to do this exercise as continuously as possible.

Practices

Solo

17.1   Feed and Drop
In the front court stand facing the side and feed a high soft ball to drop straight.

17.2   Cutting
Start by setting the ball up quite close to the front wall and

113

SHOTS

> Try to get your opponent behind you before you drop and
> don't drop from the back as a general rule.
>
> **Ross Norman**

cutting down on it from the top of the bounce. When you have this action established, cut the ball continuously just above the tin. Crouch down, move for each stroke, and use a compact swing, a firm wrist and a fast backswing.

17.3   Feed and Crosscourt Drop
Stand on the short line to the side of the T, feed high and soft directly off the front wall, and drop crosscourt. Start with touch and gradually introduce more cut.

17.4   Corner Exercise and Drop
Practising drops can seem a static and boring exercise but when the corner exercise, double corner exercise, screw drives and boasts (*see* practices in Chapter 20) are used to keep the ball firing round the front corners it can be very dynamic and rewarding. Start by grooving one particular shot. In a practice session you do not have to practise each drop (forehand straight and crosscourt; backhand straight and crosscourt). If you like, finish the practice with a short game by yourself, mixing different feeds and drops.

1   *Forehand Straight Drop*   Feed forehand crosscourt front–side; backhand crosscourt front–side; straight drop and repeat.
2   *Backhand Straight Drop*   Feed backhand crosscourt front–side; forehand crosscourt front–side; straight drop and repeat.
3   *Forehand Crosscourt Drop*   Feed backhand

crosscourt front–side and forehand crosscourt drop. Repeat.
4   *Backhand Crosscourt Drop*   Feed forehand crosscourt front–side and backhand crosscourt drop. Repeat.

Pairs

17.5   Driving and Dropping
1   A feed drives straight to the service box for B to straight drop.
2   A feed drives straight for length for B to drop straight.
3   A feed drives crosscourt to the service box for B to crosscourt drop.
4   A drives straight or crosscourt; B straight drops.

17.6   Boast, Drop and Drive
A boasts; B drops and drives (that is, plays two shots). This is an excellent exercise to practise movement and drops off the boast (which is a basic combination) and to keep the ball warm.

17.7   Boast, Drop, Drive Exercises (Diagonal Movement Exercises)
1   A boasts, B drops, A drives; B boasts, A drops, and so on. (Change sides at half-time in the practice so that each shot is practiced on both sides.)
2   A boasts, B drops, A drops, B drives; A boasts, and so on. (Change at half-time.)
3   A boasts, B drops, A drives, B drives from back; A boasts, and so on. (Change at half-time.)
4   A boasts, B drops, A drops, B drives, A drives from back; B boasts, and so on.

17.8   Feeding and Drop
1   A feeds straight for B to straight drop, then crosscourts for B to crosscourt drop. (Change places, and sides.)
2   A feeds anywhere for B to straight drop. B starts on the T; A has to cover both front corners. This exercise can necessitate quite a bit of movement and some skill from A in judging appropriate feeds. See how many drops B can make without a mistake.

Condition Games

17.9   Front Game
Play a game within the front half of the court – soft shots only allowed.

17.10   Front and Back
A can hit any shot to the back court, B any shot to the front court.

17.11   Drop off Boast
A normal game is played but a straight drop must be played off a boast, or the player loses the point. This is used to practise a basic combination.

17.12   One Short, Stay Short
A normal game is played but once the ball is played to the front half it must stay short.

Practice Games

17.13   1   Play your normal practice match and restrict your attacking play to particular shots or opportunities (for example, the straight drop and the crosscourt drop) or try to force a weak boast with a good crosscourt and then straight drop.
2   It can be useful to arrange some of your practice games against weaker opponents so that you can practise shots. You may be able to go out and concentrate almost totally on your front-court game.

18
The Boast

Squash has many ingredients, but one of them is unique in major racket sports. It is a game of angles. Its basic rebound principle allows shots to be rebounded off any wall, on to the front wall. For the creative player this opens up a whole range of opportunities to use angles. Angles can be used to attack, defend, work and confuse an opponent.

The most important of the angle shots is the boast. It is a principal recovery shot and often the only way to retrieve the ball from the back corners. As an attacking shot it ranks with the drop as a major ingredient in the attacking game.

When to play the boast is one of the key tactical decisions that you will make in squash. Along with the crosscourt, it is the loosest shot in the game. Its use must be calculated and disciplined.

The boast is an impressive shot that rebounds with precision and accuracy off two or three walls and technically it has one great advantage: it is easy to practise in pairs and forms a part of many practice routines.

Tactics

Some players feed the boast up for their opponents, putting themselves at an immediate disadvantage in a rally. Their opponents quickly learn to keep the rallies going and prise out or wait for these opportunities. Other players play boasts of the same quality and their opponents are beaten or just scrape the ball up. The key tactical point on the boast is, when do you play it?

Back-Corner Boast

As a general rule do not boast from the back except as a recovery shot or to take advantage of an opening to attack.

1 As a Recovery Shot
When you have developed the skill, it is easy to boast from the back corners. That is the problem: you should not. If you are under pressure in the back corners your opponent is probably on the T, in the best position to cover your short shots and take advantage.

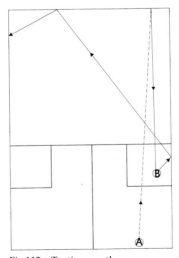

Fig 112   Tactics: use the attacking boast when you have a short straight ball and your opponent is in the back.

> If I see my opponent's face and I can see that they're tired then I use the boast more and make them run.
> **Jansher Khan**

As a recovery shot, boast only if you have to. Try to straight drive. Work at it. Use the practice where A is in the front corner and crosscourts side–floor–back for B in the back to attempt a straight drive and then boast (or just boast if unable to straight drive).

In a rally try to get your opponent in the back so that you can recover the T.

In short, the back-corner boast is an important recovery shot but do this only as a last resort.

2 As an Attacking Shot
Boast to move an opponent when you have a special reason to attack. These reasons will include an opponent who is back off the T; a front-wall watcher; an opponent who has his feet pointing at the side (not in a ready position), making it difficult to turn quickly; a very tired opponent; wrong-footing an opponent still moving back; breaking the pattern of play after a long rally of deep shots; if your opponent is very predictable (for example, crosscourting every boast) or lacks any proficient short shots.

Fig 113 **The Attacking Boast**

(a) While Chris Robertson looks on Stuart Hailstone shapes for a shot that could be a backhand straight drive.

(b) Hailstone holds the ball letting it pass him slightly to a position for the backhand boast.

(c) The follow-through while maintaining balance.

Attacking Boast

1 Boast when you have a short straight ball and your opponent is behind. This is one of the standard combinations of the game. It catches your opponent out of position.

2 Volley boast when you can intercept a straight ball and your opponent is behind and move him on the diagonal (the furthest you can make him run). Look for this opportunity in your game. Set up a straight rally and wait for it.

3 Take the ball early on the bounce and boast before your opponent has had time to recover the T. Some balls that may travel for length can be taken early, on the rise, and boasted. This is a difficult shot to time but you may be able to catch an opponent out of position.

Covering and Following Up

The boast is one of the shots in the game where it is easy to sit back and see how it is going and how your opponent is doing in getting to it. It is important not to fall into this trap. A drop off the boast is a standard combination your opponent should consider and one you must cover. Try not to boast unless you can cover all your opponent's alternatives. As soon as you have finished the boast, keep moving until you are on the T.

Think ahead from your boast. Work out countermoves to your opponent's alternatives. If your boast pressurizes your opponent, he may respond with a lob or use a crosscourt. Try to volley these.

Remember: Cover recovery boasts and follow up attacking boasts with volleys.

Fig 114   **The Forehand Boast**

(a)   Del Harris shapes for a full forehand straight drive.

(b)   Holding the ball he lets it come back past him and brings his racket down to hit through the ball.

(c)   A later impact point than the straight drive and a slight turning of the body guides the ball into the side.

(d)   The follow-through while still in a balanced position.

117

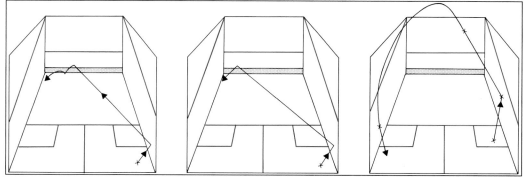

Fig 115 Types of boast. (a) The two wall or dying boast. Try to get the second bounce to die in the nick. (b) The three wall or nick boast aimed to land in the nick. (c) The skid boast hit hard, high and at a narrow angle.

Target Area

There are two target areas for the boast. The two-wall or dying boast is played at an angle so that the second bounce will die just before the side or on the side. The three-wall or nick boast is hit at a sharper angle and travels right across court to land in the nick.

Technique

Path, Position and Stance

It is important on the boast to move to your position in such a way that the impact point is behind the body. Shape up as for the straight drive and let the ball come back a little.

Swivel on the hips and knees to let the body face backwards slightly so that you can use the classic side-on action.

From the T, moving backwards on the forehand may entail stepping back on the right foot and sidestepping to position, resulting in an open stance. This quick movement can allow you to

Fig 116 The Backhand Backcorner Boast

(a) Striding into the corner Jansher Khan takes a path that places him to the side of the ball and allows room for the ball to come off the side wall. Note how he is already preparing his racket.

(b) Jansher points his toes into the corner and squats down into a strong backcorner stance.

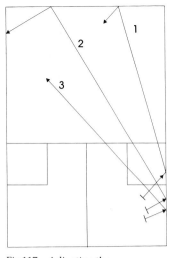

> As well as a recovery shot from the back corners the boast can be used as an attacking shot from the mid-court if an opponent hits a short shot – fade the ball into the nick on the second bounce.
>
> **Lucy Soutter**

take advantage of an attacking opportunity. On the backhand, stepping across and getting into a basic stance will give better balance. Deliberately stepping back and/or facing the back corners will obviously telegraph the shot.

Swing

Generally, on the boast you will use a compact swing for control. Often you will have to pull your shot because the side wall is in the way and obstructing your follow-through. You can do this by breaking your swing sharply immediately after the impact point. Alternatively, you can hit the ball at an oblique angle, applying sidespin, turning your racket along the side of the ball parallel to the side wall when you obviously cannot play through the ball along the line of the shot.

If you use the basic stance the impact point will be nearer the back knee than the front. Hit up and through this point with an open face. This will give it a little height to clear the tin.

Adjusting the Angles

The correct angle into the side wall can be found with a little experimentation. Adjust the

Fig 117 Adjusting the angles: adjust the angles of your boasts by experimentation. (1) Too far up the wall brings the shot out into the middle, (2) The correct angle to find the nick on the second bounce. (3) Too sharp an angle into the wall doesn't take the boast to the front.

(c) Impact for the boast is behind the body. The swing comes down and up through the ball lifting it into the side.

(d) Jansher pulls out of his shot and pushes back to the T.

Problem	Cause	Solution
1 Boast does not reach the front wall.	The angle is too sharp into the side wall. The ball has been let go too far back past the body; you are positioning too far in front.	Aim further along the side wall towards the front. Position more behind the ball.
2 Boast comes off the front, out into the middle of the court.	The angle is too far towards the front. The ball is in front of the body at impact. Positioning too much behind the ball.	Aim further back – more into the side wall. Position more to the front of the ball.
3 Boast too high above tin.	Hitting upwards too hard. Hitting too high on the side.	Hit softer. Hit through the ball more and not up so much. Let the ball fall to a lower impact point. Use a slight downward cutting action on very high balls.
4 Boast goes in the tin.	Going over the ball in the stroke. Closed racket face. Not hitting up and through the ball. Not allowing for the fact that the ball will fall (lose height) over its path. No margin for error.	Hit up and through the ball. Use an open racket face (check grip and wrist action). Allow a margin for error on the front wall.

angle for each boast until you get the ball to die in the nick on the second bounce. The boast-and-drive exercise is an ideal practice to work at this. Concentrate on one particular type of boast at a time and try and get this grooved and rhythmic.

The chart provides a simple analysis of the angles and how they should be adjusted. This is the way you should think while practising. Keep concentrating. Talk to yourself in terms such as 'Aim forward a little', 'Hit up', and so on. Remember that the angle at which you strike the ball into the side wall will vary

depending on your distance from the front wall.

Variations

Hard Boast
This beats an opponent with speed. It is important to get it to sit low in the front so that it can stretch an opponent and force a weak return.

Three-Wall Boast
This is usually played from the

back corners (from the middle and front, the path of the shot takes too long). Hit at a sharp angle (which you are sometimes forced to do in the back corners with a difficult ball), and aim directly for the nick. Do not attempt this shot exclusively when boasting but save it until you feel you are perfectly positioned. If it is a little off target it can be a very loose shot, and provide an opportunity for your opponent. The boast and

When I'm playing Jahangir or Dittmar, I'm very careful when I boast because they can counter with the drop. Boast when your opponent is in the back.

Jansher Khan

crosscourt exercise is ideal to practise the three-wall boast.

Recovery Boast – and High Three-Wall Boast

When a ball has passed you to the extent that it cannot be angled for a floating or skid boast and your position is poor for a back-wall lob, a high boast will get it back and give you time to recover the T, but you have to be very quick to recover what will be an easy shot for your opponent. Use this only when there is no other alternative.

The high three-wall boast travels up along the cut line and rebounds off the opposite wall and out into the middle. Again use this only as a last resort. Its one virtue is that it gives time.

Floating Boast

This is a touch shot played high to drop down off the front wall. It gives the striker time to get right up on the T and look for the volley intercept. The floating boast is very effective with a cooler ball and can be used to create time for recovering.

Boasting on the Rise

It is useful to be able to cut down on a rising ball (getting it before the back), therefore taking it early before an opponent has had a chance to recover fully.

Deceptive Boast

Shape up as for a straight drive and hold. Swing, keeping your body in the straight-drive position, hold the wrist back and push the racket head into the side.

Skid Boast

Hit high, hard and at the narrowest angle you can into the side wall. The objective is to get the ball to travel high across court and hit the side wall near the back corner, the floor and then the back. This will be difficult for your opponent to volley and will come off the side wall at a sharp angle.

The skid boast is worth practising as it can be very effective with the right opponent in the right conditions. Practise with a partner, driving straight to yourself and picking a ball to skid boast for your opponent to repeat on the opposite side.

Practice Progression

Solo

Hand Feed and Boast

Stand on the 'sideline' just forward of the back of the service box.

Throw the ball high off the side to land on the back line and boast into the side about 60cm (2ft) behind the intersection of the short line and the side wall.

Racket Feed and Boast

Feed a straight ball high and soft to land in the service box and boast.

Racket Feeding and Boasting

Feed straight and boast. Run and retrieve the boast (it may bounce twice) and feed straight balls until you have moved back to the service box, then boast.

Repeat this practice.

Pairs

1   A in the front court feeds a high, soft ball to the service box. B feeds straight to the service box (one or more balls as necessary). B boasts. A self-feeds (for control, one or more balls). A feeds straight to service box.
2   A self-feeds and feeds to service box. B boasts.
3   A feeds to service box. B boasts.
4   A drives straight. B boasts.

Practices

Solo

18.1   Driving and Boasting

1   Drive feed to the service box and boast. Retrieve and drive feed on the opposite side to the service box and boast. Practise as continuously as possible.
2   Drive straight for length several times and boast.

Recover the ball and repeat.
3   Drive several times, boast, retrieve with a drop feed and/or straight drive. Drive several times on the opposite side and repeat.

18.2   Front-Court Boasting (Side-to-Side Exercise)

1   Boast high so that the ball rebounds off the front and side without bouncing.
2   Boast continuously so that the ball bounces before the side and rebounds to be boasted again.
3   Forehand boast; straight backhand drop into the corner to rebound off the side; backhand boast, straight forehand drop into the corner to rebound off the side.

Pairs

Boast and Drive

This is the basic and most important pairs practice from which a whole series of practices is derived. It provides

121

useful practice for the beginner and the professional and it is ideal for practising both shots and movement.

18.3 Boast and Drive: Length
A straight drives for length; B boasts.

Often it is useful to concentrate on one aspect of the shot at a time. A could start with preparation and footwork, then length (often it is useful to start with overlength), and then width. The target could be to try and hit the side wall behind the back of the service box. A should move back from each shot towards the T so that he is not just moving from side to side but is practising the movement he would use in a game. B should concentrate on one type of boast at a time and get that grooved in.

18.4 Boast and Drive: Service Box
A straight drives to the service box; B boasts.

This is the area from which attacking boasts are played and it is a useful way to practise them. It is a good workout on movement for A, who can gradually work up to hard low drives and kills.

18.5 Boast, Drop and Drive
A drops and straight drives; B boasts.

A practises a standard combination which gives B more time allowing him to come to a ready position on the T and therefore practise the movement he would use in a game.

18.6 Boast and Crosscourt
A crosscourt drives; B boasts.

A drives a crosscourt for the side, floor and back and B boasts. A must move several paces back from each shot so that he can practise his positioning. It is often useful to use a small target or marker for the crosscourt.

18.7 Boast and Lob
A lobs; B boasts.

This is a good exercise to complement the preceding one and is best used once the crosscourt has been grooved in and the ball is quite warm.

18.8 Boast and Alternate Straight and Crosscourt Drives
A plays alternate straight and crosscourt drives; B boasts.

18.9 Boast and Straight Drives from Front and Back
If we take our basic boast-and-drive exercise and add a straight drive from the back, we introduce more movement and a wide range of possible practices. Pairs practices are an excellent way to groove shots and work systematically on movement. Extra movement, while not always desirable, has its place but should not result in scrappy shots or tiredness affecting the rest of the session.

1   A straight drives from front; B straight drives; A boasts; B drives, A drives; B boasts; and so on (one straight drive from back).
2   A straight drives; B straight; A straight; B boasts; A straight; B straight; A straight; B boasts; and so on (two straight drives from back).
3   A straight drives; B straight; A straight; B straight; A boasts; B straight drives; A straight; B straight; A straight; B boasts; and so on (three straight drives from back).

Volleys can be introduced in any of the above exercises in place of drives from the back. This is a useful way of practising the follow-up principle of the boast.

4   A drives straight; B volleys straight; B boasts; A drives straight; and so on.

18.10 Boast, Drop, Drive Practices (Diagonal Movement Exercise)
1   A straight drives; B boasts; A drops; B straight drives; and so on.
2   A straight drives; B boasts; A drops; B drops; A straight drives; and so on.

18.11 Introducing the Crosscourt
1   A crosscourts; B straight drives; A boasts; B crosscourts; and so on.
2   A crosscourts; B boasts; A drops; B crosscourts; and so on.
3   A crosscourts; B straight; A boasts; B drops; A crosscourts; and so on.

18.12 Introducing the Volley
A crosscourts; B volleys straight; A boasts; B crosscourts; and so on.

18.13 Introducing options
1   A drives straight or crosscourt; B boasts; and so on.
2   A drives straight or crosscourt; B straight; A boasts; B drives straight or crosscourt; and so on.
3   A straight drives; B boasts; A straight drops; B straight drives or crosscourts; A boasts; B straight drops; and so on.

18.14 Two-Shot Practices
1   A drops and straight drives; B straight drives and boasts; and so on.
2   A drops and crosscourts; B straight drive/volleys and boasts; and so on.

18.15 Feeding
1   A feeds short drops from side to side; B boasts.

This is an excellent exercise for lunging and recovering.
2   A feeds anywhere in the front half; B boasts.

This is an excellent speed

and movement exercise for lunging, recovering, turning, changing direction and keeping on your toes.

3   A feeds anywhere; B boasts.

While A is feeding he should allow some time for B to recover the T. A counts the total number of boasts B can perform without a mistake.

Condition Games

18.16   Back Corners and Boast

A hits anywhere in the back corners (or half).
B boasts (between the tin and the cut line).
Score: Players win a point if they hit a winner into the target area or if their opponent makes a mistake.

18.17   Back-Court Game and Boast

A: normal game. B: back half and boast; or back half, boast and volley boast.

18.18   Diagonal Game

A and B can play only in one front quarter and the diagonal opposite back half (or corner).

Scoring can be used in many of the pairs exercises by selecting appropriate target areas to make the competition equitable. For example, with the boast and straight drive, drive to the corner and boast above the tin and below the cut line. American scoring to 10.

Areas and rules on scored pairs practices can be adjusted to facilitate competition for different standards.

Practice Games

18.19   To practise the boast, self-imposed practice games can range from playing as many boasts as possible to restricting shots to the basic game, plus boasting at the correct time and following up.

19
The Back Corners

The key to winning squash is not found in spectacular winning shots but in the back corners. It is the ability to get the ball into the back corners and to get it out that is the vital element of the game. This is where the battle is won and lost. The player who is forced into the corners most is usually the one who loses. This is where mistakes are made, openings created and players forced out of position. When tactics at the World Championships are considered it may be seen that the very elite players are better at getting the ball into and out of the back than other top players.

For a beginner, the basic consideration in the whole game is how to get the ball out of the back and how to stop it going in there. This is a problem of skill and in a match situation it involves movement, anticipation and speed. Sensible tactical decisions in this area require considerable patience and discipline.

This chapter looks at how you develop the required skills through good technique and by using squash's great advantage – the facility to practise.

Tactics

There is a time to attack and a time to defend. The back corners constitute a defensive situation. You are at a positional and a time disadvantage. As a general principle you should try to win the T before attacking. There may, however, be opportunities or special reasons which may justify attacking at other times, but it is best to regard these as exceptions to the general rule.

If you are in the back corners and your opponent is on the T he is in the best place to cover your shots and take advantage of them. If, for example, you boast, he could quickly counter with a drop while you are still out of position. Likewise a crosscourt could be intercepted and volley dropped.

The straight drive is your best choice from the back. Put your opponent in the back corner and take control of the T. If you cannot straight drive you will be forced to boast. (This is one of the problems you try to give your opponent when you drive.)

One of the weakest shots in the game is a crosscourt from a poor position at the back. Do not attempt to flick the ball across if you are not in the best position for the shot. Play safe, and play straight. Use the crosscourt when you sense that your opponent is hanging in, looking to volley your straight drive. As a general rule, attacking from the back is dangerous and often puts your opponent at an advantage. You can, however, consider boasts, drops, kills and reverse angles if your opponent is back out of position, a front wall watcher, not in a ready position, on his heels or with

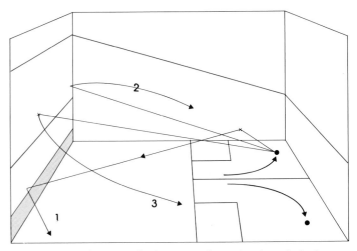

Fig 118   The back corners: the three main alternatives from the back corner (1) boast (2) straight drive and (3) crosscourt. Generally try to play straight, use the crosscourt as a variation and the boast if you have to.

Fig 119   Ross Norman takes care with a clinging drive from Mir Zaman Gul. Note the racket under the ball preparing for a high straight drive.

his toes pointing at the side, tired, or if you sense an opening to break the pattern of a rally. Be careful and remember; the odd undisciplined shot can lead to a lapse.

Your decisions on shot selection should depend on these basic principles plus your experience of the particular match situation. Keep them simple and discipline yourself to follow them.

Key Points

1   Endeavour to straight drive from the back corners.
2   Consider the crosscourt only when you have the right ball and can beat an opponent with width.
3   As a general rule do not boast from the back unless you are forced to.
4   Do not attack from the back. Exceptions to this depend on special opportunities and your experience of the match.

Target Areas

Boast
There are two options on the boast. Endeavour to get the ball to die in the nick, on the second bounce or better, the first.

Straight Drive
Aim for good length and width. Try to angle the ball in to hit the side wall behind the back of the service box, and to bounce and come off the back. If your opponent is standing up the court, or looking for the volley, then try to angle the

> From the back play mainly straight.
> **Ross Norman**

ball into the side at the point where he would wish to volley.

Crosscourt
The crosscourt must beat an attempt at interception by your opponent. Aim low and hard for dying length to the nick, or the floor behind the service box, or higher and wider into the side to beat the volley.

Technique

When working on the three basic shots out of the back corners it can be useful to start by standing and throwing the ball off the back. Even for the experienced player it gives time to experiment with the angles and to find the most comfortable position. First we will look at playing the shot in position, and then at the movement and path to this position.

Fig 120   Ross Norman prepares for a full drive from the back court while Mir Zaman Gul looks on.

125

Fig 121   **Backcorner Impact Points**

(a) Boast

(b) Straight

(c) Crosscourt

(d) Reverse angle

Boast

Position
Stand outside the sidelines facing the back corner and throw the ball high and soft to bounce off the back and land between you and the corner.

Stance
Use a strong stance evenly balanced on both feet with your toes pointing into the back corner. Bend down, using your knees.

Swing
In the back corners your swing will often have to pick the ball up from the floor. As the ball will lose some height over its flight it is necessary to lift it.

Often you will need to use a more compact swing than on the full drive, a lower backswing and a more open racket face. This swing more than any other travels in a big U shape, travelling down more vertically, under, through and up on the ball. Think of swinging under your back knee to allow enough room to

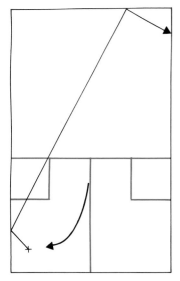

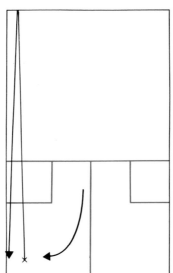

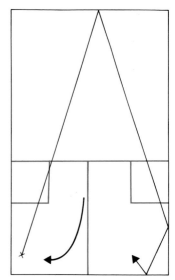

Fig 122(a)   Boast: as a general rule don't boast from the back unless you are forced to. Fig 122(b) Position: on the boast, the toes point into the corner and the ball sits between you and the wall. Use this shot when the ball doesn't come off the back enough to be hit straight.

Fig 123(a)   Straight Drive: endeavour to hit straight from the back by positioning down to the side of the ball. Fig 123(b) Position for the straight drive by moving to the side of the ball. Hit it when it's between you and the side.

Fig 124(a)   Crosscourt: look for opportunities to crosscourt when the ball has come off the back enough to allow you to position behind it. Fig 124(b) For the crosscourt position behind the ball and to the side, allowing it to come past you so that you can get enough angle on it to hit the front, then the opposite side.

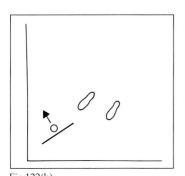

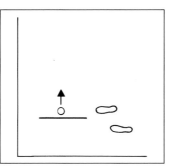

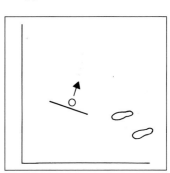

Fig 122(b)

come up on the ball rather than getting too close and hitting down on it.

Wrist Flick
The restrictions of the back corners, do not always allow you to play a smooth and full swing. Often the racket head must be accelerated and the racket face opened by means of the wrist.

Fig 123(b)

The Difficult Ball
Retrieving the difficult ball may involve positioning further to the side and facing directly to the back. From low in your crouched position the racket will reach to the back-wall nick. Swing right down into the nick and use wrist flick to lift the ball into the side of the court.

Early racket preparation is

Fig 124(b)

crucial as this saves time. Often more experienced players will shorten their grip on very difficult balls, sliding it to the top of the handle and thus gaining greater leverage over the racket head. This technique can be used to boast virtually irretrievable balls or to lift balls straight which otherwise would need to be boasted.

127

Straight Drive

Position

Stand outside the sidelines facing the back corner and throw the ball high and soft between you and the side wall. This may mean shuffling down to the side of the ball more than on the boast.

Stance

Use the same strong stance as for the boast but swivel a little on your feet, knees and hips to bring the body round to face the side wall at impact. The more behind the ball you get, the more power you will be able to put into the shot.

Swing

The impact point is between you and the side wall at approximately a right angle. Make sure that your swing gets behind the ball enough to get it straight. Swing across your body, get under the ball and lift it high onto the front wall.

Crosscourt

Position

When throwing the ball to practise a crosscourt shot, throw high and hard so that the ball comes out past the body. Position in to the side and behind the ball. It must come out past you so that you can get the correct angle.

Stance

Use the same stance as above and shuffle sideways or swivel to get behind the ball with an impact point in front of the body.

Swing

If you are not well positioned for the crosscourt do not attempt it and risk a weak shot. Do not flick or twist – swing smoothly across your body.

Now, throw the ball and see if you can get behind it enough to hit the side, floor and back.

Fig 125   **The Forehand Straight Drive**

(a)   Del Harris in position to the side of the ball with racket ready.

(b)   Swinging down to an impact point between himself and the side Del comes under the ball and lifts it onto the front.

(c)   A full follow-through, swung right across the body.

Fig 126   **The Straight Drive**

(a)   Hailstone on the T watches Nicolle prepare and shape for a straight drive. (Note the ball is rebounding back into the court from the back wall.)

(b)   Nicolle's swing impacts with the ball at a right angle with the side.

(c)   Hitting up through the ball he starts to step back and circle to the T. Hailstone moves in.

Fig 127   **The Crosscourt Drive**

(a)   Hailstone watches as Nicolle shapes for his shot.

(b)   Nicolle gets behind the ball leaving it a little in front.

(c)   He hits crosscourt, swinging up through the ball.

Fig 128   The Forehand Straight Drive

(a)   Under pressure Jansher Khan steps into the back corner on the back foot.

(b)   Bending, he swings down and manages to get his racket behind the ball.

Fig 129   The Backhand Straight Drive

(a)   Jansher moves into the corner to the side of the ball and starts preparing his racket.

(b)   Endeavouring to get the ball straight he works to the side of the ball. Note the backcorner stance and the racket preparation.

(c)   Using wrist he flicks it straight.

Path, Preparation and Movement

One of the key problems in the back corners is that players run to the ball, crowding their shots, which can lead to cramped strokes, a tendency to hit down on the ball and a failure to get the correct angle into the side or front. This problem is compounded by the fact that the ball may rebound off both the side and back walls and out into the player.

Allow yourself room in the back corners. From a ready position on the T, turn or swivel and move forwards to the corner and to the side of the ball. If you think of moving to the side of and behind the ball this will create the room you can use to adjust your position for the boast, crosscourt and straight drive. It can be useful to think of moving down and then in but you must of course leave room

(c)   Swivelling a little he manages to get his swing behind and under the ball enough to hit straight.

(d)   Jansher swings up through the ball lifting it high to come back deep.

131

for your opponent to recover from the corner.

Prepare your racket as you move, so that if the ball bounces in an unexpected way your racket is ready to swing and you can deal with the problem immediately. Often improvisation is necessary and half the time it takes to hit the ball is saved by early preparation.

Your final position will depend on which shot you have decided to play. Impact for the crosscourt is in front of the right angle, for the straight drive just slightly behind (at a right angle for a parallel shot), and for the boast behind the right angle.

A stance evenly balanced on both feet will provide a stable platform from which you can make slight adjustments to your final position by swivelling your feet, knees and hips to the best position for the shot. You will also be able to reach for the shot while retaining balance.

It would be very useful to shadow-practise this. From standing on the T, turn and take a step or two, jump, preparing the racket as you do, so that when you land you are ready to swing. When under pressure you may already have started swinging before you land.

Bending your knees will help you use them as if they were shock absorbers, braking you and giving you balance.

Recovery

The strong bent-knee stand you use in the back corners is not just for balance but also for recovery. The back corners are where you get into trouble and are caught out of position. How quickly you can recover from here back to a ready position on the T is crucial.

Your body performs a rhythmic action as you stroke, with the knees bending slightly and then with the weight pulling up as you swing. The best players use this momentum from the bent-knee position to push up, turn, swivel and step towards the T in one movement. This is a sophisticated piece of co-ordination and if you mistime

Fig 130 Rodney Martin facing into the backcorners for a boast or forehand straight drive crouches slightly to get under the ball.

Fig 131 England's Stephen Meads about to straight drive from the back corner. Note how his weight is about to transfer onto the front foot. Simon Parke watches from the T.

it, it will spoil your shot, but it is well worth developing and practising.

Your movement into and from the back is as important as your stroke. Use the solo practices in the practice progression to practise stroking and use the shadow practice and pairs practices to practise movement.

Shadow Practice

From a ready position with your weight forward on the balls of your feet, swivel on the outside foot (left when moving for a forehand), turn and step towards the back on the foot nearest the corner (right for a forehand), pointing your toe at the back wall. Follow with a jump to land evenly balanced on both feet, in a position to the side of the imaginary ball and facing in between the back and the corner. As you jump, prepare your racket, swing through on landing, and pull out of your stance, stepping back towards the T on your left foot (toe pointing at the T) and walk briskly back to a ready position.

Repeat this movement to various points in the corner and for imaginary straight drives as well as boasts. Sometimes more than one step will be necessary.

One or both corners can be used and this practice made into a fitness exercise – perhaps 20 corners or however many can you do in a minute.

Pairs Movement Practice

Boasting and driving is an excellent exercise to practise for working in the back corners but generally results in the back-court player moving from side to side. When competent in the back, it is very useful for this player to start working on movement to a ready position on the T and then back down for the boast again. This can be a rather rushed operation when boasting and driving, so it's useful to use an exercise that gives the back-court player B time to work on movement. This is achieved when the front-court player A drops and then drives.

Example

A drops and drives straight; B moves from a ready position to the back, boasts and recovers the T.

To practise hitting straight from the back, the back-corner circling exercise is excellent practice and should be a regular part of pairs practice sessions. A drives straight from the back, and circles via the half-court line back to the T. B moves in and drives straight and repeats A's movement. Obviously, when driving straight from the back room must be left for your opponent to get access to the ball and this necessitates this movement towards the half-court line which often incorporates sidesteps.

Another exercise that gives more time and room to practise movement when straight driving is for A in the front court to drop and drive, while B straight drives and boasts in the back court. This gives B time to return to a ready position on the T.

Variations and Recovery Shots

Varying the Pace

There is a full range of paces that can be used from the back corners. Too often players attempt to fight their way out with hard drives and end up just playing loose shots. Use the paces available to apply pressure, create time, surprise an opponent and break the pattern of play.

Varying the Length

Good length is the tactical foundation of the game. Losing it can result in your control in the rallies falling apart. When good length has been achieved with some consistency (and can be retrieved when lost), then you should look at varying it (along with the pace). One of the basic problems you give your opponent is deciding whether to take the ball before or after the back.

Straight Lob, High and Soft from the Back

Use a compact swing, open your racket and get under the ball. This is best played to be tight on the side around the short-line area if a volley is threatening. It can be played a little shorter than a full length (as it gives time to cover the T), and, if tight, can force an opponent to dig a difficult shot out of the back. This shot can give you time to get right up court, to hang into the side and look for the ball to volley. If your straight lob is dying, this may restrict your opponent to a boast or straight return (that is, not a crosscourt) and allow you to anticipate these.

Hard Dying-Length Drive

This hard, low drive can be used to break the pattern of play. The ideal is to hit it fast enough to make your opponent let it go past, but short enough for it to tend to die and beat him or force a boast.

Angling In

An opponent's shot that has come out from the side presents an opportunity to angle the ball in to die on the side as well as the back.

Fig 132   Jahangir Khan having improvised a straight shot out of the back corner from a ball that was behind him starts to push back to the T.

Because of the loose ball, your opponent will be pushed a little wider (to the side and off the T) and hence be less likely to volley the straight ball. This allows you to play a narrower ball that does not bounce out from the side but is continually moving in.

Your opponent is out of position and will not be able to take the ball off the side or off the back (if played for dying length). Use this shot when a serve or crosscourt hits the side and back on the full and bounces out into the court.

Kills and Low Drives
These are dangerous because they will leave you out of position. Select the opportunities carefully, picking the balls that come right out of the back so that you have the best chance to kill and to cover the shot. You must decide from your experience of the match whether it is to your advantage or not to use these shots.

It is better to keep a pattern of good length interspersed with occasional kills and low drives than to try too much and lose control of the rallies.

Drops
Drops from the back are exceptions to the basic tactical rules so if you have to use them, do so sparingly and with caution. Straight drop with touch and cut, and put cut on your crosscourt drop for the nick. Try to use them only when your opponent is tired or back on his heels.

Reverse Angle
This is a favourite attacking ploy from the back. It can be easily disguised since the position and preparation are similar to a crosscourt and many players do not read the shot until the ball comes off the front.

Pick the shots that come well off the back, step in behind the ball, and angle it across to the opposite front corner side wall to rebound onto the front. The shot should be played hard and is better played further back rather than forward on the side so that on rebounding it stays closer to the front and does not bounce out. It should die on the same side of the court as the striker but before the side.

Crosscourt Lob
The key ingredient on the crosscourt lob from the back is width. This shot, which is a little like a lob or semi-lob service with your opponent on the T, must beat your opponent's attempted volley but has the advantage of dying in the back and giving you time to recover the T.

There is a danger of hitting out, of course. Picking the ball that comes far enough off the back is crucial so that you can get behind it. Use a short swing for control, a very open face and a little wrist flick when necessary.

Skid Boast
The skid boast is a very useful shot, quite underrated and underused. With a warmish court and ball this shot can be made to travel high and wide across the court at a wide angle. It travels across a player more than the crosscourt so a

134

volleyer is hitting less down the line of the ball. This makes it more difficult to volley and the sharper angle into the side can lead to a more difficult bounce which can surprise. Ideally, the skid boast will travel right to the back of the court to hit the side, floor and back.

Only attempt the skid boast from close to the side and hit upwards, hard, at a very narrow angle. You need to get your weight behind the shot and position more as for a straight drive if possible.

If the skid boast comes across the court too much you have hit it too far out from the side wall, at too sharp an angle. Try to just skim the side. If the boast comes too narrow (a less common problem), then you need a slightly sharper angle. Generally, you will need quite a hard upward stroke to get the ball to carry, so if it's not going back enough hit it higher and harder.

The skid boast tends not to get much practice and if it is not played accurately it can go out or end up a weak shot in the middle. It is, however, worth practising and worth playing. You will find that there are some opponents who it will throw completely and it can be a major asset when used against them.

Practise the skid boast with a partner. Straight drive to yourself and pick a ball coming well off the back or one fed to the service box and then skid boast. Your partner does the same on the other side and returns with a skid boast.

Occasionally your opponent will put you in a position where you cannot crosscourt and moves to the side, trying to intercept your anticipated straight return with a volley. This is the time to skid boast.

Sometimes your opponent restricts you to a boast and

Fig 133 **The Backwall Boast**

(a) Nicolle has passed Hailstone with a drive. It won't come off the back so the last resort is to rebound it off the back wall.

(b) Hailstone sprints to the ball and lowers his racket in an attempt to get under it.

(c) He hits upward firmly on the ball so it will carry to the front wall and give him time to recover the T.

moves to the front court in anticipation. Again, this is a good time to consider a skid boast, putting the ball over your opponent's head and behind him.

Back-Wall Boast (Back-Wall Lob)

This is the last-resort recovery shot and should only be used as such. When the ball has passed you and will not be coming off the back (or not enough to allow a side-wall boast), use the back-wall boast.

On the forehand side of the court, you will use a backhand stroke straight into the back wall and of course a forehand stroke on your backhand side. Move as much to the side of the ball as you can, get under it, open your racket and hit firmly-to-hard upwards. Aim the ball to travel crosscourt to hit the front wall, bounce and then cling. With a little practice it is surprising how often this can be achieved.

If the ball does not travel to the front wall you are too far from the backwall (and not hitting hard enough) or not hitting it high and hard enough. Make sure you are getting right under the ball and getting it as high as possible on the back wall.

One of the advantages of this shot is that it allows you to move up the court and look for opportunities to volley and still have a last resort if the ball passes you. Another advantage is that it gives you the time to get up on the T to cover your opponent's return.

If the ball clings, look for the straight return you can intercept.

Practise solo by driving straight to yourself and then back-wall boasting. A good exercise for a coach to use is to feed the ball in front of the short line for the pupil to drop straight and then drive deep, feeding for the back-wall boast, then feeding short again. This way the pupil is moving up and down the court and approaching the back-wall boast in a situation similar to that encountered in a game.

Practice Progression

Boasting

1 Throw and Boast
Stand outside the service box width facing the back corner, throw the ball high and soft to rebound off the back between you and the corner, and boast.

How many can you get up out of 10?

2 Gradually move away from the corner and throw lower and softer, so that the ball does not bounce out as much and you have to move several steps to get in position for it. Boast.

3 Racket Feed and Boast
Hit a high shot off the front to bounce and rebound off the back and boast.

Boast-and-Drive Pairs
As soon as possible, move to the boast-and-drive pairs practice. Initially it will be useful for the front-court player to self-feed then drive straight.

It may also be helpful for the player boasting to drive straight once or twice until he is well placed for the boast.

Driving

Throw off the Side and Drive
Stand halfway behind the service box and the back on the sideline facing the side. Throw a high soft ball to bounce between you and the side, swing under it and lift it high onto the front to land in the area behind the service box.

How many can you get out of 10?

Throw off the Back and Drive
Stand outside the service box width facing the back corner, throw the ball high and soft to rebound between you and the side and straight drive.

How many can you get into the area behind the service box out of 10?
Gradually move back, throw lower and softer so that you must move several steps down to the side of the ball, bend to get under it and drive.

Hit the ball high and soft off the front to bounce and rebound off the back. Drive again. Some shots may bounce directly off the back, some before, some may bounce twice and some can be picked up and thrown off the back. Initially this practice is where

you should concentrate. Try to be as continuous as possible. A fast ball (a red or blue dot) can be useful to start with.

Continuous Driving
Gradually build up proficiency and develop a rhythm. This is one of the most important practices in squash.

How many continuous shots can you play that bounce and come off the back to be driven again?

Before and After
Play one shot before the back, and one after the ball has rebounded off the back.

Practices

Solo

19.1 Continuous Driving
1 Straight drive continuously for length from the back corner.
2 *Before and After* Play one shot before the back and one after the ball has rebounded off the back.
3 *Hard Drives* Drive hard out of the back, developing a rhythm as you do so.
4 *Hard and Soft* One hard drive, one soft.

19.2 Drive and Boast
1 Drive for length and boast; retrieve the ball, drive again several times on the same side and boast.
2 Drive and Boast; feed several straight shots on the opposite side and drive and boast; and so on.
3 Drive, boast, drop, drive, boast, and so on.
4 Drive, boast, drive, boast.

19.3 Straight Drive with Variations
This is best practised by first using one of the continuous driving practices (above) until a rhythm has been developed. It is best to drive several times (keeping the ball warm and keeping a rhythm) and then fit in the variation, retrieving the ball and then continuing this process again.

1 Drive and straight drop.
2 Drive and crosscourt drop.
3 Drive and play a reverse angle.
4 Drive and kill (straight and crosscourt).
5 Drive and crosscourt.
6 Drive and crosscourt lob.
7 Drive and skid boast.

Pairs

19.4 Serving and Receiving
A serves and B receives. 10 shots each.

19.5 Boast and Drive
1 A straight drives; B boasts.
2 A drops and drives straight; B boasts and recovers to the T.
3 A drops and drives straight; B straight drives and boasts and recovers to the T.

19.6 Boast and Crosscourt
1 A boasts; B crosscourts. (Target: side, floor, back.)

2 A (in the back court) drives straight and boasts; B drops and crosscourts.

19.7 Boast and Alternating Drives
A boasts; B alternates straight and crosscourt drives.

19.8 Boasts and Straight Drives
1 A straight drives from the front, B straight drives, A boasts, B drives, A drives, B boasts, and so on (one straight drive from the back).
2 A straight drives, B straight, A straight, B boasts, A straight, B straight, A straight, B boasts (two straight drives from back).
3 A straight drives, B straight, A straight, B straight, A boasts, B straight drives, A straight, B straight, A straight, B boasts, and so on (three straight drives from back).

19.9 Circling
Both A and B straight drive, taking the ball off the back. Lift the ball above the cut line and move in a circle via the back wall to the half-court line, then to the T. This allows the striker to move directly to the ball.

19.10 Diagonal Movement Exercise
1 *Boast, Drop, Drive* A straight drives, B boasts, A straight drops, B straight drives, A boasts, and so on.
2 *Boast, Drop, Straight, Straight* A boasts, B drops, A straight drives, B straight drives, A boasts, and so on.
3 *Crosscourt, Straight, Boast* A crosscourts, B drives straight, A boasts, and so on.
4 *Crosscourt, Straight, Straight, Boast* A crosscourts, B drives straight, A drives straight, B

boasts.
5 *Boast, Drop, Drop, Straight, Boast* A boasts, B drops, A drops, B drives straight, A boasts, and so on.

Condition Games

19.11 Circling
Straight condition games down one side.
1 To the area behind the short line.
2 To the area behind the service box.

19.12 Boast and Drive
A drives to the area behind the service box (back corner); B boasts above the tin and below the cut line.

19.13 Front and Back
A plays any shot to the front of the court; B, any shot to the back half.

19.14 Back-Court Game
Both or one of the players is restricted to playing shots into the back half of the court. This is good practice at getting the ball into and out of the back corners.

Practice Games

19.15 To practise back-corner play in a practice match, emphasize driving straight from the back corners. Perhaps concentrate on the straight drive, attempting to hit everything straight. If you are the better player, extend the rally or agree to compete by playing the backcourt game. It would be excellent back-corner practice for you to play someone better who is restricted to the backcourt game. You would get a lot of practice digging the ball out of the corners. Seek out a better player for a practice session.

20
Angles And Attack

Squash is an unending search for the shots that your opponent can't attack and can't get to. First learn and impose the defensive part of your game and then devote time to developing shots to beat your opponent. Build up a repertoire. Copy, collect, experiment with and devise ways of winning points. Don't restrict these to drops, boasts and attacking volleys but also use angles, nicks and surprise shots.

Explore all the angles so that they will be available to you in different situations. Use the angles to move the ball away from your opponent and to throw it unexpectedly at him.

Learn to play winners. Practise them. Become familiar with shots that your opponent just won't get to. Use the nicks.

As well as nicks, develop tricks. Use disguise, deception and variations to surprise your opponent. Work out little routines that you can pull out in the right situation. Save them up for the right time. Become familiar with them, so that when you sense an opening you can improvise a new response.

Use whatever works. Improvise and adapt to the situation. Most of all, be positive.

Angle (Front-Corner Boast)

An angle is a short shot played into the side wall at a narrow angle. The ball is played into the side and comes off the front travelling as much across the court as down it. This means that an opponent has to move further up the court in order to retrieve it. The angle is also called the front-corner boast and, if played softly, the 'tickle' boast.

The real advantage of the angle is that it can be disguised so well. A full swing for a straight or crosscourt drive can be suddenly slowed. A straight drop can be turned into the side at the last moment, sending an opponent the wrong way.

To play the angle, shape as for a straight drive, keeping the ball between yourself and the side. Delay the shot a second, allowing the ball to come through, and as you swing down hold your wrist back, turning the ball into the side. The impact point is as for a boast but this may have to be adapted when the ball is further forward by using the wrist to angle the ball into the side. If the ball is close to the side, the racket can run along the side of the ball, imparting sidespin and angling it into the wall.

The angle should be used with discretion because if it's read by an opponent who gets onto it early it can leave you out of position. It is best used as a variation when mixed in with drives and drops, may be best saved for later stages of the match rather than early on and is very useful against a tiring opponent.

Angle from Deep

This is a shot that has moved into 'softball' or international squash from the American hardball game. Ross Norman uses it occasionally when he shapes for a full swing from the back and then breaks his swing, turning it into the side wall near the front. The shot has a shorter path than the boast, loses pace off the walls, and, if used sparingly, comes off at an awkward angle.

Hard Deep Angle

The Australian Tristan Nancarrow slams a similar shot a little higher and as hard as possible, so that it rockets right across court in a lower kind of skid boast, providing a strange and awkward angle for an opponent.

Reverse Angle

The reverse angle is like an exaggerated crosscourt played across the body directly into the side wall. Play the ball sharply into the side so that it rebounds across and stays close to the front wall, rather than bouncing out.

To play the reverse angle, take the ball between yourself and the front, stroking it across your body. Deception can be added by shaping for a straight drive and using the wrist to flick the ball across into the side. Although the body is facing the side, keep the impact point forward, allowing

Fig 134 Tristan Nancarrow improvises a reverse angle against Jansher Khan.

the backswing, downswing and through part of the swing to be the same as for a drive but with room for the wrist to turn the shot at the last minute.

The reverse angle can be practised by feeding the ball up into the middle of the court and then playing the shot. Progress from this to playing it continuously near the front before it gets to the side and also after it comes off the side.

Reverse Angle off the Back

To play a reverse angle from the back, pick a ball that comes right out from the back wall, allowing you to get in behind it for the required angle. Shape as for a drive and use the wrist to flick the ball across.

Set up a rally of deep drives and then throw the reverse angle in as a surprise shot, or wait until you sense that your opponent is lagging back before using it.

Corkscrew

The corkscrew lob and service are the most spectacular and sophisticated uses of angles in the game and are well worth having in your repertoire.

To get the appropriate angle, play the shot from the central area of the court, position behind the ball, hit it high and hard, aiming as close to the side on the front wall as possible. The ideal target is to get the ball to rebound off the front and side and travel across the court to hit the side wall near the back. The spin imparted by the two-wall impact can pull the ball out parallel to the back wall (perfection is getting it to cling), making it very difficult to get behind and often forcing a back-wall lob.

Use the corkscrew on the serve but be careful not to foot-fault or hit the side wall first. Step wide and hit under and up very hard. Use a backhand serve from the right box and a forehand from the left.

The corkscrew is best reserved for warm conditions with a bouncy ball.

Half-Volley

The half-volley is an opportunist shot. It allows you to take the ball early, depriving your opponent of the time that the ball takes when bouncing. Use it when the ball bounces in the middle and your opponent is caught out of position.

Play the half-volley with a closed racket face and a

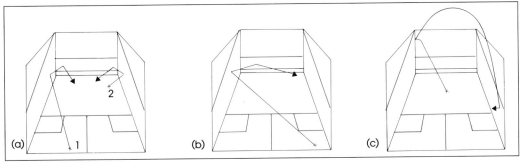

Fig 135 Angles and attack. (a) (1) the angle from deep (2) the frontcorner trickle boast or angle. (b) The reverse angle from deep. (c) The corkscrew can be rebounded parallel to the back wall.

Fig 136 Jansher Khan prepares to apply cut to a drop against Rodney Martin. The high open racket is about to cut down across the back of the ball.

topspin action, smothering the ball as it comes up after hitting the floor and deflecting it in a soft, lobbing path just above the tin.

The half-volley is easy to practise. Feed the ball at about the cut line to land just in front of you and play a half-volley just above the tin. Feed and repeat.

The topspin action is rarely used in squash but it can also be used for deception to turn a full swing into a topspin drop and as a means of bringing the high ball down, instead of cutting down through it.

Kill

The kill is the finishing shot in squash. Take the ball high and cut down through it, aiming just above the tin. Try to get the ball to die as short and quickly as possible. See if you can get it to die before the short line.

Play the kill early and move

it away from your opponent. When crosscourting, angle it wide but get it to die before the side. A good angle to practise at is to aim between the front outside corner of the service box and the side.

Fade the straight kill so that it dies on the side. Don't angle it in so much that it bounces out.

Practise the kill by having a coach or partner feed high soft balls that bounce up. Start with a high backswing and swing diagonally down and through the ball.

Nick

The ultimate attacking shots are played straight into the nick. Practise this. Don't hold back when the right opening is there. On crosscourt drops, occasionally on kills and boasts and on attacking volleys, especially those overhead, aim right in for the nick and try to get the ball to roll or bounce awkwardly for your opponent.

Pick your shots carefully, so that you know you can make it before you hit. It's easy, on the nick, to be lured into attempting the spectacular rather than calculating the percentages. Don't play shots that will leave you out of position, which could bounce out behind you and give away a stroke, or which involve a high risk of a mistake.

Disguise

You disguise your shots by shaping (preparation, position, stance) in the same way for a number of different variations, so that your opponent doesn't know where the ball is going until it is actually played. When you have time in the front court, position and prepare in the same way for

the straight drive, the crosscourt and the angle. By preparing early you can keep your options open until the last second.

Zaman was the master of disguise. From a comfortable backswing and an open stance he could direct the path of his swing to drive or drop, either straight or crosscourt, as he was playing the shot. Disguise is useful especially when blended with a clever use of variations, but it must be remembered that it is really secondary to playing the best shot you can.

Deception

Squash is for the magician as well as the runner. The racket is faster than the eye and this allows you to use 'sleight of racket' in your game. Express yourself with this and sprinkle a little magic into your game.

Show your opponent you are going to play a particular shot, get him to move off for that shot and then change it. This is deception. Use deception to wrong-foot an opponent. Lure him into moving or at least transferring his weight, making it difficult to turn or change direction.

Delay is necessary for deception. Give your opponent time to move. Prepare early for the 'show' shot, hold it, and then change.

Use the wrist to deceive. Position, prepare and swing as for the 'show shot' and then change it at the last minute.

Use your body to deceive by moving with the 'show' shot, using the wrist for the actual shot. For example, to change a straight drop into a crosscourt, prepare and shape as for a straight drop. Perhaps exaggerate the positioning to the side a little. Prepare early and leave the ball a little

Fig 137   Jansher Khan disguises his front corner shot to keep Rodney Martin guessing. Is it an angle, is it a drop or will he power it straight with a wrist flick?

Fig 138   Deception by Jahangir Khan. A straight shot but all the body language says crosscourt.

further forward, and just before impact break the wrist slightly and flick the ball crosscourt.

Deception can take many forms and often a player, if he uses any at all, will use only a few. Search for, experiment with and learn as many deceptive shots as you can. Try them out in practice and practice games.

Shape to hit straight, exaggerate your positioning and preparation, delay and then flick the ball across. Keep your body to the side; even turn and look for an imaginary ball behind you. Don't spoil the effect of your deceptive shot by moving immediately you have connected with the ball. Your opponent may not

have picked it up immediately, so don't help him. Practise this when boasting and crosscourting, boasting and alternating straight and crosscourt drives, and with a front-and-back game.

Shape to hit across and hit straight. Exaggerate your front-on positioning and the turn of the body across court. The trick is to position for a crosscourt but leave the ball a little wider to the side so that a slight delay will allow it to come through to a more suitable impact point for the straight drive. Let the wrist come through first and hold the racket head back for a later impact point while the body and head swing round for an imaginary crosscourt shot.

Practise this with the boast and straight drive exercise.

Shape for a full drive, wind up, turn your shoulder, swing down and as you do so brake and play a delicate drop. Practise this by using the touch exercise (described in Chapter 17) with a full swing. This deception can be practised easily with A boasting and B dropping and driving.

Shape to play short and flick long. Take your racket down low and prepare to drop. Hold it. Delay. Try to hear your opponent moving. Now accelerate the racket head with your wrist and flick the ball high to die in the back.

These are the four main areas of deception: shaping to hit

141

Fig 139 **Disguise and Deception**

(a) Jansher shapes up in the front court.

(b) Impact.

(c) It's a straight drive.

(g) Jansher shapes for a drive in the front court.

(h) Playing an angle.

(i) Jansher uses deception by turning his head for a straight drive.

(d)   Jansher shapes up in the front court.

(e)   Swinging through.

(f)   It's a crosscourt.

(j)   Jansher shapes up for a drive in the front court.

(k)   Instead he plays a deceptive little crosscourt drop by using his wrist.

(l)   Uses deception by feinting for the straight drive.

Fig 140   **The Deception**

(a)   Briars frontcourt with Harvey back on the T shapes for a straight shot and holds it.

(b)   Holding his position for the straight shot he flicks across deceiving his opponent.

(c)   Harvey moves late for the ball.

straight and then hitting across; shaping to hit across and hitting straight; shaping to hit long and hitting short; and shaping to hit short and long.

Use them and bits of them and any other variations that will work. One of my opponents catches me time and again by swinging and missing and then swinging again. Try shaping for a boast and driving, shaping for a drive and boasting and shaping for a straight shot and throwing in a reverse angle. Experiment. Develop deception. It's one more weapon you can use to defeat your opponent.

Variation and Surprise

From each part of the court you have different options. The more alternatives you have from each position, the less predictable your play and the more weapons you have to beat an opponent. Ideally, you will position so that you have a choice of shot and select the one that suits your tactical requirements at the time. This will often mean playing away from your opponent.

The more variations you have at your disposal in any one situation, the more chance you have of beating your opponent. Use the diagrams opposite to work out the best alternatives in order of preference if your opponent is in positions BCDE.

Use disguise and deception with surprise. Of the total number of variations you have at your disposal you will use some more than others. Your play will follow a pattern. Set up this pattern, repeat it, let your opponent expect it and then suddenly bring in a new variation. Now, it may be that your opponent will learn

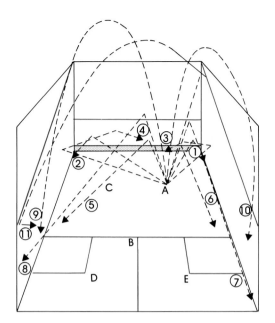

Fig 141   Variations from the front court.

1. Straight drop.
2. Crosscourt drop (also the deceptive 'faded' crosscourt drop).
3. Front corner boast.
4. Reverse angle.
5. Crosscourt kill (also kill to crosscourt nick and crosscourt low drive).
6. Straight kill (also straight low drive).
7. Straight drive for length (also for dying length).
8. Crosscourt drive for length (also for dying length).
9. Crosscourt lob.
10. Straight lob.
11. Corkscrew lob.

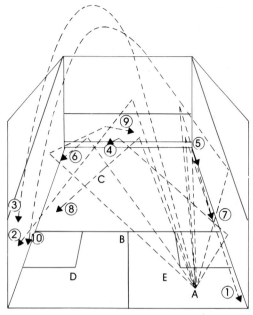

Fig 142   Variations from the back court.

1. Straight drive.
2. Crosscourt drive.
3. Crosscourt lob.
4. Boast (and nick boast).
5. Straight drop.
6. Crosscourt drop (and also the deceptive crosscourt drop).
7. Straight kill.
8. Crosscourt kill.
9. Reverse angle.
10. Skid boast.

Of the available variations work out the best alternatives in order of preference if your opponent is in position B, C, D or E.

quickly from this. Your problem is to work out how quickly. How many times can you surprise him before he is really onto it and expecting it? You don't, of course, want to race through all the surprises you have been saving up for him all at once and you do want to get your money's worth out of each one.

I try to change my game for the different opponents I have. With the top players I like to play a long game. For example, against Dittmar I try to keep it back and tight so he can't do anything. I get all his shots and then he becomes impatient so I can counter-attack with winners. I try to play long games with Dittmar and with Rodney Martin too.

Jansher Khan

Fig 143   Jansher improvises a drop against Peter Hill.

Practices

Solo: Front-Court Practices

20.1   Corner Exercise
Forehand crosscourt front–side to screw out for a backhand crosscourt front–side to the opposite front corner and repeat. This excellent figure-of-eight exercise is used to practise ball control, grooved technique and angles, as well as fast preparation and fast strokes. Start early, develop a rhythm, and then build up the pace. Practice can be above or below the cut line.

This continuous exercise is an excellent way to feed the ball up for drops and attacking shots. It can also form the basis of a solo front-court game when mixing in all the angles and shots.

20.2   Double-Corner Exercise
This exercise involves a double shot to each front corner. Forehand crosscourt front–side; backhand straight front–side; backhand crosscourt front–side; forehand straight front–side; and so on.

Again this practice is an excellent control, technique, angle and fast stroke exercise, but it also involves movements which are valuable footwork practice. This practice too can be performed above and below the cut line.

20.3   Screw Drives
Straight drives front–side to screw out into the middle, on the forehand side and the backhand side.

This shot must be hit hard to screw out enough to allow continuous practice. Technique tends to break down under pressure, resulting in shots that are less consistent and accurate. This exercise will help groove technique for the pressure situations. It is also useful to feed balls for shot practice and in the solo front-court game.

20.4   Reflex Drives
Straight drives, hard and low, played in front of the cut line. Use a compact swing and sharp preparation.

Again, this is excellent practice at grooving technique under pressure.

20.5   Reverse Angles
1   Forehand crosscourt side–front to bounce, hit the side and repeat.
2   Forehand crosscourt side–front to bounce and repeat (that is to say, hitting the ball before it hits the side).

146

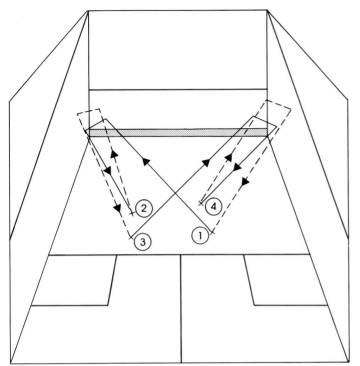

Fig 144   Double Corner Exercise: (1) forehand crosscourt front/side;
(2) backhand straight front/side; (3) backhand crosscourt front/side
and (4) forehand straight front/side.

20.12   Length, Drops and Variations
Drive several balls for length, establish a rhythm, and pick balls to drop straight or crosscourt. Try other variations (see 'Straight Drive with Variations' in Chapter 19).

20.13   Kills
Feed the ball to the service box and kill straight. See if you can get the ball to bounce twice before the cut line. Retrieve and feed again. Don't attempt a kill unless you have the right ball – feed again.

An advanced practice is to kill the ball off the back wall. Feed length drives until you have the right ball and kill. Use cut and keep practising – it's not easy.

20.14   Nicks
Nicks can best be practised by feeding the ball up high and soft off the front wall or by using a front–side feed and the corner exercise to keep the practice continuous.

Pairs Practice and Condition Games

20.15   Angle (Feeding)
1   A feeds straight short balls from side to side for B to angle.
2   A random feeds short for B to angle.

20.16   Boast and Angle
(Diagonal Exercise)   A feeds a straight (or crosscourt) length for B to boast, A feeds a short straight ball to B to angle, and so on. This strenuous exercise can provide a good workout or fitness routine for B. It can be timed or the total shots counted.

20.17   Disguise
1   A feed-drops, B straight drives. Initially, this exercise can give time to develop the consistent early backswing that it necessary for disguise.

20.6   Front-Court Boasting
Continuous boasting side to side.

20.7   Touch Exercise
Soft continuous drops played close to the front wall. Crouch down, use a stroking action parallel to the floor and a firm wrist.

20.8   Cutting Exercise
As above, but cutting each drop firmly.

20.9   Drops
The solo exercises given in Chapter 17 provide some examples of continuous dropping as well as feeding and dropping practices. Most of the above exercises can be used to feed balls for different drops. Work on one drop for a while and try to get it grooved in, then move on to another.

20.10   Solo Front-Court Game
Often players are at a loss when considering front-court practice, but it doesn't have to be static, cold and boring. With the practices given above, variety, pace, movement and shots can all be mixed into a dynamic exploration of the angles and possibilities in the front corners. Make it a little game, rally against yourself, and go for winners. See if you can beat yourself.

20.11   Drive, Angle and Reverse Angle
Drive several balls for length and pick one that comes off the back enough to reverse angle.

Experiment with a few 'angles from deep'. To practise this, feed the drive towards the middle so that it comes outside the service box width.

147

2 *Boast and alternate straight or crosscourt drives* A boasts; B alternates straight and crosscourt drives. In this exercise B attempts the same positioning, preparation and stance for each shot.

3 *Front and back* A plays any shot to the backcourt; B any to the front. A attempts to practise disguise when he can, so that B cannot easily anticipate and volley. When A is under pressure he will play the best defensive shot he can (for example a lob) and not worry about disguise.

20.18 Deception

1 *Boast and drive* A boasts, B drives straight. B practises shaping for a crosscourt but drives straight.

2 *Boast and crosscourt* A boasts, B drives straight. B practises shaping for a straight drive but crosscourts.

3 *Boast and option of straight or crosscourt drive* A boasts, B has the option of a straight or crosscourt drive. B attempts to pick balls suitable for disguise and keep his partner guessing.

4 *Front and back* The above practice is developed into a condition game. A can play any shot into the back court; B any short shot.

5 *One short all short* Both players play a normal game, but once the ball goes short all shots must be short.

6 *Front-court game* A and B play a game in the front court only.

20.19 Variations

1 *Feeding for variations* A feeds from behind and B plays variations: straight drive; crosscourt; lob; kills; straight drop and drive; angle and drive.

In this practice B is working through the variations available to him from a particular position and combining disguise and deception. A keeps feeding the ball up either on one side or both.

2 *Boast and option of straight or crosscourt* A boasts; B hits straight or crosscourt.

3 *Drive and drop or boast* A drives; B drops or boasts.

4 *Boast or drop; straight or crosscourt* A combination of the two exercises above.

5 *Front and back* A can play any shot into the back court; B any short shot.

20.20 Surprise

Surprise can be worked into any of the exercises given above that allow options. Remember: set up a predictable pattern, then break it and try to catch your opponent unawares.

'Practice doesn't make perfect; perfect practice makes perfect.'

It's very easy to go through the motions when practising, to just hit the ball around, get a bit bored and move on to play a game. For practice to be effective you need to work out exactly what you are trying to do and be able to answer the basic questions: 'Why am I practising? When should I practise? What should I practise? How should I practise? These are answered in Chapter 21.

The message at the top of the page could just as easily say 'Effective practice gets results'. The great advantage of squash is that it is designed for practise, unlike tennis and badminton. You can get results by taking a ball on court and exploring the walls and angles by yourself or with a partner. *The Squash Workshop* includes a vast range of practices. They include technique practices, movement practices, practice, practice progressions, solo practices, skills, pairs practices, coaching and feeding exercises and also new threes and fours practices.

Chapter 22 examines condition games, the step between practice and matches, and covers shots, tactical rules and scoring, as well as methods you can use to develop your own exercises. The formats of the ten basic condition games are fully explained.

Your squash programme could, with a little simplification, be divided into four categories – solo practice, pairs practice, practice games and matches. Chapter 22 also covers *practice games* and shows how to get full benefit out of friendlies by emphasizing in a game situation the shots you have practised.

Practising is something we do by fitting practices together into practice sessions. Chapter 24 explains how you can go about this and summarizes the key ideas on practising.

21
Why, What, When and How

Why Practise?

To improve your squash there are three main parts of your game you can work at improving; shots (more accurate, consistent and powerful shots from more positions and under more pressure), getting to the ball (fitness, speed and movement) and putting shots together in rallies (tactics and temperament).

Better shots are built on better technique and skill. The cut and thrust of a squash match is a very poor place to work on these. Here practice is unsystematic and spasmodic. To get results in learning a skill repetition is the key – repetition and feedback through knowledge of results. This is achieved through systematic practice.

You will be more effective in your practice if you can specify exactly what you want to achieve. Answer the question 'Why do I practise?' Write the answer down. Effective practice will give you results. These results will make a difference to your game. They are your goals or targets. Set goals for your practice.

Setting Practice Goals

The more specific your goals are the more chance you will have of success. The purpose of this book is to provide the appropriate steps towards your goals.

> On the day of a match I try to get down to the courts, have a warm-up for half an hour or forty minutes and practise hitting the ball. I take my time, concentrate on getting good length, practise getting it tight and then run through some shots at the end.
>
> **Lucy Soutter**

Goals must be realistic and relate to your needs – your needs in matches and in your development as a player. The things you want to do better in matches must be translated into specific practice objectives. Some examples are given below.

Example 1

Need   I don't seem to volley in my game. This means I'm not dominating the T and I'm not getting the pressure I should into my game.
Goal   To volley in a game situation.
Practice objectives   Refer to Chapter 16, 'The Volley'. Select your level on the practice progression and work on solo practice to develop competence. Refer to the volley practice section and select pairs practices that will have you moving and volleying. Play condition and practice games on the volley and then try it out against easier opponents.

Example 2

Need   My forehand is inconsistent, resulting in loose shots and lack of control. I need to improve my technique and if possible groove my swing.

Goal   Better control and a grooved swing on the forehand.
Practice objectives   Use the technique practices (Chapter 10). Work at service-box drives and build up from drives above the cut line to one above and one below, and then to all below.

Example 3

Problem   I don't drop when I'm put short.
Goal   Dropping when short.
Practice objectives   Work on the solo drop practices in Chapter 17, especially the boast, drop and drive; boast, drop, drive exercises; front and back; drop off boast, one short, stay short; games and practices.

Example 4

Problem   I always volley crosscourt, often hitting straight back to my opponent.
Need   A straight volley in a game situation.
Practice objectives   Practise a straight volley. Use the practice progression in Chapter 16. Give yourself a target, for example to volley twenty times straight behind the short line without a mistake. Use the pairs exercise crosscourt, volley, boast (Chapter 18).

PRACTISING

Fig 145 **Circling**

(a) Jansher Khan on the T with Del Harris in the back straight driving.

(b) Del circles around to the T and Jansher moves into the corner to drive.

(c) Jansher straight drives and circles back to the T.

Fig 146 **Corner Exercise:** Ross Norman practices the corner exercise slowly with footwork.

(a) Forehand crosscourt front/side.

(b) Forehand follow-through becomes the backhand backswing as the ball rebounds.

(c) Backhand crosscourt front/side etc.

How successful you are depends in part on how appropriate your goals are and on how well you select your practices to achieve these goals. There is a massive amount of information in this book. Work with a coach in setting targets. He will have the experience to help you pick the right goals and set the right steps.

Your goals can be general or specific. General goals will be improving all shots, working on the volley, developing winners, getting better length or more power, and so on. The more specific you can make these goals, the more effectively you will be able to practise and the more clearly you will be able to evaluate your results. From this evaluation you can reassess goals and redesign practices where necessary.

> Try out the shots you have practised in an easier game, where you are not under pressure, and concentrate on the things you have practised. Then try them out in a match.
>
> **Lucy Soutter**

Remember results take time. Set long-term and short-term goals and then go into action.

What to Practise

I know the sounds and rhythms of practice and whenever I hear them I peep over the gallery or through the glass back. What do I see? More often then not it's someone practising his favourite shot or favourite exercise.

It's frustrating to work on weaknesses, but improve these, set goals in this area, and you will improve your game. After setting these goals, work out which practices will help you achieve them, design a sequence round these and work at a level that is best for learning.

As well as overcoming weaknesses, you can develop your game in a number of areas. With your coach, think through your game, analyze what your needs are and select or design practices to work on them. Use the practice progressions in the shots chapters and then pressure to work at a level that's appropriate for you. Relate

Fig 147 **Alternating Volley Exercise:** Jansher practices alternating forehand and backhand volleys straight to the front wall.

(a) Preparation for the backhand volley straight to the front wall.

(b) Backhand volley

(c) The follow-through moves through to the backswing position of the forehand volley and so on.

153

'what to practise' as closely to your game as you can.

Below are a number of areas you can consider practising which are important to your squash development.

Technique

Technique gives you consistency and accuracy on your shots. Practise it and get it into your practice sessions. Read the technique chapters and use the technique practices in Chapter 10. Your game is built on basics. Don't ignore this part of your practice. Even at a professional level, how grooved a swing is, how quick and cleanly the ball is hit is vital.

Overcome Problems and Weaknesses

Work on the problem areas and work at eliminating weaknesses. Use the technique practices, practice progressions and shot exercises. Work with your coach or develop your own exercises.

Develop Your Shots

This is the longer-term part of your practice. Work on shots that you're not using or not using well enough in your game and develop these. Use the practice progressions in the shots chapters and solo practice to improve control and then build on this with pairs practice and games.

Groove Your Shots

As we have discussed, a game is a poor place to develop and groove shots. It is often the case that you can play a shot but it's a little wayward – too short, too narrow, or inconsistent. A surprisingly small amount of work on this problem can groove it in again

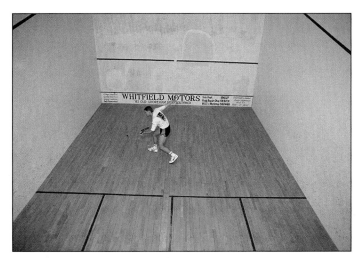

Fig 148   Chris Dittmar working alone on court perfecting his shots.

and brush it up so that it's firing consistently and accurately into its target area.

This is one area in which regular practice sessions are recommended for all players. All practices can be used, especially the pairs routines. Start easily, line the ball up, groove it into your target area and then progress it.

Groove Your Winners

A match provides very limited opportunities to practise winners. These shots, however, have much more significance in your game than the number of times they are played. Put time aside to groove them in. Even if you don't think of yourself as an especially attacking player, they are still important. Practise them. It's important that before and during a major tournament your winners are grooved in and waiting to be used.

Use the solo front-court practices in Chapter 20. Feed and practise winners and use the solo sequences, drops and front-court practices.

Use the front game, front-back game, back game plus short shot and refer to the condition games in the shots chapters.

A day or two before and during a tournament don't be tempted to do any hard training. A light workout on 'lining the ball up', grooving the drives in and running through your winners is most beneficial.

Movement

Squash movement is often disjointed and pressurized. In a game you have other things to think about, but just as a dancer practises steps to learn a dance so you can improve your squash movement. Your taking off, moving, positioning, footwork, path, braking for the shot, bracing, balancing, pulling out, pushing back and recovering position on the T can all be worked on. Consider your movement when you practise. Make improved movement one of your goals. Train your feet so that your movement fits into the regular rhythms and patterns of a champion. See Chapter 8 on movement and balance and most pairs exercises.

Pressure

I despair at players and coaches who think a pressure session is the answer to all squash practice and training. It has its place, however. It is pointless being able to play nice grooved shots if you can't do it in a game and can't do it under pressure. Get a balance between these two.

When put under pressure, it's possible to work harder than you would in a game. If you've got control under this sort of pressure you have a good chance of reproducing it in a game. When practising under pressure you don't want to work at a level where your strokes will break down. Try to hang on to the grooved stroke you have developed while you gradually increase the pressure.

Good practices include the feeding progression and pressure exercises in Chapter 26 and the diagonal practices in Chapter 20.

Tactics

There is so much happening in a game so quickly that you can't work out and think through each situation as it happens. To order your game tactically you need a plan, rules and shot combinations for automatic responses. These are discussed in Chapter 6. Practise the rules and combinations until you are familiar with them.

When to Practise

We like to play and compete. It's difficult fitting practice time in. Playing tends to come first and we don't get round to practising. It's important, therefore, to know why you practise and what to practise before deciding when to practise.

When the questions are answered and you're clear as to what to do, you can then look at the question of when and how often to practise. How many practices can you fit in? It's not always easy, unless you're a professional and can play in the day, to get practice courts but I do know players who practice solo at lunch times and play matches in the evening.

As well as booking time exclusively for practice, you can combine practice and games (a practice session followed by one game or a best of three); practise solo with two on a court, working one down each side; and practise at the weekends when you have more time and court space. Plan your practice times, partners and goals. Make a realistic decision on what you can fit in. Establish regular times.

The balance you establish between playing and practising will depend on your needs and also the stage in the season. Off season it is not crucial to be moving smoothly and have all your shots grooved in. This is the time for thinking in the longer term and building the skills and shots you will want to utilize in the coming season.

Pre-competition is the time to prepare and bring together all the different elements of your game for competition. Start to fit them together tactically and under pressure. During competition your emphasis will be on having all shots and winners working well and ready to use. Building up to a tournament will involve practice, matches and a lighter workout a day or two before, perhaps involving solo practice to sharpen up on winners and shots.

The table below shows what could be suitable emphasis in your practice for each stage in the season.

How to Practise

Now you have worked out what, why and when to practise, how are you going to go about it? I see players so often going through the motions and serving time when practising.

Remember that it is perfect practice that makes perfect. Here are some ideas to help you practise effectively and get results.

OFF SEASON	PRE-COMPETITION	COMPETITION
Technique	Movement	Grooving shots
Developing shots	Pressure	Grooving winners
Developing variations	Tactics	
Overcoming problems and weaknesses		

Targets

One of the main reasons you practise is to improve the accuracy and consistency of your shots. You can't be accurate unless you have worked out exactly where you want the ball to go – a target. Use a physical target when practising – for example, half a squash ball (painted), a paper or cardboard marker on the floor or stuck on the wall, chalk lines or a racket head cover. If you don't use a physical target, use a mental one when you practise.

Line the Ball Up

Practise playing the best shots you can. Eliminate casual shots. Line the ball up. Have everything ready and wait for the ball to fall to the impact point you want, then swing.

Feedback

Think of exactly what you want out of each of your shots. Look where it's landing. Work out how you can adjust and correct every ball to get the next one right. Concentrate on this. If it's short, think. 'Longer; up a bit.' Continually monitor your shots. Adjust. Talk inwardly to yourself: 'Up a bit. Over. Get round behind it. Too close. Still short–higher. Let it come back. That's it.'

Front Wall

Translate your calculations on the accuracy of your shot into what you need to do on the front wall – both horizontally and vertically. Think in simple up-and-down, back-and-forth terms.

Feel

Be aware of your swing, body and movement when practising. As well as consciously analyzing the activity, we learn by getting a feel for the shot. Use the feel check on the swing and the freeze check on your movement.

Rhythm

You will feel when the parts of your stroke start to come together. You develop a 'flow'. At first it will be just one shot. As soon as you get this feeling of rhythm, hang in there and work for it again. Sometimes when working on technique and shots you can concentrate on rhythm alone and not worry about the target so much. You practise to get into a rhythm on your stroke in which everything happens easily and your body and swing flow together.

Grooved In

There is a stage in practice where shots land in the target area easily and consistently. The mental effort is a little easier and adaptions in court position are accommodated automatically. This is what you practise for. When you have your shots grooved in, hold on to this, as you increase both movement and pressure.

Start Easily

Start your practices easily. This may involve gentle feeding and limited movement. It gives you a chance to get control, to concentrate on one thing at a time, make the adjustments needed to find your target, develop feel and rhythm and get grooved in. Start your practices easily and then build up. The build-up on an exercise is called a progression.

Progression

Once you have your shots grooved in or at a good level of control, you then want to increase the movement, choice, pace, pressure and competition so that you can reproduce it in more game-like and pressured situations. A simple progression is to use the practice progression initially and then move on to solo, pairs practices, condition games, practice games and matches.

Levels

Practise at a level where you can get control and then progress this. Practising easier exercises has its place if you are really working on a particular aspect of a stroke but it can lead to just going through the motions.

Practising at a level that is too difficult can lead to control and technique breaking down and may not prove much other than being a workout. The practice progressions in the shots chapters are to help you find the most appropriate level to work at.

Movement

Movement is easiest practised in pairs starting with a feeding or front-to-back exercise (for example, boast and drive) and then moving into a diagonal movement exercise. Start easily, learn the steps, develop a rhythm on your movement and then progress this.

Pressure

This is most easily introduced by a coach pressure feeding from an anchored position (see chapter 25).

Concentrate on One Thing at a Time

Keep your practice simple. Concentrate. Pick out one aspect of your stroke and practice to get this working. Don't try to do too much. Once this is working easily, move on to something else while trying to hold onto the first achievement.

22
Condition Games and Practice Games

Condition Games

Competition focuses concentration. Condition games introduce competition to practices. They do this, as in all competitive games, by using rules. These rules or conditions can apply to one or to both players. Sometimes different conditions are applied to each player. These conditions can involve:

1 Area
2 Shots
3 Tactical rules
4 Scoring

Condition games are most effective if the elements being practised have been honed first. This is best done in practice – solo practice and co-operative practice with a partner. Condition games are the next step – the step between practice and matches.

Each of the shot chapters includes examples of condition games. The rules or conditions you make must be adapted to the standards, needs and goals of the competitors. Be flexible. Conditions which are too strict may not allow rallies to develop. Most of all, make them work. Let's look at the type of conditions you can apply.

Areas

Court lines provide the easiest and most useful definition of court areas, but additional boundaries can be made with chalk or tape. Areas are sometimes made by reducing the width of the sidelines or placing a line across the front of the court for the attacking game.

For the sake of simplicity I have introduced names for commonly used areas. This is a form of code or shorthand that should save having to define areas every time they are used.

Front court (Front) area in front of the short line.
Back court (Back) area behind the short line.
Back half (Half) (also called half side or back side) area behind the short line and within the service box width.
Corner area behind the service box and within the service box width.
Back quarter Back quarter of the whole court – behind the short line and within the half-court line.

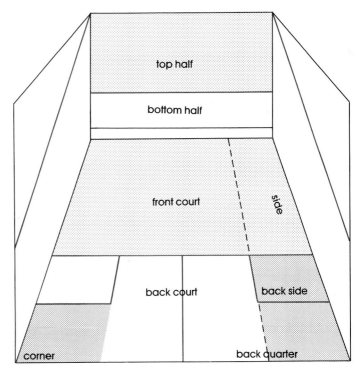

Fig 149 Areas of the court.

Del Harris

There are two main things I did to get better. I used to practise on my own all the time and my manager, Norman Norrington, used to take me to visit pros at other clubs for hard games. That helped me no end.

I used to travel to school on the bus and after school I'd get the bus to drop me off at the squash courts. I'd practise and then go home. Mostly I'd practise on my own.

When I went full-time I started getting on court twice a day. For example, in the morning I'd have a game and in the afternoon I'd hit the ball on my own for an hour or an hour and a half. I worked on a regular practice sequence.

For players learning the game and wanting to get better it's important to get your technique right at the start. After that there's no substitute for practice.

You've also got to play regularly to get better. In your games, concentrate on getting the ball into the back corners and practise to get it out. Hit hard to the back and attack when you've got the opening.

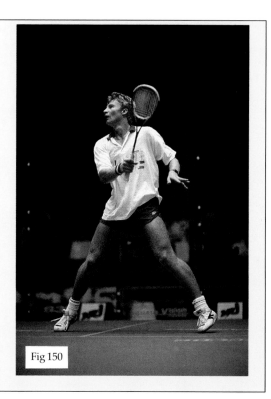

Fig 150

Middle half area between a line drawn halfway between short line and the front, and the line joining the back of the service boxes.
Side area within width of the service box (or a chalk line).
Top half (Top) area on the front wall above the cut line.
Bottom half (Bottom) area below the cut line and above the tin.

Shots

As well as restricting play to particular areas, condition games can restrict play to particular shots.

1 Let us take the front-back game. Conditions can be applied that would restrict this purely to the boast and straight drive or allow any number of shot options and areas.
Examples
(a) A front; B back (A can play any shot to the front court and B any shot to the back court)
(b) A front; B back half
(c) A front; B corner
(d) A front; B back half, straight shots
(e) A front; B corner, straight shots
(f) A boasts; B back half, straight shots
(g) A boasts; B corner
(There are a whole range of possibilities. Unless particular shots are specified, any shot to that area can be used.)
2 A good way to concentrate on a particular attacking shot is for one or both players to play a back-court game plus one or more attacking shots.
Examples
(a) Back-court game and drop (continued)
(b) A back-court game and drop; B normal game
3 A player can win a rally only with a particular shot (a drop, for example) but still lose it with a mistake.
4 One or both players may be required to play either all hard or all soft.
5 Restrictions can be placed on particular shots, for example volleys.

Tactical Rules

As well as placing particular conditions of area and shot on players, condition games can be used to practise tactical rules. Depending on the type of rules, these may – as with lets and strokes – be agreed between players, but some may need a referee (a fellow player or coach) to rule. Rules are best developed for the individual requirements of a player.

The referee may call 'Stop' if a rule is not adhered to and award a hand out or point accordingly. The following is not a comprehensive list of tactical rules for games, rather some ideas that may be of use in developing rules relevant to your game.

Lob the short ball.
Drop off the boast.
Play straight from the back.
Hit away from your opponent (no two consecutive shots allowed in the same quarter).
Attack only if the ball lands in the middle.
Play short only when your opponent is behind you.
Return service straight.
Boast only when the ball is short and your opponent is behind.
Volley long when your opponent is in front.
Volley short when your opponent is deep.
Take opportunities to attack.
Receiver can play the back game only.
Server can play the front game only.

Scoring

Scoring condition games should be simple, clear and adaptable. You should keep in mind the purpose of the exercise and adapt the rules accordingly.

I have found the easiest way to start many of the exercises is to hit the ball off for the first shot in the exercise and give the receiver the option of not taking it if it's too difficult. This allows a quick start to the practice, encourages rallying and makes the server start in a co-operative way.

Here are some ideas on scoring:

Serving
Just hit off rather than stopping for a formal serve each time. Remember that you cannot win a point on the service unless it has been accepted.

If your opponent is in the front, hit to the back.

Ross Norman

American or Point-per-Rally Scoring
Don't make the games too long. Often up to 6 will be suitable, although you can play to 9, 10, 15, or what ever.

Handicaps
One idea when one player is better than another is that A is on normal scoring and B on American scoring.

Penalties
Playing particular shots or combinations of shots may involve losing the point. For example, if you hit the tin you lose two points.

Bonuses
If you hit a particular shot, combination or target area you win a point. For example, in the circling exercise, hitting the side wall behind the service box could be an automatic point.

Ten Basic Condition Games

High Game
Only shots above the cut line are allowed. This game trains players to use the height of the front wall to obtain length and to vary the pace.

Back Game
Only shots into the back court are allowed. Excellent practice for the defensive game, concentrating on length and width.

Front Game
Only shots into the front court are allowed. Great practice for many of the attacking shots that you would have the opportunity to play only occasionally in a match.

Front-Back Game
A practises shots to the back court and B to the front court. Good practice at developing shots, looking for openings and playing shots consistently while not having the same pressure and movement as in a match.

Volley Crosscourt Game
Each player volleys across to the opposite back quarter. The rally continues back and forth until a ball lands in the opponent's quarter and a point is won. If the ball misses, a point is lost.

Back Game plus Short Shot
Only shots to the back court are allowed, plus one or more short shots. This practice allows players to concentrate on the defensive game and look for openings to attack with, for example, a drop. The number of attacking shots used can be built up. It can be useful to make a rule that only shots to the front court can be played from the back.

Normal Game plus Tactical Rule
For example, a normal game plus a lob every short ball. A wide range of tactical rules can be applied to the normal game or the back game – for example, a crosscourt rule (all crosscourts must hit the side), or a drop off the boast (all boasts must be straight dropped).

Normal Game versus Condition Game
A plays a normal game; B plays a game with conditions. This is ideal practice when B is the stronger player. This principle can also be used with two-

Fig 151 **Ten Basic Condition Games**

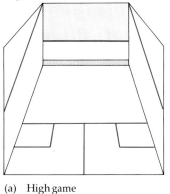

(a) High game

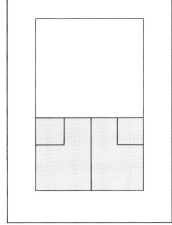

(b) Back game

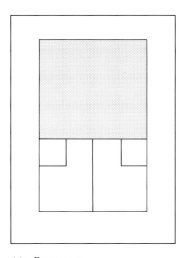

(c) Front game

condition games, in which one player has more restrictions than the other.

Middle Game
If the ball lands in the middle half of the court the point is lost. Excellent practice to make both players concentrate on not hitting the ball in the middle – that is, to avoid playing weak shots.

Side Game
The ball can be played anywhere up and down one side of the court within the width of the service box. Ideal practice at straight shots, keeping the ball tight and at straightening up your game.

Variations on this are, of course, the many circling games involving both driving and volleying, sometimes to different areas.

Designing Practices and Games

Much of the reason for the very full discussion on practices is that a fuller understanding of the principles behind practicing will help you adapt and design practices of your own. Combine, extend and develop practices to suit your needs. Experiment. But most of all make them work.

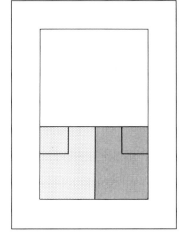

(e) Volley crosscourt game

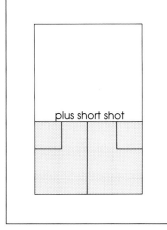

(f) Back game and short shot

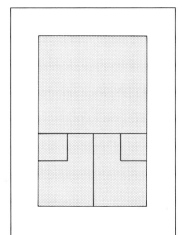

(h) Normal game v condition game

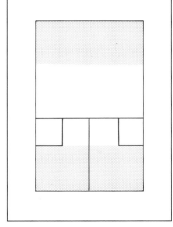

(i) Middle game

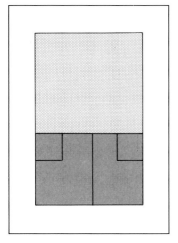

(d)   Front/back game

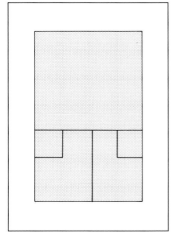

(g)   Normal game and tactical rule

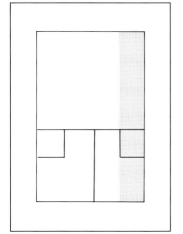

(j)   Side game

Fig 152   **Side Game**

(a)   Jansher Khan drives attempting to get the ball past Ross Norman.

(b)   Ross volleys to keep the T.

(c)   Jansher moves to the corner to drive again.

Practice Games

Matches are about winning. In them you concentrate on what you do best, what you are most consistent at, and what is familiar. Matches are not the place to take risks, experiment or concentrate on parts of your game that do not have immediate benefit.

Think long-term about your game. Not all games have to be matches. Some can be used to practise particular parts of your play by using self-imposed or informal rules (as opposed to the formal rules of the condition game). For example, a player may concentrate on playing drops, forgoing other attacking chances and trying to set up opportunities on the drop. Many more drops would be used than would be tactically astute in a match but this would be excellent practice at improving the drop in a game situation.

In practice games try to concentrate on one thing at a time. Extend rallies to create opportunities.

Designing Practice Sessions

Practice sessions, like coaching sessions, need not just be a loose collection of practices. Best practice and best results are achieved by building on basics and working to a theme.

Plan your sessions. Write them down. Use a quick shorthand method of listing and planning exercises. Provide alternatives for different practices and be prepared to adapt on the day.

Make time at the start of a practice session to work on technique and lining the ball up. Once you are aware of your technique and have 'grooved in' your stroking, move on to practice shots and movement. Try to groove each shot before moving on to the next practice. Ease your way into each exercise.

Design sessions that fit around a theme, so that you are building on earlier practices and adjusting and adapting them to different situations. Build sessions from simple shots and themes to increased movement and difficulty. Balance the static and moving practices so you don't tire too early and are still practising for quality at the end of your session. Finish with a practice that relates to a game situation.

Summary

1   Systematic practice using repetition and feedback will give results.
2   Set specific practice goals.
3   Relate your practice goals to your needs.
4   Practise weaknesses.
5   Practise to get the basics right.
6   Practise to develop your shots long-term.
7   Practise before competitions to groove shots and winners.
8   Establish regular practice times.
9   Plan different practice goals and sequences for the off season, pre-competition and competition phases.
10   Practise with targets.
11   Practise lining up the ball, getting a feel for your shot and establishing rhythm.
12   Start easily and then increase movement and pressure.
13   Concentrate on one thing at a time when practising. Get this working well and then move on.
14   Select the practices from *The Squash Workshop* that are the most appropriate for your needs and goals.
15   Use condition games to practise shots in competitive situations.
16   Develop your own condition games using rules on areas, shots, tactics and scoring.
17   Learn the ten basic condition games.
18   Use practice games to emphasize the shots and tactics you have practised.
19   Plan your practice sessions by using a theme to fit practices together into a practice sequence.
20   Use and adapt the practice sequences.

Coaching aims to assist and guide learning. People learn differently, at different rates, and have different needs and problems. The coach adapts his teaching, instruction and training to players' individual needs. It is important therefore that a coach has some idea of how pupils learn. A coach utilizes his own knowledge of the game to help pupils learn. This learning is mainly through doing. These aspects are examined in Chapter 23, 'Coaching Basics', which also looks at how players can become coaches, the attributes a coach should possess and the skills he will endeavour to develop.

A coach's main task is to get his pupils doing things – things that will help them learn and improve. Activities must be at the right level to produce results – they must follow a progression. This is the subject of Chapter 24, 'Coaching Routines'.

Chapter 25, 'The Lesson', covers some of the initial coaching problems – what to start with and how to get started, the goals of lessons and the range of activities involved. *The Squash Workshop* is full of ideas and activities you can adapt for your lessons.

Chapter 26, 'Coaching Tools', lists some of the methods you can use in coaching, including group coaching exercises, and encourages you to develop and experiment with your own methods.

23
Coaching Basics

Learning a Skill

Players learn skills by imitating others (children are particularly good at this), by consciously analyzing movements, by getting a feel for the skill while performing and by a combination of these. Coaching is always recommended when learning squash as it is a game of habit. If bad habits are picked up in the initial stage, unlearning may be necessary before progress can be made. During this phase, retrogression (a decrease in performance terms) occurs with resulting motivational problems.

Initial skill learning in squash involves developing ball control and developing good technique. Skill learning takes time. Practice and patience are essential. Repetition is the key. Once a skill is developed, repetitive practice leads to reliability. A game is a poor place for initial learning, and obviously doesn't provide repetitive practice at a particular skill. Coaches help select, develop and monitor practices at the appropriate level for the pupil.

Once basic skills are learnt they should then be subject to stress and be practised in a variety of contexts so that they don't remain isolated from the players' game.

Coaches aid skill learning by watching, analyzing, criticizing and helping pupils practise. Skill learning is greatly assisted by the coach's feedback (often called 'knowledge of results') to the pupil. A coach can help pupils practise properly and therefore achieve 'best' learning.

A clear idea of what and how to practise is useful. Coaches can help with this and with setting goals. Specific realistic goal setting gets results. One effective and efficient method of teaching skills is the whole-part-whole approach. The learner first attempts the whole skill, then various sub-skills, and then integrates these into the whole skill again.

Learning to Coach

The Squash Workshop can help you learn to coach. With the right attitude – one focused on the pupil's needs, not the coach's 'system', theory or ego – activities and methods can be learnt that will help pupils learn. With experience, coaching will become easier, the basic tasks being automatic, allowing time for activities such as correcting faults, incidental learning and fitting shots into a tactical framework.

One of a coach's main tasks is to get pupils to perform the activities that will help them learn. A coach needs to be familiar with these activities and to adapt them for each pupil. The wide range of skills an expert coach possesses is not going to be developed instantly. Take these basic steps and you will be on the right track.

Learn the Practices
Learn and become familiar with the basic solo and pairs practices. These are the exercises you will eventually adapt for your pupils. They have been covered in Parts 2, 3 and 4.

Learn to Feed
Feeding is a basic coaching skill. Practise this with partners, learning to feed for the basic technique practices and shots.

Learn the Basics of Technique and of Each Shot
Learn the key points on technique, the fundamentals of each shot and the basic

principles on tactics. Write them down (you may find it useful to use pieces of card) and memorize them.

Design and Adapt Exercises
The coach adapts each exercise to a level appropriate to the pupil. Generally these are called progressions; they are described in the next chapter.

Watch Coaches at Work
Watch coaches, how they instruct, set up the practices, and progress them. Take some coaching yourself.

Attend a Course
Most squash associations run courses in coaching. If you are serious about wanting to coach, apply to attend one of these. It is impossible to take in all the course content at once and the more preparation (the more of the above steps) you can do before the course the more you will get out of it.

The Coach

The coach's role ranges from instructing on the basics, analyzing faults, and teaching tactics and practices to overseeing a player's long-term programme. One thing, however, stands out – getting results. Pupils have different needs and different things work for different pupils. Part of the coach's job is assessing these needs, analyzing them, selecting what's important and relevant, and then working on them. At an advanced level the coach working with a pupil will try to find a balance between long- and short-term development. He will become involved in a player's programme.

As a coach you will need to develop a thorough knowledge of the game and to become familiar with technique, shots, practices and tactics. You need to be able to get involved at different levels, from explaining basics to advising on tactics and playing the right shot at the right time. Most of all, a coach needs to learn and use activities and to adapt these to each pupil's individual needs – needs he has been able to analyze.

Develop the ability to analyze. Observe. Take your eye off the ball and study the pupil and the parts of his stroke. Is the position correct? Is it comfortable? Does the stance give good balance? Does it allow a transfer of weight, give a comfortable position for the swing? Is the swing controlled? Is the path of the swing appropriate for the shot? How do the parts fit together and how do they affect the shot? With this understanding, this analysis, a coach is ready to go into service.

Develop methods. Use the coach's tools and expand your toolbox. Use the 'ideas' method, become familiar with it, master it and then adapt it to your needs.

Develop the ability to explain clearly and concisely. Develop phrases and points that are succinct. Collect them. Try 'Don't run to the ball, move to the place you want to hit it from', 'You're under pressure; create time, lob', or 'Stop for your shot'. Repeat clear points. Summarize, Emphasize themes. List the key teaching points clearly. But remember: don't talk too much. Demonstrate clearly, using the whole-part-whole method.

A coaching session may be on basic technique or shots, but it shouldn't ignore what's happening in a player's game. To be useful it must relate back in the long term to the player's practices and to his game.

The coach then needs to get results – long-term results. Coaching in itself won't make a pupil better; it's what the pupil does with that coaching that's important.

24
Coaching Routines

The difficulty of coaching exercises can be increased or decreased in exactly the same way as with the practice progressions given in the shots chapters.

Gradually build up your routines. Start easily, practising lining the ball up, and get the shots grooved in before gradually increasing the pressure. If the shots are inconsistent there's no real point in increasing pressure – they can only get worse. First establish consistency and accuracy, and then try to keep this while gradually introducing more movement and pressure. Ideally, pressure can be built up so that the shot or shots can be placed under as much pressure as in a game, or even more.

The degree of movement and pressure is controlled by the type of feeding and the design of the routine (more side-to-side, front-to-back and whole-court movement).

Start coaching routines easily and then build up movement and pressure.

1   Practise without the Ball
It is best to run through the preparation, positioning, stroke and recovery at a specific point on the court and practise adjusting to this point. Use a marker on the floor, or a ball held in the coach's hand. See Chapter 10.

2   Practise with the Ball
Gradually introduce movement by varying feeding placements. Instruct on technique, shot and target area.

3   Practise from the T
From a ready position on the T, have the pupil move to a striking position, play the shot and recover to the T. Use solo feeds and slower feeds to allow the pupil time to do this.

4   Introduce Movement and Anticipation
Introduce more movement and anticipation by feeding long and short, side-to-side, or by using three-quarters of the court.

5   Practise under Pressure
Gradually build pressure up with more difficult feeds and quick volley feeds before a pupil has had time to recover the T from the previous shot.

6   Practise Shot Selection and Tactics
The pupil practises anticipating, moving and selecting the most appropriate shots from a range of choices set down by the coach – for example forehand straight drives, straight lobs when under pressure, killing the easy ball and volleying where appropriate.

7   Practise with Competition
Use condition games designed for a particular theme or shot. For example, the pupil can only hit to the back court; the coach can use the whole court.

Designing Coaching Exercises

One of a coach's principal tasks is to design exercises to work on particular aspects of a player's game – technique, shots, movement or tactics. Exercises can be set up in several simple formats, as outlined below, but within each is an almost infinite number of variations. A coach's real skill is in selecting the particular shots, target areas, tactics and the like, so that effort is concentrated on the activities that are most relevant to the player; in instructing during the exercise; in gradually increasing the amount of movement and pressure; and in relating the exercise back to what is happening in a player's game.

It is not useful to allow any shot in an

167

exercise. Remember that improvement comes from repetition. Select one shot, repeat it, work on it, groove it in, improve it and then move on. Gradually progress the exercise to include more shots and variations.

Keep your objectives simple and clear. Set them out at the beginning but adapt and develop as you go on. It is not too difficult for a coach to give a pupil the run-around. The challenge is to select areas that are important to the pupil's game and to improve them.

These basic coaching formats are fairly simple. The coach feeds for the pupil to a particular area (say, corner or quarter) and has the ball played back to him. These are often called 'anchored practices', because the coach is anchored in one place. If the area the coach feeds to is increased this can increase the movement, the range of shots and the pressure.

The activities listed below are not a complete list; rather they are examples that the enterprising coach will be able to extend.

> I like to be organized, to know when I'm training and that I've got a rest day to look forward to. That's how I get the best out of myself. If you're casual and just decide what your going to do each day you can't build up a system. You need a routine.
>
> **Lucy Soutter**

Rear Feeding

Basic Feeding Exercises

Straight Feeding

Initially the pupil may stand in the front court facing the side until a technique or shot is grooved in. Then he will generally work from a ready position on the T.

Initially the coach will feed high and soft until the shot is grooved in. Then placements, height and pace can be varied.

Activities
1 Technique practices.

Fig 153   The coach feeds from behind for a forehand volley straight.

2 Straight drives for length and width, to bounce off the back and cling.
3 Dying-length drives to the back of the service box, hard.
4 Straight lobs: low backswing. Keep under the out-of-court line.
5 Kills off balls that sit up.
6 Volleys: good length; dying length; volley kills.
7 Drops: drop and then drive.
8 Any combinations of the above: with straight drives, dying-length drives and kills; with length volleys, lobs.

Crosscourt Feeding

The pupil will generally start in a ready position on the T and be turned to watch the coach.

The coach can feed directly to the front or by boasting. (Initially this can be high and soft.)

Activities
1 Crosscourt drives to the side, floor, back; and also medium-pace drives higher and wider.
2 Dying-length crosscourts – hard, low drives targeted for the floor just behind the service box.
3 Kills off balls that sit up.
4 Volleys – length, dying length and kills.
5 Lobs: various.
6 Drops: drop and then drive.
7 Any combinations of the above: lobs and volleys; drives, dying-length drives and volley kills.

Front-Court Feeding

Front-Court Feeding
The pupil starts in the ready position on the T, ready to move either side.

The coach can feed directly to the front, straight, or crosscourt, or boast, anywhere in the front court.

Activities
Any combination of the activities in the basic feeding exercises above – for example, straight and crosscourt drives for length;

straight and crosscourt volley (the coach feeds higher); forehand straight drives, kills and volleys, backhand lobs.

Variation
A variation of the above exercise can allow shots down both sides of the court. This means that the coach is no longer anchored and has to move side to side.

Activities
Any shots to the back court can be included. Remember all the volley possibilities.

Examples
1 Straight drives: the coach feeds anywhere in the front court for the pupil to hit down either wall. Options are to straight lob, use dying-length drives, kills and to vary the pace.
2 Straight drives and crosscourt lobs: the pupil crosscourt lobs when under pressure; otherwise straight.
3 Tactical theme – hitting away from your opponent: the pupil plays the ball to the side opposite the one from which it was played, moving the coach on every shot and therefore practising hitting away from an opponent.

Half-Court Feeding

The pupil starts in the ready position, ready to move forward or backward. When driving from the back court, the pupil will generally circle as in a game and in the circling practice.

The coach can feed short or long. The ball will need to be quite warm when hitting to the back court. It may be useful to do a little circling practice to establish movement patterns and get the shots grooved in. Pressure feeding is easily achieved by volley feeding.

Activities
Any combinations of basic straight feeding shots, plus straight drives from the back. Include variations of pace and length.
2 Circling – for example, straight drives (with the coach feeding anywhere down

the side); straight drives and straight lobs; straight drives, lobs and volleys.

Three-Quarter Feeding Exercises

With the pupil in the ready position, the coach can feed the ball anywhere in three-quarters of the court (Fig 153, *shaded* area). Generally the coach tries to provide feeds that are suitable for the shots that have been practised. Pressure is easily applied with volley intercept feeds (volley boast, volley, drops and volley drives).

Activities

A full range of the straight, front, back, crosscourt shots already described are available. Select combinations of shots that have been worked on and progress these.

Whole-Court Feeding Exercises

The pupil starts in the ready position. The coach moves from side to side and can feed anywhere in the court.

Activities

Any shot to the back court can be used, with all the previous possibilities applicable. Shots can be all straight or straight and crosscourt and can include volleys. Movement involves the whole court.

Examples

1 Straight drive, lobbing, straight where necessary; volley straight (on crosscourt) where applicable.
2 Straight from the back, hit away (volley or drive) from the coach in the front court.

Front Feeding

Basic Feeding Exercises

Straight Feeding (Fig 154)

The pupil stands outside the service box and drops or volley drops.

The coach initially feeds high and soft to the short line but then builds up movement, feeding alternately and then randomly shorter and longer, with the pupil moving up and down to the side of the ball.

Activities

Straight drops, volley drops, and combinations of these.

Crosscourt Feeding – Short

The pupil stands on the short line between the service box and the T.

The coach feeds crosscourt for the pupil to crosscourt drop.

Activities

Crosscourt drop, angle, boast.

Crosscourt Feeding – Long

The pupil stands just inside the half-court line facing the side.

The coach drives crosscourt for the pupil to boast.

Activities

Boast, crosscourt drop, crosscourt volley drop, volley boast

Side-to-Side Feeding

Drops

With the pupil on the T, the coach feeds straight for the straight drop and crosscourt for the crosscourt drop – generally higher softer balls to give the pupil time to move for the shot.

Activities

Straight and crosscourt drops.

Boast and Drops

With the pupil on the T, the coach feeds straight for the pupil to straight drop and crosscourt for the pupil to boast. Feeding is alternating or random.

Activities

Straight drop, boast.

Fig 154 Front feeding for the forehand straight drop.

Whole-Court Feeding

Front Court – One Corner
With the pupil on the T, the coach feeds to any part of the court but uses a number of soft feeds and high soft feeds to create time for the pupil to recover the T.

Activities
Any shot to the front right corner: straight drops, straight volley drops, crosscourt drops, crosscourt volley drops, boasts, volley boasts, angles, crosscourt kills for kick.

Front Court – Both Corners
As above, but now the coach has to move from side to side. All the above activities could be used but this is a particularly good exercise for concentrating on straight drops or boasts.

171

25
The Lesson

Getting Started

It is a coach's job to pitch coaching instruction and activities at a level that is suitable for the pupil to learn. This he does with activities by using the coaching progression. Initially, however, the coach must decide a starting point. Three things help. First he must discuss his wants with his pupil; second, assess his needs; and, third, select what themes and activities to work on.

Discuss

Briefly discuss with your pupil what he feels his needs and problems are. Does he know the basics? Are there any particular problems in his game? Is his game stuck and not improving?

Ask questions that will provide you with information on a player's background, level, frequency of play and goals. This information will help you make decisions on changing and adapting technique, setting practices and planning a course of lessons.

Ask: How long have you been playing? How often do you play? Are you in the club leagues? Do you practise by yourself? Are you able to practise? What things do you want to do? What are your problems? Have you had coaching before?

Assess

Assess your pupil's level and needs. Remember that he may not want to become world champion, just get better at squash and be set on the right course. Pupils' perceptions of their problems (invariably beginners have problems with the high backhand return of serve and in getting the ball out of the back corners) and their real needs (building on basics) may be quite different.

Assess strengths, weaknesses and limitations.

Use the knock-up to assess pupils. Observe footwork, positioning, balance, grip, swing, and so on. Check for faults that may be apparent.

Analyze your pupil in a short game. (I often use American scoring to 6 or 9.) Feed the ball to various parts of the court and make a mental list of points you can make. When analyzing better pupils, use some of the more pressurized coaching and pairs practices. With advanced pupils, watch them play a match and make notes or use match analysis techniques.

Select

Select themes and activities that are relevant to the pupil's wants, needs and long-term development. Ideally plan a course of lessons.

Create the Right Learning Situation

Do not be too eager to rush into instructions and correct all your pupil's faults at once. First create the right atmosphere in which your pupil is receptive and can feel successful, then move on from there. Go through these steps.

1 *Rapport* Introduce yourself and get to know the pupil.
2 *Relax* Give your pupil time to settle down and relax.
3 *Encourage* Everyone responds to encouragement. Praise your pupil at the start.

Ignore nervous mistakes. Use a 'Good shot', 'Well done', and 'It's going well'.

4 *Feed* It is your job as a coach to give your pupil the very best chance to hit the ball.

5 *Analyze.*

6 *Instruct* Instruct in a step-by-step manner that will allow your pupil to concentrate on one thing at a time. Often coaches provide more information than pupils can use and just end up confusing them.

Basic Control

The first thing to look for when assessing a pupil is consistency of shot. If this is missing after you've given a pupil time to settle down there is no point in moving on to more advanced topics. Basic control must be established first.

Lack of control can be a basic co-ordination or technical problem. Slow your pupil down, take time and start easily with ball control exercises (bouncing the ball on the racket, patting, gentle stroking) and the basics of technique (see Chapter 5).

Once basic control is established you are ready to move on.

Lesson Structure

Often the coach and the pupil approach a lesson with a vague idea of what they are going to do. The clearer this idea becomes, the greater the chance of success and the greater the relevance to the pupil's game and long-term development.

The clearer the goals set for a lesson, the more likely you are to be successful. The main theme of a lesson should be related to practical activities, covering specific points on technique, practice, target areas and tactics.

For example, a player may not lob when under pressure and this may be selected as the general theme of a lesson. Specific points should be brought out by the coach and ordered in a logical sequence in the lesson structure.

1 *Technique* Use early preparation and a short backswing to save time and help touch. Emphasize an open racket face to help lift the ball.

2 *Shots* Practise straight and crosscourt lobs.

3 *Target areas* Specify the target area.

4 *Practice* Practise each shot, gradually building up the pressure. Use the three-quarters feeding exercise to practise straight lobs, crosscourt lobs and straight drives from the back.

5 *Selection* Introduce shot selection into the practise where the pupil lobs when under pressure.

6 *Game* Practise lobbing in a game or condition game situation.

7 *Summarize and practise* Summarize key points, including relating the shot to the pupil's game. Revise exercises the pupil should practise.

This session takes a common problem and a clear theme for a lesson and sets out a simple sequence of events. Start simply with control, emphasizing technique, target areas and shots. Practise shots, gradually increasing movement and pressure. Relate back to the game. Finish with some homework.

IDEAS

One common approach to lesson structure is the 'IDEAS' method. Use this to plan your lessons. Make notes (perhaps on cardboard). Plan alternatives. Adapt and jump over activities. If something is working, hang on to it. List the key points in your instruction (teaching points). How can you make these memorable and concise? Don't try to be comprehensive.

Introduction

Discuss wants, background and what a pupil needs. Establish an easy rapport. Relax. Start slowly. Encourage the pupil to warm up before going on court (and perhaps have a knock-up by himself). Don't rush into instruction. Use the knock-up, moving exercises, or a game to make your assessment. Set goals for the lesson and agree them with the pupil.

Demonstration

Demonstrate the key shots or techniques fully and clearly. People learn by seeing and doing (visualization and imitation), not by hearing you talk about it. Use the whole-part-whole method: demonstrate the whole shot, then the parts, then the whole shot again. Stand the pupil in a good position to see the demonstration.

Explanation

Explain the key points. Use simple, clear, concise terms. Use a step-by-step approach and number the steps. Develop key points on technique, tactics and target areas from Part 2 and Part 3. Practise your explanations so that they are clear.

Activities

Use the previous chapter and the practices in the shots chapters to design a progressive series of exercises. Start early, establish control, get the shots grooved in and then progress. Finish with a game or game-type activity. Instruct as you practise, giving reminders and feedback. Include revision and regular activities.

Summary

Finish the session by reviewing what you've done and summarizing the key points. Relate the theme of the lesson to what's happening in the player's game. Provide homework in terms of practice for the player. Fit the lesson and practice into the player's programme.

Lesson Plan

The instructional content of your lessons is fully covered in Parts 2, 3, 4 and 6. Use this information to work out your aims for and the content of each lesson. The expert coach adapts this information to the level of his pupil and his needs at the time.

Write down the main instructional points for each lesson and the activities you may use. Perhaps include more activities than you would actually need and then select the most appropriate at the time. This is your lesson plan.

Sample Lesson Plan – Straight Drives: Forehand

Aims
1 Instruct on the basics of grip, stance, swing and positioning.
2 Instruct on movement and the ready position.
3 Develop concepts of length and width.
4 Practise the tactical idea of playing mainly straight.
5 *Practice* Solo practice forehand straight drives.

Introduction
1 Knock up.
2 Relax the pupil and assess his ball control.
3 Try to get the pupil to stop for the shot and take time. Once this is established, the pupil will find it easier to adapt to changes in technique and the shot.
4 Check and instruct on grip, open face, racket preparation, stopping, balance and lifting the ball above the cut line.

Demonstration
1 Stand the pupil on the side wall facing the coach and demonstrate the forehand straight drive. Demonstrate movement from the T with shadow movement.

Explain
1 The V grip.
2 Racket preparation, the open racket face and the swing.
3 Balance, the side-on stance, distance from ball.
4 Positioning and vertical and horizontal angles.

5 Movement from the T and the ready position.
6 Target area.

Activities
1 Forehand straight with the coach single feeding.
2 Forehand straight with the coach continuous-feeding.
3 Forehand straight, moving back and forward a little.
4 From the T to front court.
5 From the T to back court.
6 From the T to the front and back court.
7 Solo practice (high and soft).
8 Backhand straight: front court.
9 Forehand and backhand straight, with the coach moving from side to side.
10 Game: mainly straight.

Summary
1 Revise the main instructional points.
2 Summarize the theme of playing mainly straight.
3 Key points for pupil to remember.
4 How to practise.

A Basic Course of Lessons

1 Straight drives: forehand
2 Straight drives: backhand
3 Crosscourts, forehand and backhand
4 Lobs
5 Service
6 Return of service
7 Volley
8 Boast
9 Drop
10 Back corners and tactics

26
Coaching Tools

Feeding

Some claim that feeding is an art, but a less pretentious description of this basic coaching tool would be as an important part of the coach's craft – something to be worked at.

The ball you feed for your pupil to practise should be the most appropriate to the task. At the beginning this must give your pupils the best opportunity to play their best shots.

Don't use a full swing or a squash stroke; rather use a side-on patting-type action, with a short swing and an open racket face. Lift the ball high and soft so that it travels slowly and bounces high, giving the pupil time to prepare and position. Don't feed too close to a pupil; it's easier for him if he has to take a step or two towards the ball.

Progress exercises by feeding further

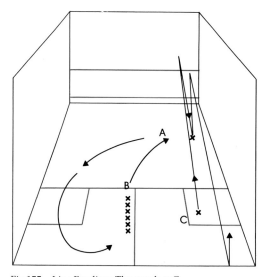

Fig 155   Line Feeding: The coach at C feeds for a group who hit straight in turns and circle to the back of the line.

away from the pupil (this can still be high and soft, giving him time to move) or by hitting harder and earlier (pressure feeding). If a pupil is having difficulty you can make your feeding easier. This is how you control the level a pupil works at. Much of the success of a lesson depends on the appropriateness of your feeding.

Feeding Progression

Hand feeding (throwing off the front or side); single racket feeding (one shot at a time); continuous feeding; double hand or racket feeding (with two balls).

Hand feeding is used by the coach close to the front or in the back corners. Along with single racket feeding it is a useful tool for groups not experienced in continuous feeding.

Pressure Feeding

Hit hard and volley-feed to apply pressure. Volley-feeding is particularly useful when used to intercept balls before a pupil has recovered position (shots the coach can predict). Push these away from the pupil – volley to length, volley boasts and volley drops.

Targets

Define target areas clearly. Do this in terms of court lines and positions so that a pupil can work on them when you are not actually providing physical targets. Keep it simple – side, floor, back; hit the side behind the service box; bounce and cling; and so on.

Also define targets in terms of what effect

you want the shot to have on an opponent. This is really the key – forcing the opponent to take it off the back, playing wide to beat the volley, and so on.

Use physical targets (paper, matchboxes, racket head covers) on the floor and pin targets to the wall (use Blu-Tack, tape and chalk).

Front-Wall Grid

In squash we have two target areas – one on the front wall and one within the court. Explain target areas in terms of where the ball should be on the front wall and explain how a pupil can alter his shot to hit higher (get under it, open the racket, use a lower backswing) and further across the wall (by positioning).

Use the high game (only shots above the cut line allowed).

Correcting Faults

Analyze and isolate the faults. Use the fault-finding chart. Develop simple practices to concentrate on this area without pressure. Simplify the technique, stroke or shot. Use different 'tools' to slow the pupil down and make him aware of what he is doing. Practise with a correct technique. Establish control and consistency at a simple level. Gradually build up the ability. Provide practices. Fault correction needs practice and repetition because technique will break down under pressure.

Above the Line
Use the cut line as an aid to get length. If a pupil is playing short, instruct them to hit above the line.

Advice between Games
Keep this simple. Coaches usually try to do too much. Follow these steps:

1 Encouragement
2 One or two things to concentrate on.
3 One or two opponent's weaknesses to exploit or tactics to counter.

Make arrangements on who is going to talk to a pupil well before the match.

Overcorrecting
Sometimes pupils find small adjustments in placement very difficult. If they become stuck here try overcorrecting. If a service just won't hit the side, a drive won't go in the back, or a drop won't go low in the front, hit it straight into the side, the roof, the floor or the tin. Radically change the position and angles (just as an exercise without pretending it's a shot) and then come back to the target area again. It works.

Percentages
Use simple percentages or numbers out of ten to focus attention and to provide clear goals and feedback – for example, 'How many serves can you get to hit the side, floor and back?'

'Freeze'
Get your pupil to freeze occasionally in technique practice so that you can point out faults on particular aspects of his technique.

'Stop'
Use the 'Stop' command in a coaching game so the pupil 'stops' in their position, allowing tactical errors to be pointed out. Games can be interrupted in this way by a coach to make quick instructional points ('Come on back to the T', or 'Get me in the back') and started again as soon as a pupil is back on the T.

Watch Practices
Watch your pupil's practice. Criticize, comment, suggest and provide the next step or target.

The Programme
What are the activities a pupil should use to get better – solo practice, pairs practice, practice games, matches, coaching, fitness activities? How often should they be scheduled? Don't get carried away. What is realistic? When? Timetable it. How long should he do this for? Four-week cycles?

FAULT FINDING

Faults	Problems
Rushing	Off balance, moving while hitting, mistiming, inaccuracy, inconsistent shots.
Moving while hitting	Inaccurate and inconsistent shots. Difficulty recovering after shot.
Swinging your body	Inaccurate and inconsistent shots. Moving your head and taking your eye off the ball. Pulling the shot round.
Too close	Cramped. No room for a full swing. Leaning back while hitting. Head coming up, eye off ball. Too upright. No transfer of weight.
Too upright (not bending knees)	Poor balance. Difficulty braking. Poor transfer of weight. Not getting down to the ball.
Poor positioning	Poor balance, excess body movement. Often compensated for with a less accurate, wristy shot.
Too large or wild swinging Excess follow-through Uncontrolled swing	Missing, mistiming, loss of touch. Less control and consistency. Dangerous. Difficulty in corners and close to wall. Often necessary to rush shot. Hit down on ball. Difficulty in reacting quickly.
Poor racket preparation	Rushing, missing, mistiming, a less grooved swing.
Poor preparation	No time to line the ball up.
Loose/dropped wrist	Weak link, less racket head control. Inconsistent swing.
Rolled wrist Closed racket face Grip slips	Ball goes low or down. Drop shots into tin. Poor lobs and back-corner shots. Miss or uncontrolled shot.
Eye off ball	Missing.

Check

Use the checks in Chapter 5 – grip, racket head, stance. Teach pupils to check themselves and develop new checks of your own.

Questions

Check your pupils' understanding with questions: 'Can you remember the five points we've covered?' Invite questions from pupils: 'Do you have any questions?'

Solutions

Stop for your shot. Use the stop and freeze techniques in solo practice. Wait until the ball comes to you. Hit only soft shots. Try walking. Develop good racket preparation. Create the time you need. Vary the pace. Recover to a ready position on the T. Play tighter shots. Watch your opponent.

Practise slowly concentrating on balance. Use the stop and freeze checks. Check your positioning. Use your knees to brake.

Check positioning. Stop and stay on balance for your shot. Practise straight driving and hold your shoulders facing the side.

Check positioning. Prepare early and stop. Wait for the ball to come to you. Reach out for your shot. Use your knees. Move up and down the middle, keeping your feet out of the service box width. Practise straight drives keeping outside service box width. Try to keep out of this area in a game. Use the pairs practice, boasting and driving. Move away from a ball that comes at you.

Leave room between yourself and the ball (see above). Use knees. Practise stances. Do some footwork and stretching exercises.

Don't run for the ball. Do move to the place you want to hit the ball from. This is positioning. Use solo and pairs practices and concentrate on positioning.

Use a swing that is appropriate to your level of skill. Use a compact swing when learning. Practise: without ball, with ball, a compact swing, quick reflex drives, reflex volleys. Don't sacrifice control for pace. Start your backswing lower. Swing through the ball.

Don't wait until the ball has bounced before you move your racket. Prepare your racket as you move. When practising, take the racket back when the ball hits the front wall.

Get into position early and wait until the ball is just in the right place before you hit it.

Keep the wrist cocked throughout the swing. Use the feel check. Practise without the ball and with the ball. Use a short swing.

Use grip and feel checks. Don't let the grip creep around and close the racket face. Practise hitting through and up on the ball. Use V grip and checks. Hold the grip firmly but not too tightly. Check grip every time play stops. Change racket grip regularly. Use a grip aid.

Keep watching until you have finished your swing. Freeze and check that you are still looking at impact point after shot.

Shut Up

The number one fault of coaches and teachers is that they talk too much. Get your pupils doing things. Explanations should be clear, concise and if possible memorable. Repeat them, emphasize a theme, but don't get into long explanations. Demonstrate, explain, then do.

Instructions

Keep these simple and clear. One- or two-word commands can be very useful, for example, 'Ready position'. As well as practising this position, this command puts a pupil on the T, ready to move and awaiting the coach's next command or feed.

Racket Preparation

A useful time to practise this is when the ball hits the front wall.

Pause

To assist a pupil to take time for a shot and to avoid rushing, try to get him to pause in between being prepared and in position, and hitting.

Praise

Pupils are encouraged by praise. Try to be positive. Look for the good things to emphasize. At times be specific if you can. Say 'Good length', or 'Nice change of pace', as well as 'Good shot' and 'Well done'.

Video

Use videos of technique to show pupils exactly what they are doing, and of games so that they can analyze their own tactics. Have pupils go through the video to perform their own match analysis – mistakes, length, and so on.

Debriefing

After competition it can take time to relax and return to the patterns of normal everyday life. Immediate post-mortems may not be useful. Allow one or two days and then discuss the performance. Learn from competitions. All the information is there. Target weaknesses for practice. Set goals for the next competition.

Develop Methods

Try things. If it works, it's useful. Save and adapt it. Think in terms of your pupil's problems and needs. Try to solve and satisfy these. The methods suggested here are not comprehensive; rather, they are ideas and examples. Develop your own and borrow from other coaches.

The key tactical problem in squash is selecting the right shot at the right time. Part 6 examines what is important and provides a framework to help you make these decisions.

The Points
What are the important factors in deciding where the points come from? How do winners and errors affect the final result? How can you solve the problem of unforced errors in your game? See Chapter 27.

The Plan
Your plan (Chapter 28) provides a tactical framework for what you are trying to do. It helps you balance the different types of play.

The Rally
The instant-decision making of squash, the shot-by-shot decisions of your game are made in rallies. Chapter 29 examines how to select the right shot and type of play, plus setting up rallies.

The Match
Match play, considered in Chapter 30, is where you have to modify the plan by adapting to a particular game and opponent. Troubleshooting provides solutions to tactical problems you may experience.

Practising Tactics
Chapter 31 covers how you can go about practising and developing your tactics.

Tactical Summary
Chapter 32 provides fifty tactical rules to follow that will help your tactical play and ten tactical errors to avoid.

27
The Points

To win at squash you need to win points, not lose them. Points are won on your winners and your opponent's mistakes. They are lost on your mistakes and your opponent's winners. Points build to big points and games, and games win matches. Winning points is your goal at its most basic. How well you achieve this is simply calculated by recording the final result of every rally with the score. Victory or defeat is in the balance of winners and errors.

$$\text{Your Game} \left\{ \begin{array}{l} \text{winners} \\ \text{errors} \end{array} \right.$$

$$\text{Your Opponent} \left\{ \begin{array}{l} \text{winners} \\ \text{errors} \end{array} \right.$$

Match Analysis

Match Analysis is simply working out where the points come from and why. This is the crucial data of your game.

1 Where are your winners? Can you play more, more effectively? Are you taking your opportunities to win points?
2 Where are your mistakes? Can these be minimized or eliminated? What is the reason for them?
3 Where are your opponent's winners? How is your opponent getting opportunities to play these shots? Can you change your game to eliminate them?
4 Where is your opponent making mistakes? Can you pressurize him into more?

Tactics

Tactics are the ideas behind the events that lead to winners and errors.

Your winners are looked at in attacking play. Your errors are considered in defensive play, and in the selection of attacking opportunities. Your opponent's winners can be minimized by denying him the opportunity to play them. This is the defensive game. Your opponent's errors can be encouraged and forced if you concentrate on pressure, positional play and his weaknesses.

		Tactical Area
Your Game	winners	attacking play
	errors	defensive play
Your Opponent	winners	defensive play
	errors	pressure and positional play

These are the areas where points come from. Understanding them is the key to taking control of your game.

Winners and Errors

The matches you win and those won against you are a balance of winners and errors. This is just as important for the top professionals as it is in your game. Let's look at three examples.

Example 1

In the 1987 World Open semifinal in Birmingham, Jansher Khan beat Jahangir Khan in a 1¾-hour match 4–9, 9–3, 9–7, 9–7. The match consisted of 148 rallies (including 37 lets and 12 strokes) and each player played 1,360 shots. Jahangir played 27 winners to Jansher's 24 but he also made 33 errors to Jansher's 27.

183

1987 World Open Championship
Semifinal: Jahangir Khan v Jansher Khan

	Winners	Errors
Jahangir Khan	27	33
Jansher Khan	24	27

Jahangir, we see from the above table, hit 3 more winners but made 6 more mistakes than Jansher. These mistakes cost him the world title.

Example 2

In the 1989 British Open final at Wembley, London, Jahangir Khan won his eighth consecutive British Open title defeating Rodney Martin in the one hour forty-nine minute final 9–2, 3–9, 9–5, 0–9, 9–2. Jahangir won a total of 62 rallies and Martin won 59.

1987 British Open Championship
Final: Jahangir Khan v Rodney Martin

	Winners	Errors
Jahangir Khan	25	23
Rodney Martin	36	37

The facts are simple. Martin hit 11 more winners than Jahangir but made 14 more errors. This is the crucial statistic.

It's interesting to note that the scores in each game were decisive and that in the climactic fifth game Jahangir made only 1 error while Martin made 7.

	Winners					Errors				
Games	1	2	3	4	5	1	2	3	4	5
Jahangir	8	1	6	5	5	5	5	3	9	1
Martin	4	13	7	9	3	8	10	9	3	7

Good play and bad often come in groups caused by lapses in concentration confidence and physical condition as well as by changes in tactical policy. An interesting fact to come from the above balance of winners and errors is that Rodney Martin made the final move (playing a winner or error) in the majority of rallies (in 73 of the 121 conclusive rallies).

Fig 156   After losing the fourth game 9–0 to Rodney Martin in the 1989 British Open final Jahangir Khan comes out to take the fifth 9–2 and collect his eighth British Open title.

Example 3

In the 1989 World Open, the Australian Chris Dittmar achieved his first ever victory over Jahangir Khan but lost in the final when Jansher Khan regained his world title. Errors, forced and unforced, were a key factor in the victory and in the defeat.

1989 World Open Championship
Semifinal: Chris Dittmar v Jahangir Khan

	Winners						Errors					
Games	1	2	3	4	5		1	2	3	4	5	
Dittmar	10	8	10	5	7	40	0	2	4	3	6	15
Jahangir	9	13	5	12	7	46	5	4	5	4	8	26

Final: Jansher Khan v Chris Dittmar

	Winners						Errors					
Games	1	2	3	4	5		1	2	3	4	5	
Jansher	5	5	9	11	8	38	8	6	1	2	4	21
Dittmar	7	9	3	9	6	34	5	1	6	4	7	23

> Your straight drives have to be accurate and when I'm a bit rough I find I'm playing a lot more crosscourts. As the season goes on and I get grooved in and my game straightens up.
>
> **Ross Norman**

You should know in your game how many winners and errors you are making. Perform the analysis exercise on page 183. Now you have the material to make decisions on your game and can start improving it.

Unforced Errors

Squash matches are won and lost on mistakes. The lesson we could draw from the examples above is symptomatic of the key tactical problem in squash – how do you play winners and play positively while minimizing errors?

Unforced errors (as opposed to the ones you are forced to make) are often the crucial area in winning and losing. To improve your game it is important to know where they are being made, to analyze their causes and then to decide on a course of action.

Take the following steps to minimize errors in your game:

Step 1   Are unforced errors costing you matches?

You should know the answer to this question. If you don't, you must find out. Have your coach or a friend note down the number of mistakes you are making and what they consist of. The most common form of mistake is a shot into the tin, but also included are mishits, balls that are out and strokes.

In what part of court, off which shots and in what situations are you making most of your errors?

Fig 157   With Jansher Khan back out of position Ross Norman improvises a backhand straight drop.

Step 2   What is the cause of these errors?

Once you know what and where your mistakes are, you can work out their cause and then start to do something about it. This is the sort of precision you want to develop in thinking about your game. Once you can do this and you've grasped the basic tactical ideas in this chapter you will be thinking tactically and solving tactical problems.

There are four areas in which to look for the causes of errors. The technical, tactical, temperamental and physical areas.

Step 3   What are you going to do about it?

It's all very well if you're sitting there flicking through your squash book looking at the pictures of Jansher Khan and Ross Norman and thinking, 'Well, perhaps I do make rather too many mistakes'. What are you going to do about it? If you've taken steps 1 and 2 then it's time for step 3. Action.

TACTICS

Problem Solving: Unforced Errors – Causes and Solutions

Causes

Technical Area

Mistakes are easily diagnosed in the technical area due to the uncontrolled, inconsistent and inaccurate nature of the shots. Repetitive mistakes in particular areas of the court and on particular strokes are due to basic faults.

1 Mistiming
Under pressure the ineffective connection of the moving racket, ball and player is often caused by poor racket preparation and rushing. Other basic problems include poor ball control, poor racket control, an inappropriately sized swing and moving while hitting.

2 Taking Your Eye off the Ball
This is a basic fault that can become a problem particularly if you are too close, off balance or swinging your body with the shot.

3 Grip Problems
One of the problems of an unorthodox grip is that it can lead to faults in your stroke. A particular problem is the closing of the racket face, resulting in the ball going down. Errors often result from a grip twisting or slipping.

4 Faults
Inconsistent strokes, resulting from poor technique, will of course be prone to error. Common basic faults are considered on page 178–9.

5 Problem Areas
Most players have relative weaknesses and some real problem areas in their game. Examples are the volley, especially backhand high, the back corners, the forehand drop and the boast.

Physical Area

In squash there are tired mistakes – balls you get to but mishit, lose concentration on, calculate wrong or just become rash with, in an effort to finish the rally.

Solutions

Technical mistakes can be eliminated with practice and coaching. This may mean a return to basics, concentrated practice in the problem area and a gradual building up of the technique so that it doesn't break down under pressure.

1 Preparation Gives Time
Practise racket preparation with solo practice by taking the racket back when the ball hits the front wall. Build this ability up by using the practice progressions in the shots chapters. Eradicate rushing by getting a stop in before you hit. Refer to Chapters 5 and 10 on other basic timing problems.

2 Eyes on the Ball
Try to keep your head still while swinging, especially when under pressure and when the ball is close to or rebounding off the side wall.

3 The Correct Grip and the Right Equipment
Grip faults are best corrected early on (*see* Chapter 5). A slipping or twisting grip is a reminder to hold the racket firmly through the stroke.
    Sweaty grips can largely be overcome by some experimentation and good preparation. Change your grips regularly and especially before competitions, use grip aids, wrist bands, and have a comparable racket available with the same grip.

4 Good Technique
Technical faults are best analyzed by a coach and corrected with basic practices. Faults appear under pressure when technique breaks down. Creating time for a shot and adapting the swing size can minimize them.

5 Practice
Problem areas should be analyzed and then practised. Don't practise your favourite shots; practise your weaknesses. Take care when you are moving into a potential danger area – aim higher, prepare, use a shorter swing, emphasize control and don't take chances.

Pace yourself through a match and a rally. Vary the pace. If you are tired, you are more prone to error so pick your shots and allow a greater margin for error.

186

Tactical Area

The player who makes errors in the tactical area either fails to understand tactics, fails to 'read' the tactical situation on court, or fails to see the summation of all the small decisions – the patterns of play. Careful calculation of the risks involved in a shot are thrown away due to impatience, overeagerness, desperation, carelessness, poor decision making or just a poor awareness of the match situation.

Mistakes from tactical errors fall into three categories.

1   Attacking the Wrong Shot
Attempting overambitious shots and attacking difficult balls leads to errors. Sometimes a player makes a decision to play a particular shot before assessing whether it is really the right opportunity. There has been no calculation of the risk involved.

2   Attacking at the Wrong Time
Attacking when an opponent is in position on the T forces you to lower margins, forces more errors and leaves you open to counterattack.

3   Aiming Too Low
There is a very simple reason why players hit the tin – they aim too low. It never occurs to many players that the reason they hit the tin so often is because they aim an inch above it.

Temperamental Area

1   Anxiety
Excess nervousness and anxiety can cause muscle tension and cloud thinking. This can cause mistakes through mistiming and also through poor or panicky tactical decisions.

2   Lapses in Concentration
Mistakes often occur in patches. Here concentration is a major cause. One mistake should ring the alarm bells and bring a player back on course. (See Danger Areas . . .)

3   Impatience
Impatience is a major cause of tactical errors. It comes from an overeagerness to win points rather than set up rallies.

Tactics are about discipline. If the shot is risky, don't play it. Be a little dogmatic. Give yourself clear rules and standards. Eliminate the areas of play where you are making mistakes. This may sound severe but it works. Just don't play them. Practise tactics in practice games to become familiar with tactical rules and combinations. Concentrate on just one or two areas at a time. Set them up and repeat them.

Use feedback from tactical analysis and debriefing after a competition to help you learn from your mistakes.

1   Attack the Easy Ball
An easy ball is a weak shot that gives you time to position, prepare and play your best shots. Wait for and set up these opportunities. You will know before you hit that everything is right, ready and waiting.

2   Attack when your Opponent is out of Position
If your opponent is out of position there is less chance that he will get to the ball easily and therefore you can aim a little higher and safer.

3   Allow a Margin for Error
Aim high enough above the tin so as not to make mistakes. Adjust your aim depending on the difficulty of the shot – the more difficult the shot, the greater the margin for error.

1   Preparation and Positive Thinking
Good match preparation should help avoid nervous errors. Refer to Part 7 of this book, use the knock-up checklist and start your match with a playing-in period. If nervous mistakes creep in, return to a playing-in period and direct yourself to concentrate on positive coping thoughts.

2   Concentration and Danger Signals
Avoid lapses by recognizing danger areas and concentrating positively on the next rally rather than dwelling on past misfortunes. Use a regular checklist when serving and receiving to avoid lapses. Monitor each shot and each rally. Talk to yourself. Memorize the danger areas. Test yourself now.

3   Rally
To overcome impatience, practise longer rallies. Perhaps try two matches on end. Develop clear rules and work within these.

28
The Plan

The balance between your winners and errors is the key statistic in your game. Tactics are about how you balance and control the events that lead to these winners and errors. They explain where the points come from.

Squash is not just a shot-making shoot-out; winners and errors are not isolated and unconnected events but are the result of what has gone before.

Squash is a game of rallies, rallies that end in winners and errors. It is because squash is a rallying game that tactics are important.

A Rallying Game

In a rally there is the urge to win points and the temptation to take chances. A player is forced into instant decision-making while the exploration of shots, paces and angles, the search for openings and opportunities, and the probing of strengths and weaknesses continues.

With all the events that occur in a rally, what is really important in deciding where the points come from? What are the key ideas a player should be concentrating on?

There are five simple steps a player makes in avoiding errors and attempting to win points. These steps are a player's most basic line of thinking. For the best players, we could say that they are instincts.

Five Steps to Winning Points
(and Not Losing Them)

1   The first thing you must do in a rally is get to the ball. This involves movement, fitness and positioning and brings in the crucial role of the T. The very best players

are the best at getting to the ball and getting back on the T.

2   The second step is to get the ball back without making a mistake. We have already looked at this area. Of course it's rather elementary but if you can get to every ball and get it back without making a mistake it's impossible to be beaten.

3   The third step is to deprive your opponent of the opportunity to hit winners – that is, eliminate weak shots.

4   The fourth is to create openings and force mistakes by using pressure and positional play.

5   The fifth is to play winners.

These are the crucial steps you should take in a rally to win points and not lose them. We divide the type of play you use to do this into four game types – defence, pressure, positional and attack.

The T

The first battle in squash is for control of the T. We could say the T stands for Time and Territory.

The experienced player knows that opportunities to play winners and force errors will come along in the course of a match and that the first task is to take control of the rallies. A player in control of the rallies has time on the T – time to think, time to get to the ball and time to play the shot of his choice.

Squash is a battle over territory controlled from the T. The player in control conducts the game – its direction and its pace. He is in the best place to take advantage of any positional openings.

In a rally, possession of the T swops back

Fig 158   **Winning the T**

(a)   Hailstone in the back corner prepares to straight drive for length in and endeavour to get the ball past Nicolle.

(b)   Finishing his drive he steps back towards the half court line and prepares to take the T.

(c)   The drive forces his opponent into the back and allows him to win control of the T.

189

Fig 159   Ross Norman eyes the ball closely and takes charge of the middle against Chris Robertson.

Fig 160   Lucy Soutter volleys to keep control of the T against Liz Irving.

and forth. The player who controls it most is in control of the rallies. Make your first priority in a rally getting control of the T. The rest happens from there.

You will win control of the T by putting your opponent out of position in the back corners. This is the defensive game.

Defensive Play

Defence is the key to winning squash. It is not merely retrieving and avoiding errors. Good defence will provide problems for your opponent, as well as giving you the T. It will deprive him of opportunities to attack, put him out of position in the back corners and limit his options. At best, it will force weak balls and mistakes.

The ingredients of defensive play are length, width, recovering the T, watching, good court coverage, no mistakes and varying the pace. There are three main shots used – the straight drive, the cross-court drive and the lob.

Bury your opponent deep in the back corners. Play good length and make him wait for the ball to come off the back. Angle it into the side behind the service box so that he has to scrape it off the wall. Angle crosscourts for the side, floor and back (or floor, side and back), limiting options and forcing weak straight balls or boasts. Lob crosscourt and straight so that the ball will

> Free shots are loose balls that give your opponent an attacking opportunity. This is a particular danger on the crosscourt as it travels through the middle and can be volleyed.
>
> **Ross Norman**

Fig 161 **Varying the pace**

(a) With Briars right behind him Harvey moves in for the ball with a low backswing.

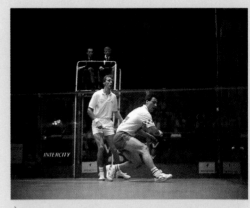

(b) Opening the racket he comes under the ball. Briars is on his toes.

(c) Harvey gets the ball high giving him the T.

(d) Briars is forced into the back corner and Harvey takes the T.

die, forcing your opponent to play a desperate volley or a hurried return. Give your opponent these problems while you take control of the T.

The minimum requirement when in a defensive situation is, of course, a safe return. The more pressurized, off balance, stretched, twisted and poorly placed you are, the less controlled the shot. Adapt your swing size, prepare your racket, and try to hold yourself steady through the impact point. Lob to create the time to regain the T.

Court coverage is an important part of your defensive game. Fitness and movement are covered elsewhere in this book. Defence needs to be sustained throughout a match. If it fails, the foundation of your game has gone and you are heading for defeat. Work hard to cover your weak shots.

Keep your squash simple and get the defensive part of your game working at the start of each match, game and rally. Put your opponent out of position in the back and deprive him of opportunities to take control of the T. Remember, the player with the strongest defensive game usually wins.

191

Pressure Play

Time is a key element in squash – time to get to the ball and time to play good shots.

Deprive your opponent of this time so that he may not get to the ball before it has bounced twice; so that if he gets there he's stretched and hasn't time to line the ball up and play good shots. Force him to play weak shots which you can attack and pressurize him into mistakes.

Get pressure into your game by taking the ball early, by volleying and by hitting hard. The sooner you hit the ball, the less time this gives your opponent to get back in position. The harder you hit it the faster it goes and the less time an opponent has to play it.

Pressure is often the cumulative effect of several shots or rallies, where an opponent has been struggling to recover the T in time

Fig 163   Jahangir Khan applies the pressure with another volley against Chris Robertson.

for the next shot. Apply and build on it when you can. Follow up. Turn the screw. If an opponent has become a little ragged in his shots, anticipate, volley, take the ball early and hit hard. Look for the tactical errors and openings that will allow you to up the pressure. When your opponent tires, push him into oxygen debt, keep the pressure on and don't let him get away.

Apply pressure when you are dominant in the rally and have the mid-court. If you are out of position and not in control of the rallies, attempting to apply pressure can deprive you rather than your opponent of time and therefore put you at a disadvantage.

The Volley

Dominate the T with the volley and anticipate volleying opportunities.

One of the things you should try in all your play, including your defensive game, is to limit your opponent's returns. For example, a crosscourt, lob or dying-length

Fig 162   A loose ball from Adam Schrieber gives Del Harris the opportunity to apply pressure by turning on the power.

Fig 164 **Look to Volley**

(a) Jansher Khan under severe pressure manages to get it straight.

(b) Robertson looks for the opportunity to volley.

(c) Robertson's move is for a volley as Jansher attempts to recover.

Fig 165 Sarah Fitzgerald volleys to
apply pressure against Danielle Drady.

impact with a wall and on bouncing. Take
the ball before the side and back and early
on the bounce (including the half-volley)
when you sense that your opponent is a
little out of position. It is then that it is
worth sacrificing a little control to increase
pressure.

Hit Hard

Hit hard to deprive your opponent of time
and to provide a more difficult return.

Hard hitting is often less controlled, so
it's important to pick the right time. There
is little point in bashing and dashing
around the court if this is going to put you
at a disadvantage.

Hit hard when driving from the middle
area of the court. Here you don't need the
time a good length shot gives you. Pull the
ball shorter for a dying length and angle
kills wide for a dying width.

Jahangir Khan's game is based on relent-
less driving. He works hard to get in position
where he can punch the ball consistently
deep and hard, following up with more
pressure or placements and then winners.

Positional Play

Squash is a simple game that's difficult to
play well. It is a battle over territory –
territory controlled from the T. In it you use
shots of different paces and angles to out-
manoeuvre your opponent.

Two players of equal ability can enter
a court and one leave tired and defeated
although his shots were as good as his
opponent's. In the tactical squash battle
he has been forced to work harder than
his opponent, forced out of position more
often and then moved over a distance. The
victor has mastered squash as a positional
game and he has played the right shots at
the right time.

There are two simple rules on where to
play the ball in squash.

1 Play the ball safely into the back.
2 Hit the ball away from your opponent.

straight drive may not come out of the back
enough to allow a crosscourt, and hence
the return is limited to a straight drive or
boast. This will allow you to hang in to the
side, anticipating a straight return while
still covering the boast.

Volleying opportunities will, of course,
come up all the time. Take them. Don't,
however, attempt to slam every volleying
opportunity into the nick. It's not an all-or-
nothing game.

Taking the Ball Early

As well as volleying, create pressure by
taking the ball early. Take it before your
opponent has recovered the T. If he is not
there waiting and is even a little out of
position, there is an opening to be ex-
ploited. Deprive him of time and limit his
options.

A squash ball slows dramatically after

Fig 166 Susan Devoy moves Martine Le Moignan over the diagonal with a forehand straight drop off a short crosscourt.

Fig 167 **Combination: crosscourt drop the short straight ball.** Move the ball to the corners away from your opponent.

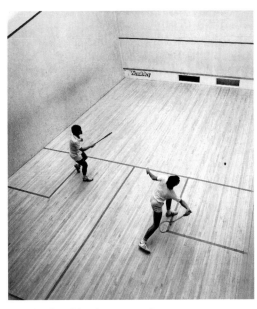

Fig 168 **Combination: return the serve straight.** Although there are other alternatives develop the straight return as an automatic response and change it when opportunities present themselves.

195

Fig 169 **Combination: straight drop the short crosscourt.** Seize opportunities to hit the ball away from your opponent. Look for short crosscourts and when your opponent is back out of position play a straight drop.

Fig 170 **Combination: drop off the boast.** Force your opponent to boast from the back and then counter with a drop to force him to move over the diagonal.

We have been studying all the shots and variations of shot you can use to achieve this. In most situations you have alternatives. Try to keep your decisions on which alternative to use simple. Use variations and deception and wrong-foot an opponent, but don't let these spoil what should be a simple tactical decision. Use the alternatives that will move your opponent the most.

This is the third rule of placement:

3 Hit the ball as far away from your opponent as possible.

A player with tactical ability seizes the opportunities to hit the ball well away from his opponent. That's how he will play his game.

Two ideas can help master positional play – the general rules of positional play and combinations.

Fig 171 **Combination: boast the short ball.** Look for opportunities to catch your opponent out of position and then move him over the diagonal by boasting the short straight ball.

Fig 172   **Combination: volley drop the loose crosscourt**

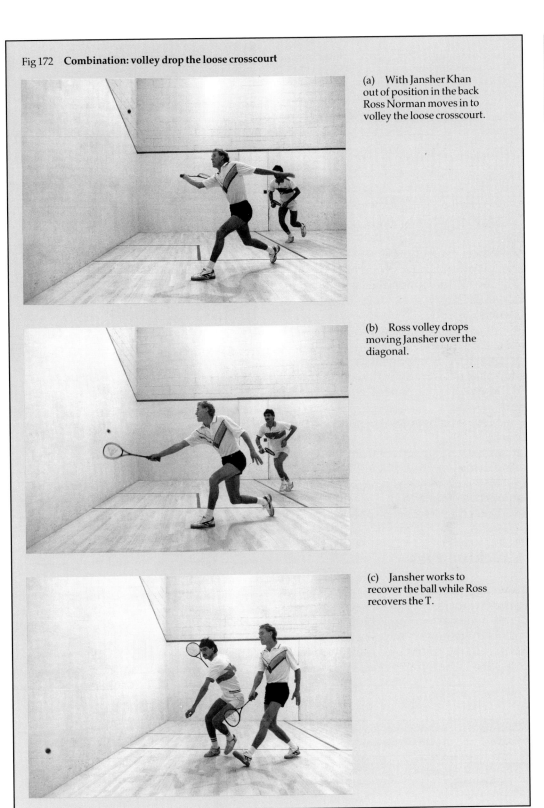

(a)   With Jansher Khan out of position in the back Ross Norman moves in to volley the loose crosscourt.

(b)   Ross volley drops moving Jansher over the diagonal.

(c)   Jansher works to recover the ball while Ross recovers the T.

> The safest shot is to hit down the wall but to work an opponent use the crosscourt as a variation. It forces your opponent to twist and turn and this is harder for him.
>
> **Ross Norman**

Fig 173   Ross Norman attacks when Jamie Hickox is deep in the court.

10 Rules of Positional Play

1   Play deep when your opponent has the T.

2   When your opponent is out of position, play the ball away from him.

3   Choose the option that will move the ball as far away from your opponent as possible.

4   When your opponent is out of position in the back, play short.

5   When your opponent is short, drive and volley deep for dying length.

6   Move your opponent over the diagonal.

7   Move your opponent up and down the court.

8   Move your opponent from side to side using dying length and dying width.

9   Play short only if you can cover all your opponent's options.

10   Don't hit back to your opponent.

Attacking Play

To win points, attack. Seize opportunities to play winners. Play positively and confidently and take your opportunities.

Create openings. Winning shots come from winning situations. Build these by using the tactical framework we have dis-cussed. Start with defensive play and then use pressure and positional play to create openings. You earn the right to attack. When you have the opportunity, don't flinch; use it.

Calculate the risk before you attack – the risk of hitting the tin and the risk of your opponent smacking the ball away for a winner. Good attacking play may mean the occasional mistake. Minimize these by using a margin for error above the tin. Work out what is an acceptable number of errors. Attempting too many winners will mean too many mistakes and tactical errors. Not attempting enough winners means that you are forgoing opportunities to win points.

Attack at the right time. There are two important conditions you need.

Attack when:

1   You have an easy ball.

2   Your opponent is out of position.

> Before an important match, I like to be by myself and to start to think about the match. I concentrate on my game, what I've got to do, on not making mistakes, and about where my opponent is weak.
>
> **Jansher Khan**

Fig 174   **Attack and deception**

(a)   Harvey scrambles back a short ball and Briars is underway.

(b)   Harvey under pressure has to step through to brake while Briars moves in quickly.

(c)   The ball sits up a little as Briars prepares and Harvey is forced to try and cover from the position he has just recovered to, rather than the T.

(d)   Briars shapes for a straight shot and holds.

(e)   Still facing the side he flicks across his body for a perfect deception.

(f)   Harvey transfers his weight the wrong way and the ball is gone.

Fig 175 **Attack the Short Ball**

(a) Adrian Nicolle's drive comes short trapping him out of position and providing an attacking opportunity for his opponent Stuart Hailstone.

(b) Hailstone attacks with a backhand straight drop.

(c) Attempting to retrieve the attempted winner.

Fig 176 **Attack the Loose Shot**

(a)   Ross Norman picks a loose shot from Rodney Eyles to drop.

(b)   Eyles is quickly onto the ball in an attempt to recover it.

(c)   Ross Norman looks to follow up quickly while Eyles tries to scramble back again, to cover the pressured shot.

Hashim Khan

From the beginning hold the racket right, swing right, stand right and hit in the centre of the racket. The main thing is not to make errors. If you make errors you beat yourself. If you hit back to your opponent you are in trouble. Try to know your opponent's weaknesses. Practise. You need to practise by yourself. For example, if you can't play a drop from backcourt, from centrecourt, or right in the front you need to practise by yourself. Make sure you can hit anywhere you want at any time.

For condition you need to play with someone better than you. For shots, to learn to hit that ball exactly where you want, then you need to practise by yourself.

This is a game like chess. You need to think before you hit. You need to watch the ball, to follow the ball, and as soon as possible to be in the right place at the right time. If you can, hit early, not from behind, and you need to hit in the centre of the racket. All four together are automatic: think, footwork, handwork, eyes.

Any time you make an error, think of the reason. Why did you make that error? Did you rush, or did you not watch, or were you not in time, or was the ball going away from you? There must be a reason. Think about the reason. Find the reason. Don't repeat it.

Any time your opponent plays a good shot there must be a reason – you have

Fig 177

given him the chance to play a good shot. Don't do the same thing. Don't do it again. It is like a chess game. Think, footwork, handwork, eyes. All the time think more. Know your opponents' weaknesses, why you make errors, why you don't reach in time, why you don't hit in time – there must be a reason. Think more. Thinking is very important in this game.

Develop winners. Work at these. Winners have a greater importance in your game than the percentage of times they are played. Practise them with solo practices, pairs practices, condition games and practice games.

Learn to recognize attacking opportunities and structure rallies to create them.

Tactical Balance

This chapter has been written to help you clarify exactly what types of play to use in a

game and when to use them. The overall strategy or plan is to get the right balance between defence and attack, between positional play and pressure and between your hard and soft shots.

An appropriate balance between defence and attack would be 75 per cent defensive shots (back quarter) and 25 per cent attacking shots (front quarter).

Plan your match. Think it through to get the right tactical balance. What you do of course depends on the individual decisions you make stroke by stroke – decisions you make in a rally.

29
The Rally

Setting Up Rallies

Start each and every rally in squash as if you are going to control it. Impose your game on your opponent. Follow a pattern in your game and a structure in your rallies. Then you are thinking tactically.

1 Start with Defence
The first battle in every rally is for control of the T. When you serve, take control of the T immediately. When you receive, get your opponent into the back before you try anything. Concentrate on this. Talk to yourself.

Set up your rallies mainly straight and look for opportunities to crosscourt. The crosscourt can be one of the looser shots in the game and overplaying it can lead to a loose game. In a right-handers' game, play mainly straight on the backhand and vary the forehand between straight and crosscourt drives. Volley to keep the T and vary the pace to give yourself time on it and time to regain it.

2 Look for Openings
Look for, anticipate and set up opportunities to move into positional, pressure and attacking play. Be patient enough to wait for these. Build a rally. Opportunities will

Fig 178   Bryan Beeson chooses an easy ball from Mark Maclean to attack.

Fig 179 **Keep your Opponent Guessing**

(a) Ross Norman shapes for a straight drive and Rodney Eyles moves to anticipate it.

(b) Ross delays his shot and uses wrist to flick it crosscourt.

Fig 180 **Disguise and Deception**

(a) Jansher Khan has time in the front corner and shapes for a drop.

(b) Improvising a little angle . . .

204

(c) Eyles moves late and Norman takes the T.

> It's important to have a structure for your game. Keep it simple. First get your opponent in the back with length. Next apply pressure and then look for opportunities to put the ball short. You have to be disciplined, keep to a plan, and you must practise it.
>
> **Lucy Soutter**

come along. When they do, seize them. Use positional play to move your opponent from side to side, up and down, and use follow-up and combinations. Use pressure so that your opponent doesn't have time to regain the T. Use dying length on your drives from the central area.

Move onto the attack and use combinations as soon as these opportunities present themselves.

3 *Follow Up*

Follow up when you have the advantage. Possession of the T changes back and forth in a rally but after an opening you will often have the opportunity to follow up with more pressure. Don't let this opportunity slip. Look for it. Anticipate it and step up the pace.

4 *Return to Defence*

Not every opening leads to the rally's conclusion. Many players disintegrate if their initial attempts at finishing the rally are unsuccessful. They fail to realize that one small opportunity has passed and persist in a reckless or defeatist course of action that puts them at a disadvantage. If one opportunity has passed, build another. This is squash – moving from defence to attack and back to defence again. You should be continually moving in and out of defence. This is the fortress you have set up – slip back into it easily and automatically.

5 *Create Openings and Use Variations*

The idea of setting up a rally is that you're in charge. You're not just reacting to events. Be patient and wait for openings, but try to create them as well. Here is a game for all your cunning.

Rather than the odd brilliant shot, set up a rally, develop a pattern and then inject sudden pace (or lack of pace) or variety.

(c) He sends Chris Robertson the wrong way.

205

Think like a bowler in cricket. Try things out. Save them up. Keep your opponent guessing.

Tactical Mode

How do you make the shot-by-shot decisions in squash? You have a plan, and a structure for your rallies, but instant decisions must still be made.

Each shot situation on court fits into one of the four main game types. It is either a defensive, attacking, positional or pressure situation. The astute tactical player knows the exact situation he is in and switches from one mode of play to another easily and automatically. Others fail to read the situation well and continually make tactical mistakes. For example, they may have a positional opening but hit the ball back to their opponent.

In a real game situation, the appropriate tactical mode may be a blend of game types.

Learning the appropriate response in each situation comes from experience and is helped by tactical planning, debriefing, and assimilating rules. When coaching I use video, an occasional on-court running commentary, and I may intrude and stop or freeze play immediately for major tactical transgressions.

Making instant decisions in the middle of a rally is helped by risk calculations, assessment of skill, assessment of ability to recover the T, feedback and the use of simple ideas and rules.

Calculating Risks

Calculate the risks and opportunities in each situation. For example, what are the choices out of ten of your opponent intercepting the ball or of you making a mistake.

Assessing Skill

Assess your skill realistically. Is this a shot you can produce satisfactorily and consistently?

Fig 181   A loose ball down the middle traps Bryan Beeson out of position and allows Dittmar to go on the attack.

Fig 182 Chris Dittmar seizes the opportunity of a loose ball from Jahangir to attack, moving the ball away from him with a crosscourt volley drop.

You're gauging the game the whole time, monitoring it. You're monitoring how you're feeling, how he's feeling, how the game's going, whether your winning or losing, everything about the game your gauging all the time.

You can only really explain by examples. You've had a long rally, where your opponent was on the wrong end of it most of the time, but won it. You realize that he won that rally, but it hurt him pretty bad, so your gauging every time there's a long rally you'll be feeling better than him.

If you hit a particular shot and he's put a few down, you keep that in the back of your mind so that when you get half an opportunity, you can put him in that situation again.

Ross Norman

Recovering the T
Assess your ability to recover the T after each shot. Has the response you have chosen given you enough time?

Feedback
Learn from your mistakes and successes. When viewing from a gallery, how often do you see a player make tactical errors time and again? Having the right temperament or state of mind to assess situations and learn from them within a match is a prime requirement for the good tactical player.

Keep it simple. Use simple ideas and rules. Do one thing at a time.

Ten Combinations and Basic Moves

Combinations are standard replies to standard situations. They don't have to be

Fig 183 Against Danielle Drady, Lucy Soutter attacks from the T with a backhand crosscourt drop.

Fig 184 **Counter Attack**

(a)   Robertson straight drops and Jansher is on to it quickly.

thought through but are instantly recognized and provide the right shot at the right time. They are worth practising in order to become familiar with them and provide one more simple device to help your tactical thinking on court. These are standard or basic moves. Variations should, of course, be used so that your game doesn't become predictable.

1   *Keep It Straight*

Keep your game mainly straight and you can't go wrong. The straight drive is the

> The main part of my game is to get my opponents back and then, when the ball's short and the opportunity's there, to go for the shot. I try to go for the right shot at the right time, always putting the ball as far away from my opponents as I can.
> **Lucy Soutter**

Fig 185 **Surprise**

(a)   Rodney Eyles straight drops.

(b)   With Robertson back on the T he counter drops.

(c)   Robertson moves in to retrieve and Jansher recovers position.

(b)   Norman counters with a soft touch drop . . .

(c)   . . . that catches Eyles by surprise.

> Your target on the crosscourt depends on your opponent and where he's standing. You must get the ball to the wall so your opponent can't volley it and so you can push him back.
>
> **Jansher Khan**

tightest and safest shot in the game. It also gives you a basic stable pattern.

2   *Return Service Straight*
Get your opponent in the back and win the T. Playing straight keeps the ball away from your opponent, who is moving to the T from the opposite side of the court.

3   *Look for Opportunities to Crosscourt*
The crosscourt is one of the loosest shots in squash but it has the advantage of beating an opponent with width and of not coming out of the back as much as the straight drive. Pick opportunities to crosscourt.

4   *Lob to Create Time*
Whenever you are out of position and under pressure, create time so that you can recover the T. Don't be tempted to attack it.

5   *Volley away from an Opponent*
Volleying opportunities often provide little time and it's easy to hit the ball straight back to an opponent. Position so that you volley away. Try to play away and use dying width and length when your opponent is out of position.

6   *Volley Drop the Loose Crosscourt*
Look for the opportunity to volley loose crosscourts when your opponent is behind.

7   *Volley Boast the Loose Straight Ball*
Move your opponent over the diagonal.

8   *Crosscourt Drop the Loose Straight Ball*
Again, move the ball away from your opponent.

9   *Boast the Short Ball*
When your opponent is behind and his straight shot has landed short, boast to move him over the diagonal. The boast is a working shot.

> Look for the volley, but, if it's difficult, let it go and take it off the back. Don't take risks.
>
> **Jansher Khan**

Fig 186   Chris Dittmar on the way to his first ever victory over Jahangir Khan at the 1989 World Open in Kuala Lumpur.

10   *Drop off the Boast*
Force your opponent to boast out of the back and counter with a straight drop.

Anticipation

Situations crop up in rallies all the time in which your opponent's alternatives are limited. One of the things you are trying to do in setting up rallies is to create these situations – situations that will allow you to anticipate your opponent's moves. This anticipation allows you to move early, be in position for a good shot and catch your opponent out of position.

Limiting situations occur because of the restrictions of the court and of your opponent's position in relation to the ball. Here are four common situations which you should look out for.

Fig 187   Ross Norman seizes the opportunity of a short ball from Del Harris to attack with the backhand straight drop. He moves the ball as far away from Harris as possible.

> I prefer the straight drop and try to get the ball to sit in tight to the side wall, giving my opponent the problem of getting it off the side.
>
> **Del Harris**

1   Your opponent is forced to boast from the back. Drop off the boast. Start moving forward early without completely committing yourself. Your opponent is likely to be caught out of position.

2   Your opponent is forced to straight drive from the back. Hang in to the side and look for the volley. The straight drive and boast are both alternatives when the ball doesn't come off the back enough to allow a crosscourt. If anticipating the straight drive, move a little to the side so that you can cover any straight return on the volley.

3   The ball is angled in tight to the side in the front. Move up and hang in looking for the straight return. Retrieving a straight drop angled in or a back-wall boast played to cling can prove very difficult for an opponent. Hang in to the side. If a crosscourt is played off the graphite part of the racket head, it is usually a fairly weak return and may easily be recovered.

4   Your opponent is forced to crosscourt. Move in and volley straight. This often occurs when an opponent is under pressure and is behind, stretching forward for the ball – for example, when chasing a boast.

As well as anticipating in situations where your opponent is restricted, try to predict an opponent's pattern of play and responses in particular situations. Look for and try to take advantage of opportunities to intercept, take the ball early and catch your opponent out of position.

Monitoring Rallies

The instant decision-making in a rally is influenced by the overall tactical plan of the game, by attempting to set up rallies, anticipating, using combinations and coping with situations as they develop.

How your play in the rallies is progressing needs to be monitored in terms of its success there and then in the match and adapted accordingly. It's no use having a nice plan and building rallies if your opponent is whipping you.

Changing and adapting your plan and instant decisions in terms of the game experience is match play.

30
The Match

The player with the most games wins. Points need to be turned into games and games into matches.

We have examined some of the tactical ideas you can use to order your game: an awareness of what's important in earning points, the plan you use to get the right tactical balance, how you construct rallies, the combinations and moves you use within them; and the rules you use to help you order your play.

This structure and the different types of play you use must be adapted in each match to your strengths and your opponent's weaknesses.

Strengths and Weaknesses

The simple rule of winning squash is to play to your strengths and your opponent's weaknesses.

It seems obvious but it doesn't always happen. How often have you come off court and said to yourself, 'If only I could play that again', or 'I played that all wrong', or 'I know I could beat him.' Your opponent's objective, of course, is to play to your weaknesses and his strengths. In between these two extremes lies the tactical battle-

ground for evenly matched players and the differences between winning and losing.

Your Opponent

If you don't know your opponent try to find out as much as possible about him before you go on court. Study his results. If possible, watch him play. Think through your overall approach to the match and then how you will handle each situation.

If your opponent is familiar to you, you will be able to evaluate previous experiences. You may even have some match analysis data. Don't let familiarity breed contempt. Learn from previous mistakes and successes.

With a new opponent, the minimum you can do is to use the knock-up and the first part of your match to assess strengths and weaknesses and adapt your game to the threats and the opportunities. Observe and make judgements on his fitness, movement, speed and position on the T. Is he looking to volley or attack on the volley? Is he better on one side than the other? Which side will you lob to and serve from? What is he like down each side? Length? Tightness? What are his best shots and his favourites? How will you counter these?

For example Susan Devoy has one of the best backhand drop shots in the women's game. For her opponents the simplest and best way of countering this is not to give her any opportunities in the front left court.

Your Game

A successful tactical player attempts to impose his game on his opponent. He doesn't

> Hit wide enough to beat your opponent's volley. Top professionals today are looking, waiting and hunting for a crosscourt from the back so they can get onto it and volley.
>
> **Ross Norman**

Fig 188 Susan Devoy has one of the best backhand drops in the game.

> Use the lob as a defensive shot. If you are really stretched with a drop or boast and you can't drop because you won't be able to get out of the way in time, then lob.
> **Ross Norman**

move him and keep the pressure on. If he is slow, take the ball early, and intercept it. If he is very fast onto the ball, delay, use deception and lob to give yourself time.

Play the game at your pace, not one your opponent would like. The superior tactical player controls the pace of the match. Build rallies that you are familiar with. Set them up. Develop a number of standard formats and then adapt these to work on your opponent.

just react but he does adapt his game to combat his opponent's strengths and take advantage of weaknesses.

Relate your game plan to the threats and opportunities your opponent provides.

If your opponent drives hard, don't try to out-hit him but vary the pace and keep it tight. If he is good at volleying, keep it close to the sides, mainly straight with no loose crosscourts, and use more low, hard drives. If your opponent is good at defence, then try to match him but still play positively and take opportunities. Take opportunities against a fit opponent and don't prolong the match. If an opponent's fitness is suspect, prolong the rallies, and the match;

Match Preparation

Develop a pre-match routine that you become familiar with so that when the match starts you have your shots grooved, you're warmed up and loose, mentally prepared and tactically familiar with your game plan.

Knock-Up Checklist

1 *Time*   Take time for your shots.
2 *Width*   Hit the side wall on the cross-courts.
3 *Length*   Play some drives straight to yourself. Make the ball bounce and then come off the back.
4 *Vary the Pace*   Try a few lobs.
5 *Volley*   Feed a few balls to yourself and volley.
6 *Drop shots*   Get these grooved in.

> Establish a structure to your game and use it to impose your game on your opponents.
> **Lucy Soutter**

> Lob when you are tired and remember, you can lob from the back as well. It buys you time.
> **Ross Norman**

213

After five minutes' practice you should have all these working smoothly and be ready to carry on with them into the match.

Changing Your Game

Don't change a winning game. You have the tactical balance right. Do change a losing game.

1 *Change the Tactical Balance*
If you are making errors or playing weak shots, tighten up and go back to basics. If you are rallying comfortably but not making an impact, try to force openings and take opportunities.

2 *Change the Pace*
Squash can be played at a whole range of paces. Your opponent who is comfortable at one may be quite insecure at another.

Pace Yourself

Pace yourself through the match. It is the best of five games. Many a match has been won through persistence, and lost through carelessness. If you have the opportunity to finish it off, take it. Don't risk your opponent's improved play or a lucky spell taking it from you.

Varying the pace and slowing the game is a basic tactic to try if you're being outplayed. Fortunes change; matches swing back and forth. If you can't change your game to dominate tactically, you can at least survive. Your opponent may mistakenly let you in by changing his game, become overconfident, lapse, or run out of energy and tire.

Hang in; it's the final point that counts. An opponent who has dominated early on by putting in a tremendous effort can fade against a player who has held something in reserve. Pace yourself to manage your physical resources so that you are still fighting when the final points are being decided.

Trouble-shooting

1 *My length is poor. I'm just not getting it in the back corners.*
Hit higher. Keep your shots high until your opponent is deep. Play above the cut line. If one ball is short correct immediately – automatically hit higher on the next. This is the 'one short, next higher' rule.

Analyze. Work out the particular areas where you are short and practise these.

2 *My game is loose.*
Practise playing tighter shots. Keep it simple tactically. Get a tight defensive base to your rallies before you move on. Keep it mainly straight. Position to the side and hit behind the right angle. Cut down on boasts and crosscourts.

3 *My opponent dominates the middle.*
Get him out of the middle and into the back with good length. Don't play short when he is on the T.

4 *My opponent dominates the middle by volleying.*
Your shots are too loose and you need to tighten up. Angle your straight drives into the side at the point where your opponent would wish to volley. Cut down on your crosscourts. When you do crosscourt, make sure your opponent is back off the T or add extra width.

Play more low, hard drives or go very high and use shots like the cling lob.

5 *I lose matches on mistakes.*
See Chapter 30. Where are you making these mistakes? Select opportunities to attack carefully. Use a margin for error.

6 *I am always on the run.*
Well, you are either rushing about or your opponent is making you run. Tighten up your game. Try to stop for your shot. Take time. Pause when you serve. Count to 5. Vary the pace and give yourself time to recover the T.

Lucy Soutter

Club players wanting to get better should be playing in the club leagues and looking to get competitive games. They should be practising, whether its in pairs or on their own, and if they're keen they should have a fitness programme – a professional player or a coach could help them devise one. If they have a goal to build up to and try to peak for, such as their club championships or their county championships, that can be motivating and can help keep them going.

Coaching is important. If a player is receiving one session of coaching a week he should be practising another couple of times. The coach will give him ideas on what to practise. He should also fit in two or three games a week around that and get a balance between practice and games.

In my game I need targets to aim at so that I keep the motivation going and so that I'm focused in on something that I'm working towards. Training is easy when I'm focused in on, say, the British Open. One of the things I really want to do is win a World or British Open before I finish playing squash. I'm motivated to do these two things so it's not a problem to go out there and do the work.

Sometimes it's easy to drift along. I like to get organized and plan what I'm going to do and write it down rather than do it on a day-to-day basis.

Fig 189

At the end of a day's training I write down what I've done so that when I've been successful I can look back in my diary and see how I've built up for that one tournament.

7 *My opponents read my game easily.*
This may not be a catastrophic problem as long as your game is tight. Work on this first.

Position for your shots so that you have alternatives, and can then vary your replies from each position. Use delay and deception and keep your opponent guessing. Don't rush your shots.

8 *My opponent is beating me with volley winners.*
Try not to give him these opportunities. Analyze. Where is he playing them from? Don't put the ball in this area. If you know you have provided an opening, move right

up to the T intersection or the front court immediately so that you can cover your opponent's shot.

9 *My serve is weak.*
Put it into the side wall. Try a little lower and firmer. Take time for the serve but then get onto the T quickly and watch.

10 *I can't get to the hard-hit ball.*
This may be because you are out of position. Recover the T quickly, get in a ready position (rock forward on the balls of your feet) and watch. If you are beaten in the front, move up on the T. If it's the back, hang back a little.

215

11 *I tire easily.*

You may not be fit enough but you could be wasting energy in nervousness, rushing, constant hard hitting and running. Relax before a game. Stop for your shot. Vary the pace. Tighten up your game. Pace yourself through a match.

12 *I can't play winners in a game.*

First build the openings. Don't rush. Calculate your opportunities. Become familiar with the basic combinations. Start with these. Practise shots and work them into your practice games.

13 *I start poorly.*

Prepare physically and mentally before you go on court. Use a knock-up checklist and a playing-in period at the start of your match.

14 *There is no pressure in my game.*

Don't try too hard and just rush. Select openings and follow up. Move in and out of your defensive and pressure games. Hit hard and volley when you have the opportunity.

15 *My opponent is beating me with winners.*

Ask yourself, 'Where is he playing them from?' Try to eliminate these opportunities. Your game may be too loose. If you do leave an opening, anticipate the response and move to cover it.

16 *I never seem to get back on the T.*

Remember that you can only stop twice in a rally. Make recovery to the T an automatic habit after each shot. Vary the pace and give yourself time to get there.

17 *I often hit the ball straight back to my opponent.*

Prepare early and create enough time for a shot so that you can have alternatives. Your opponent will tend to be between where he played the shot from and the T, or on the T. Play the ball away from this area. Use the combinations.

18 *I have a problem with left-handers.*

You will both want to attack the backhand

deep. This can lead to you playing more crosscourts and more loose shots than usual, as well as opening up the dangers of volley intercepts. Go straight when in trouble. Watch the front right for backhand straight drops and be careful not to give volley openings on loose forehand crosscourts.

19 *I don't volley enough.*

Try to set up the opportunities to volley. Set up a straight rally and hang in to the side a little. Get used to your opponent's likely responses. Anticipate. Push up on the T. Follow up. Think positively. Don't let the ball go to the back.

20 *I play too many boasts and let my opponent into the front.*

Discipline yourself to use the boast only either when you are forced to or when your opponent is behind and you have a short

Fig 190 Chris Robertson in all sorts of trouble against Jansher, following his loose shot down the middle.

Fig 191　Ross Norman goes on the attack against Jahangir Khan.

Fig 192　Danielle Drady prepares to apply the pressure against Sarah Fitzgerald.

ball. Eliminate all other boasts. Later when you have mastered the problem you can introduce occasional attacking boasts from the back.

Countering Game Types

How can the following types of games be countered?

The Slow Game

Against a slow-ball player who plays high

> Being organized and having a goal is important. If you just train without a goal, you can reach a stage where you think, what am I doing all this work for?
> **Lucy Soutter**

shots, lobs and drops, attempt to impose your own game. Don't get sucked in to playing your opponent's game, or become frustrated or impatient, or panic. Vary the pace and try to keep some pressure in it. Volley.

Volley deep, wide and safe. Don't be tempted to volley everything short. Pin your opponent back. Get right up on the T and look for the drops. Look for the opportunity to counter-drop if your opponent drops from the back.

The Hard-Hitting Game

You should never be tempted into trying to out-hit your opponent. Instead, vary the pace. Try to lift the ball high and deep whenever you are under pressure. Play positively. Move into and out of defence and apply pressure when the opportunity arises.

217

The Shot Maker

The single most important thing in playing the shot maker is to deprive him of opportunities to play shots. Keep it wide and deep, be patient and be ready to counter-attack. Take your opportunities as they come up but don't play your opponent's game and start going for a lot of shots.

The Volleyer

Deprive the volleyer of opportunities. Keep it straight and use extra width on the cross-courts. Go very high or lower and harder on drives. Recover the T quickly, especially if you have conceded an opening.

An emergency measure is to consider more short shots. A decision on this would depend on your opponent's ability at the front and your ability to cover them.

The Retriever

It's easy to become tired, frustrated and impatient when playing a retriever. You must play positively but you can't afford mistakes. Play defensively, vary the pace and continually look for opportunities to move into pressure, positional and attacking play. Follow up on opportunities so that they become bursts of activity. Attack in these bursts and pace yourself through the match.

31
Practising Tactics

Matches

The tactics you use in your matches should be planned before you play and evaluated afterwards by means of match analysis. If you have a very clear tactical idea on exactly what you are doing then you can make decisions on how successful it has been and modify or change it.

Practice Games

Use practice games to practise tactics as well as shots. Practise or emphasize one part of your game at a time, for example defensive play, or a combination, or tactical rule.

Coaching Practice Games

I have often used practice games with special tactical rules and enforced these as a type of coaching referee. The rally is stopped when a rule is broken and awarded against the player transgressing (regardless of whether or not the point was won).

The tactical errors used could include attacking at the wrong time, not taking an opportunity to volley, not lobbing when under pressure, and the like.

> If you have a couple of times in the season when you are trying to peak for certain events, then you gauge your training accordingly and build up for one event, reach a plateau and then build up again to peak at the right time.
> **Lucy Soutter**

Pairs Practices and Condition Games

The following are some of the pairs practices and condition games that can be used to practice tactical ideas. It is not a comprehensive list, but rather examples selected from some of the practices discussed.

Practices for the Defensive Game

Length
High game   Only shots above the cut line.
Back-court game   Any shot into the back court.

Eliminating Weak Crosscourts
Normal game with crosscourt rules   Crosscourts must hit the side on the full.

Lobbing under Pressure
Normal game – lob short ball   Any short ball must be lobbed.

Eliminating Weak Shots
Middle game   The ball can't land in the middle.
One short next deep   If one drive lands short the next must be hit deep. Two short in a row and the point is lost. (Length is achieved by emphasizing height.)

Mainly Straight
Circling Exercises
Side game   Any shot down one side.

Practices for the Pressure Game

Volleying across   A and B volley across to the opposite back quarters.

Circling and Volleying Drive (corner); volley (back half).

Back-wall rule The ball can't hit the back wall; it must be taken early before the back.

Follow Up
Crosscourt, volley, boast, drive.

Practices for Varying the Pace

A plays hard & soft; B only soft.
High, soft game.

Practices for the Attacking Game

Front game.
Front–back game.
One short, stay short.
Back-court game plus drop.
Back-court game plus boast.

Practices for Serving and Receiving

Server plays front game; receiver plays back game.
Server plays normal game; receiver plays back game.

Practising Combinations and Basic Moves

1 *Keep it straight* All the circling practices and the side game.

2 *Return service straight* Server serves easily for receiver to return; then his best serve.

3 *Look for opportunities to crosscourt* Normal game with crosscourt rule; drive (corner), crosscourt (back half).

4 *Lob to create time* Lob the short ball.

5 *Volley away from your opponent* Drive straight (corner); volley straight or crosscourt (backhalf).

6 *Volley drop the loose crosscourt* A feeds crosscourt from behind; B volley drops and drives.
Back-court game plus volley drop off a crosscourt.

7 *Volley boast the loose straight ball* Back-court game plus volley boast. Condition game: straight drives (corner) plus volley boast.

8 *Crosscourt drop the loose straight ball* Front–back game. Feed and crosscourt drop.

9 *Boast the short ball* (i) A drives to the service box; B boasts. (ii) Back game plus boast.

10 *Drop off the boast* A boasts; B drops and drives.

Knock-up Practice

Use and practice the knock-up check list on page 213.

32
Fifty Tactical Rules and Ten Tactical Errors

Rules

1 Don't make mistakes. Squash matches are won and lost on mistakes.
2 Deprive your opponent of the opportunity to play winning shots.
3 Use a margin for error above the tin when you attack.
4 Attack when you have an easy ball and when your opponent is out of position.
5 Calculate the risk before you attack.
6 Prepare for your match by arriving early, having sound equipment and spares, a good physical warm-up and mental practice.
7 Plan your matches.
8 Use a knock-up checklist.
9 Return to basics if you become anxious or loose, or lapse.
10 Avoid lapses by concentrating positively on the next point.
11 Be aware of the danger areas where you could lose concentration.
12 Pace yourself through the match.
13 Vary the pace.
14 The first battle in squash is for the T.
15 Recover to and dominate the T.
16 Create openings with pressure and positional play.
17 Hit the ball away from your opponent.
18 Learn the ten positional rules (page 198).
19 Use and practise the ten basic combinations (page 207).
20 If one ball is short, aim the next ball higher.
21 Lob when you are under pressure.
22 Use a short swing and play a safe shot when under pressure.
23 Start with defence.
24 Limit your opponent's returns.
25 Volley to dominate the T and apply pressure.
26 Volley, take the ball early on the bounce and hit hard to deprive your opponent of time.
27 Tactics are about the balance between defence and attack, positional and pressure play and between hard and soft shots.
28 Play 75 per cent defensive shots and 25 per cent attacking.
29 Be patient. Build rallies and look for and anticipate openings.
30 Follow up with pressure when you have your opponent in trouble.
31 Move in and out of defence.
32 Attack when you serve.
33 Defend when you receive.
34 Learn from your mistakes. Don't ignore them.
35 Play to your strengths and your opponent's weaknesses.
36 The superior tactical player controls the pace of the game.
37 Don't change a winning game.
38 Do change a losing game.
39 Hang in if you are being outplayed. It's the best of five games.
40 Hit high to get length.
41 Take time. Stop for your shot and don't rush the serve.
42 If an opponent hits a winning shot, ask yourself, where did he hit it from?
43 Eliminate weak shots.
44 Force your opponent to take the ball off the back.
45 Get in front of your opponent. The player in front usually wins.
46 Develop a range of alternatives from each position on court.

221

47 If you have a choice, take the ball early to apply pressure.
48 Never underestimate your opponent.
49 Use the attacking game to finish rallies.
50 Play attacking shots only if you can cover all your opponent's alternatives.

Errors

1 Don't attack difficult balls.
2 Don't attack when your opponent is on the T.
3 Don't hit back to your opponent.
4 Don't attack out of impatience, overeagerness, or desperation.
5 Don't attack if you're out of position and can't cover the shot.
6 Don't use too many boasts and crosscourts.
7 Don't aim too low on the tin. Use a margin for error.
8 Don't hit hard when you're under pressure. Vary the pace.
9 Don't play defensive shots when you have the opening to attack.
10 Don't leave the ball if you can volley or take it early.

Over a number of years as editor of *Squash Player International* magazine I have interviewed Geoff Hunt, the seven-times World Champion, and Jonah Barrington, the six-times British Open Champion. We have talked of players, their shots, tactics and fitness, and always behind that analysis has been the theme of mental performance and ability.

Jonah Barrington, as director of excellence in England, and Geoff Hunt, leading coach at the Australian Institute of Sport, are now responsible for the development of young players. Both were great exponents of a very physical squash but both understand that the right temperament is one of the qualities necessary for a champion and that the right mental ingredients are crucial in constructing winning performances.

Listen to Barrington talk about Rodney Martin's first game in the epic 1989 British Open final. 'He had an unimpressive start; he didn't get on fire. When he got on fire in the second I was amazed.' And again, talking about Jahangir's comeback in the fifth. 'When he had his back to the wall he managed to pull it round. That showed his strength of character.'

After seeing Jansher Khan take his first world title, Hunt commented: 'He's thinking all the time what he's doing. He's extremely mature for his age and is able to think out the game and he's extremely tough mentally.' And, on Jansher again, after he lost to Rodney Martin in the 1988 British Open: 'I think he was a bit nervous at the end.' In the semifinals of the same tournament he watched Jahangir play Dittmar and commented: 'Jahangir was a bit tentative and made a number of tins.'

Comments and analysis pour out of both men – 'determined, unsettled, frustrated, nervous, tentative, fire . . .' These quotes, ideas and analysis are the fundamental assessments of a player's performance. Each can be categorized in terms of psychological meaning.

Our own games, as with those of the great players, are affected by our mental performance. Our performances fluctuate. Outside pressures impinge. In Part 7 we explore these ideas and look at ways of understanding and improving mental performance.

Much of the material is extracted from or based on articles by Dr Frank Sanderson which appeared in *Squash Player International* magazine, and on conversations with him. Any errors or omissions are my own.

First, in Chapter 33, we consider your squash personality. Knowing yourself, your strengths and weaknesses can allow you to take advantage of strengths and work at overcoming weaknesses. The mental ingredients required of a squash player are discussed in Chapter 34 – will to win, confidence, concentration, stress and frustration tolerance and decision-making. How do you perform mentally? How do you rate yourself in each of the above categories? Discover the strengths and weaknesses in your mental performance in Chapter 35. Knowing a little more about temperament, about your own personality and mental performance is not enough. To improve you need strategies. In Chapter 36 we discuss the things you can do to improve and to take charge of your mental performance.

33
Squash Personality

In this article reproduced from *Squash Player International* magazine Dr Frank Sanderson argues that understanding your own squash personality can enable you to take advantage of your attributes and minimize your faults.

Given the necessary fitness, the way a player reacts psychologically to a challenge, to pressure, to pulling back to 2–2, to a critical decision going against him, and so on, depends largely on his 'personality'.

Some personality characteristics are negative, such as anxiety-proneness, and others are clearly positive, like will to win and ability to concentrate. But I believe that knowledge about one's own personality and the personality of others can be beneficial to the squash enthusiast, whether player or coach. The aim is to get the most out of your psychological attributes and minimize the harm that can be done by negative tendencies. In other words, 'Play to your psychological strengths.'

But first you should know what your psychological strengths and weaknesses are. Before you read on complete the questionnaire which I have adapted from Eysenck's Personality Inventory. Answer all questions spontaneously. There are no right or wrong answers.

1. Do you like plenty of excitement and bustle around you? YES NO
2. Do you often feel fed up? YES NO
3. Do you like carefully planning things, well in advance? YES NO
4. Are you touchy about some things? YES NO
5. Do you like mixing with people? YES NO
6. Do you find it hard to fall asleep at night? YES NO
7. Do you enjoy telling jokes? YES NO
8. Does your mind often wander when you are trying to attend closely to something? YES NO
9. Would you describe yourself as easygoing? YES NO
10. Do you ever get short of breath without having done heavy work? YES NO
11. Would you rather plan things than do things? YES NO
12. Do you often think about mistakes you have made in the past? YES NO
13. Do you enjoy practical jokes? YES NO
14. Do you suffer from 'nerves'? YES NO
15. When the odds are against you, do you still usually think it worth taking a chance? YES NO
16. Do you often get butterflies in your tummy before an important event? YES NO
17. Do you like working alone? YES NO
18. Have you often felt listless and tired for no good reason? YES NO
19. Do you usually stay in the background at parties? YES NO
20. Would you describe yourself as a restless person? YES NO

Your E (Extroversion) Score: Score 1 point for each 'No' response to Questions 3, 11, 17 and 19 and for each 'Yes' response to Questions 1, 5, 9, 13, 15.

Your N (Neuroticism) Score: Score 1 point for each 'Yes' response to all even-numbered questions.

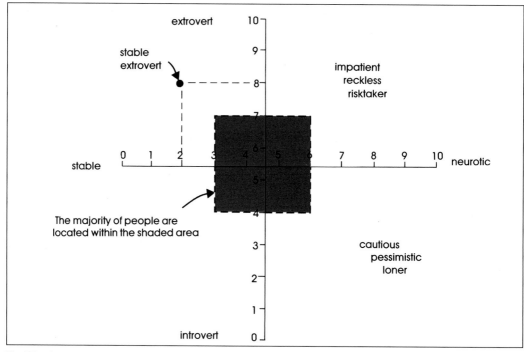

Fig 193   A squash personality graph based on two fundamental dimensions of personality: Extroversion–Introversion and Neuroticism–Stability.

Now plot your location on the graph (Fig 193) – an example is given of an individual who scored 8 on the E scale and 2 on the N scale.

Eysenck, in his theory of personality, argues that two fundamental dimensions of personality are Extroversion – Introversion and Neuroticism – Stability. Extroverts tend to be 'under-aroused' and introverts tend to be 'over-aroused'.

Hence, extroverts, in their attempts to compensate for under-arousal, seek extra stimulation whereas introverts avoid stimulation as much as possible in order to reduce their arousal levels. Those characterized by neuroticism tend to be emotionally over-aroused.

The typical extrovert is highly sociable, enjoys the limelight, enjoys taking risks, craves excitement, is easygoing, optimistic and impulsive. He much prefers to be doing things than planning them, he tends to be aggressive and can be expedient and unreliable. He has high tolerance to pain.

The introvert is a quiet, reserved withdrawn person who enjoys his own company, likes a well ordered life, is cautious and pessimistic, plans things ahead and leave nothing to chance. He is serious-minded, keeping his feelings under control, is reliable and tends to have high ethical standards. He has low tolerance of pain.

Those high on neuroticism are typically anxious, moody, frequently depressed and easily knocked out of their stride. They tend to be preoccupied with feelings of anxiety. The stable individual shows little emotional reaction to situations, being even-tempered and unworried.

Your particular location on the graph gives an indication of the ways in which you are predisposed to act and the following predictions can be made from the theory. In many ways squash seems highly suited to the extrovert player. It tends to be a highly stimulating social sport at all levels, providing opportunities for excitement, showing off, risk taking and the release of aggression. It can also be painful, which would favour the extrovert!

However, it's not quite as simple as that, because 'playing to your personality' can have both advantages and disadvantages. For example, the extrovert's tendency to employ a high-risk strategy can be spectacularly successful but can also lead to catastrophic failure, particularly when high neuroticism is present. We all know examples of exhibitionist risk-takers who regularly win the knock-up but lose the match through a succession of tinned shots and missed nicks. They are victims of their personality – going for shots too early, trying the over-difficult shot and being over-aggressive.

Introverts, on the other hand, being essentially cautious and controlled, are more prone to play negatively, playing not to lose rather than to win. They are more likely to be defensive retrievers than aggressive shot makers. Their need for order makes them more stereotyped and less able to modify their game tactics appropriately. High neuroticism reinforces the negative aspects of their play.

In terms of sportsmanship and reactions to controversial refereeing decisions, the neurotic extrovert causes more problems than the neurotic introvert. Research conducted at Liverpool suggests that poor sportsmanship is much more associated with neurotic extroversion than with calculating and cynical exploitation.

Knowing your own personality, particularly if it is in some way extreme, is useful in that you can learn to accentuate the positive and inhibit the negative tendencies. This applies in coaching as well as playing. For example, the aspiring coach who is introverted in nature may never have the charis-

Fig 194   Australian Tristan Nancarrow lapses into despondence.

ma of, say, Jonah Barrington, but he may be able to compensate for this by his predisposition to be thorough, trustworthy and reliable.

The neurotic individual faces the greatest handicaps but there are currently many methods available for reducing feelings of anxiety. Nevertheless, it is probably just as well that the majority of us are not extreme in personality, and are able to adapt reasonably well to the demands of the situation rather than be at the mercy of negative psychological attributes.

34
Mental Ingredients

Will to Win

I once asked Dardir, the Egyptian who has been associated with many of the world's leading players what the number one ingredient in becoming a champion was. He answered simply: 'Determination'.

On-court competitiveness, determination and perseverance are the qualities we most associate with will to win. Aggression of the hostile kind is not useful in squash; rather, we need a controlled aggression which is not disruptive – a hard-edged competitiveness which is channelled into the pursuit of winning.

Often squash players exhibit these very competitive attributes on court but it is not just on-court competitiveness that's important in a player's success but also the long-term consequences of this concept. Many champions exhibit a single-mindedness and total dedication in their sport. They are committed and ruthlessly pursue their goals on a long-term basis. This affects their lifestyle and allows them to train with longer-term goals in mind.

Confidence

Self-confidence can be viewed at one level as an aspect of the individual's personality make-up. Thus we can all identify individuals who we would describe as self-confident. However, self-confidence can often be a lie: there is the classic example of the deeply insecure person who hides behind an elaborately constructed façade of arrogance. Furthermore, knowing that someone is self-confident does not tell us much about how he is likely to react in a competitive squash match.

Squash confidence can be defined as the extent to which the individual believes in his ability to be successful in squash. How confident and successful you are depends very much on how you define success. Sports psychologists have identified two kinds of sportsmen in this regard: those who relate success to performing well, and those who relate it to the outcome – winning or losing. Furthermore, it has been found that winning players tend to be those whose self-confidence is focused on performing well rather than those who are over-concerned with the outcome.

The message to players is to concentrate on the task: work on confident production of the various shots and enjoy the performance. The result will take care of itself.

Don't kid yourself, but be *positive*. An insight into a positive mental strategy was provided by Susan Devoy at the British Open. 'I'm the best player around. It's just a matter of living up to it', she said.

Concentration

Good concentration, which implies full attention being given to the task, is necessary for success in squash. Losing players will often attribute their defeats to a lack or loss of concentration. For others, concentrating well is second nature, even to the extent of having 'peak experience' – an apparently altered state of consciousness in which the individual can do no wrong. Tony Jacklin has spoken of periods in his career when the hole appeared to be the diameter of a dustbin with the ball being guided on tramlines. Those who've played squash long enough will probably recall matches when 'everything went right'.

Although how well we concentrate is partly determined by our personality, there is still much that can be done to improve concentration – first by understanding what disturbs it, and, second, by examining what we can do to enhance it.

Concentration is often disturbed by psychological stress, which is defined as a perceived threat to the gratification of needs. The threat of losing is the fundamental stress and it frequently underlies lapses in concentration.

The good concentraters are stress-tolerant, able to ignore pressures associated with poor refereeing, noisy spectators, poor court conditions, and so on. At the other extreme are those whose concentration on the task is so poor that they go to pieces when the pressure is on, in some cases displaying the classic persecution complex whereby they imagine that there is a conspiracy to deny them victory.

Although all players are frequently faced with the threat of losing, this is not the only

– nor, arguably, the major – reason for poor concentration. Many of the problems can be traced to poor preparation before and poor application during the match.

Preparation for the Match

In general terms, be well prepared. Arrive early, warm up thoroughly and ensure that you and your equipment are in good condition. Get the basics right. If you are disorganized, you will of course have more excuses for losing, and you will need them, because you will lose more often. The more ill-prepared you are, the more likely you are to have other things on your mind. Do not play in borrowed shoes, or with a tatty old racket grip, or a racket that needs restringing. Such handicaps are avoidable distractions which make it harder for you to concentrate.

More specifically, preparation for the match also means, if possible, finding out in advance which team you are playing,

Fig 195   Determination is written on the face of Paul Carter as he works out with Jonah Barrington.

and who is to be your opponent. This should enable you to have preliminary positive thoughts about your match and the kind of strategy you might adopt. The twin dangers of overconfidence and defeatism must be avoided. The purpose of doing your homework is to maximize your chances of success rather than instil a high expectation of either success or failure.

This is easier said than done. If you expect an easy match, it is quite difficult to avoid complacency and lack of concentration. Conversely, preconceived notions about the invincibility of an opponent, or our dislike of a particular court, dramatically increases the likelihood of defeat. Your negative mind-set does not allow you to concentrate on what might be the best tactics in the circumstances.

Application during the Match

Typically, players appreciate neither how important good concentration is as a part of general match strategy nor how much they can control it. The player's aim should be to wrap himself in a cocoon of concentration, keeping the mind free from irrelevant thought and maintaining a positive approach throughout the fluctuating fortunes of the match. This is a daunting but achieveable aim for the player, provided that he instils in himself, over time, a set of positive strategic and tactical principles, and provided that he is able to recognize the situations which usually affect his concentration negatively.

Be positive from the outset. Use the knock-up not only to get the ball warm but to establish your match concentration. Learn about the pace of the court and your opponent's strengths and weaknesses. If you find yourself asking for lets, you are concentrating too hard!

There are dozens of situations in matches which present a natural threat to concentration – for example, playing an unforced error, having an appeal turned down, dealing with an awkward opponent, and the various reactions to winning and losing games. Players vary in what distracts them,

but many find it particularly difficult to sustain concentration after going 2–0 up, or after recovering to 2–2. But forewarned should be forearmed. If at 2–0 you think 'I've got three games to win this match', then you're not concentrating. If you're very pleased and relieved to have clawed your way back to 2–2, the chances are that you will not concentrate enough on what is required to win the decider.

The aim should always be to concentrate on the current objectives, developing a habitual routine of switching attention to the *next* rally and the *next* game. Be clinical, aiming to win with as few points conceded as possible. With this strategy, you are learning to maximize your concentration in a wide variety of situations.

Stress Tolerance

The 'champion athlete' is characterized by high stress tolerance. Not only can he tolerate pressure but he can often play at his best under pressure. He is often an overachiever who uses stress to energize himself, performs better under the stress of competition and relishes it. The 'training room' athlete is the one that can perform best when the pressure is off.

A good squash player learns to cope with anxiety, tension, nerves, frustration, as well as all the events that occur in a game, and manages to get a performance out of himself. Stress is not only coped with but channelled and utilized. Anxiety is where you are no longer stimulated by stress but become anxious and start worrying about your ability to cope. It is, of course, your perceived ability to cope that is important here, not your actual ability.

Often when watching players you will be able to note symptoms of anxiety. These can be cognitive anxiety (worry) or physiological arousal, the body's way of preparing for 'fight or flight'. Physiological arousal symptoms include heart-rate increase, sweating, an urge to go to the toilet, a dry mouth and nausea.

One way to look at and try to manage

appropriate levels of stress is by use of the arousal curve. Although this representation of arousal as a one-dimensional concept is an oversimplification, it is still useful in helping to understand the relationship between arousal and performance. The more aroused a player, the better the performance until a point where over-arousal occurs and performance decreases.

A more modern theory, called the catastrophe curve, indicates that performance improves with stress up to a critical point. At this point the player perceives the situation as greater than his ability to cope, anxiety occurs and performance falls dramatically.

Once a player has gone 'over the top', it is very difficult to get him back to a high level of performance. This is usually only achieved by considerably reducing stress levels.

Anxiety can produce muscular tension, affecting movement, and also impairs decision-making. Anxious performers also become easily distracted. They may, for example, scan an audience with a narrow focus in a desperate search for some straw to cling to – their coach and friend, one of their own players, and so on – but the performer's problems are his own and attending to distractions in this way merely clogs the system up with useless information.

To maintain performance in the face of anxiety you must either reduce anxiety or increase your stress tolerance.

Frustration Tolerance

Frustration in squash is about getting over-concerned about the outcome of a rally. It can boil over into having a negative affect on the rest of your game. If, for example, you get a series of bad decisions, try to focus on playing well rather than on the injustice done to you.

Decision-Making

Some players are better decision-makers than others. They modify their game and adjust to situations, opponents and opportunities easily. They have the ability to think tactically and make decisions. Other players do the same thing no matter who they play, using the same shots and rallies. Sometimes they win and sometimes they lose but they don't know why.

A key factor in decision-making is that you need spare decision-making capacity in the brain and one of the ways to do this is to make as many of the techniques and tactics as automatic as possible so that you don't have to think. The more you can make your game automatic, the more free capacity you have to make key decisions about strategy and about adapting tactics to frustrate your opponent. That's something you can learn. The game types, combinations, tactics and how to practise them are all in this book.

35
Assessing Mental Performance

Knowing the strengths and weaknesses in your squash personality and mental abilities will help you recognize and take control of them. These are the factors that affect your squash performance.

Mental performance is not something that's totally outside your control. You can improve it. We look at some of the things you can do in the next chapter.

First let's look at mental performance. How do you rate? The following questionnaire is not the definitive work in squash psychology; rather, it is a method to get you thinking about your mental performance in specific areas. Try it.

First, tick the most appropriate answer to each question opposite, then use the scoring system below to calculate your category scores and total mental performance.

Scoring

Score your ticks and subtotal each category.

Will to Win
Almost always, 4; Often, 3; Sometimes, 2; Almost never, 1.

Concentration
Almost always, 1; Often, 2; Sometimes, 3; Almost never, 4.

Frustration Tolerance
Almost always, 1; Often, 2; Sometimes, 3; Almost never, 4.

Anxiety Proneness
Almost always, 1; Often, 2; Sometimes, 3; Almost never, 4.

Decision-Making
Almost always, 4; Often, 3; Sometimes, 2; Almost never, 1.

Scores of 18+ for each category are good; 12 or less leaves room for improvement. All categories are compatible. Categories add to give total mental performance. Maximum score 120. Minimum score 30.

	Almost always	Often	Sometimes	Almost never

Will to Win

	Almost always	Often	Sometimes	Almost never
Is winning the main reason for playing?	–	–	–	–
Do you have long-term goals?	–	–	–	–
Do you have dreams of success?	–	–	–	–
Do you hate losing?	–	–	–	–
Do you get satisfaction from winning?	–	–	–	–
Do you keep trying even when you are well down?	–	–	–	–

subtotal _____

Concentration

	Almost always	Often	Sometimes	Almost never
Does your mind wander?	–	–	–	–
Do you dwell on past mistakes?	–	–	–	–
Do you get distracted by bad decisions?	–	–	–	–
Do you get distracted by people on the balcony?	–	–	–	–
Are you easily distracted by environmental problems – for example, poor lighting?	–	–	–	–
Do you find yourself thinking of other things not related to the match?	–	–	–	–

subtotal _____

Frustration Tolerance

	Almost always	Often	Sometimes	Almost never
Do you argue with the referee?	–	–	–	–
Do you get frustrated on court?	–	–	–	–
Do you get annoyed with yourself?	–	–	–	–
Do you get annoyed with your opponent?	–	–	–	–
Do you get annoyed with the referee?	–	–	–	–
Do you behave badly on court?	–	–	–	–

subtotal _____

Anxiety Proneness

	Almost always	Often	Sometimes	Almost never
Do you feel that you are more tense than you should be in a match?	–	–	–	–
Do you worry about the match before you play?	–	–	–	–
Do you show signs of nervousness – racing heart, palpitations, butterflies or nausea?	–	–	–	–
Do you feel confused?	–	–	–	–
Are you on edge when you play?	–	–	–	–

subtotal _____

Decision-Making

	Almost always	Often	Sometimes	Almost never
Do you vary your game according to your opponent's strengths and weaknesses?	–	–	–	–
Do you analyze your opponent's game during the warm-up?	–	–	–	–
Do you pick the right time to attack and the right time to defend?	–	–	–	–
Are you decisive on court?	–	–	–	–
Are you quick to spot a tactical advantage?	–	–	–	–
Do you vary your game according to the court conditions?	–	–	–	–

subtotal _____

Total: Your Mental Performance _____

36
Strategies

Match Preparation

When you step on court you should be physically and mentally warmed up and focused on the task ahead. Try to achieve the mental state in which you demonstrate the most appropriate levels of will to win, arousal, concentration and confidence.

Organize and create the conditions that will work for you personally, so that you are in the best frame of mind to compete. Arrive early and have your equipment prepared. Eliminate distractions and aim to be relaxed, focused on the task ahead and if possible with some knowledge of your opponent. Create a positive state of mind in which you are anticipating the game with relish. Avoid pressures and hassles, whether domestic or work.

'Psyching up' is an individual activity and individuals differ. The attention focus narrows, arousal levels rise and players start to concentrate on the task ahead.

Before major matches Ross Norman can be seen pacing up and down by himself, eyes a little glazed over, concentrating and with a channelled, focused aggression. Others need psyching down – to be allowed a quiet period of contemplation alone.

A central part of your match preparation should be mental rehearsal. This involves imagination – seeing yourself (or a model, such as Ross Norman) performing well and getting inspiration from that.

Anxiety Control

Finding the right combination of techniques to reduce and channel anxiety may need some experimentation. The coach must know his pupils, what makes them anxious and what reduces their anxiety.

Some players can reduce tension by being friendly or sociable, whilst others choose to seek solitude. Sometimes a coach may have to remove players from situations or individuals that make them nervous, even the looming presence of parents.

A clear game plan, knowing tactically exactly what you are going to do, using a knock-up checklist and having a playing-in period at the start of a match helps to overcome mild competitive anxiety.

Tapes to relax or build confidence can be tried. These may include inspirational messages, music, mood music, inspirational music, relaxing soft music, and relaxation procedures; or they might be tailor-made tapes of your strengths and weaknesses, with positive messages and reminders.

Relaxation techniques can help block anxiety. Progressive muscular relaxation relaxes each muscle group of your body in turn while meditation and behaviour therapies are useful in reducing negative self-talk and improving the self-confidence.

Improving self-confidence is an important way to reduce long-term susceptibility to anxiety. This self-confidence which is squash-specific is usually called self-efficacy. Self-efficacy is to do with desire to compete and succeed while anxiety represents fear of losing and failure.

Performance accomplishment is about success and success is about achieving goals. The more goals achieved and the more success a player experiences, the greater his self-confidence. The setting of appropriate and achievable goals is important. Unrealistic goals and unfulfillable expectations can only lead to failure, and failure to anxiety.

Imaginary or mental rehearsal, in which

Fig 196 Anxious moments for Lisa Opie on the receiving end at the British Open.

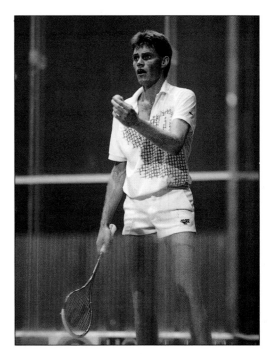

Fig 197 Rodney, frustrated by the decisions, has words with the referee.

you see yourself performing a skill successfully, helps you concentrate on your goals. Used in conjunction with progressive muscular relaxation, it can increase self-confidence and reduce anxiety. First use the progressive muscular relaxation exercises (below) for about 20 minutes and then imagine yourself performing successfully.

One of the simplest ideas in handling anxiety is over learning. If it takes a certain amount of time to learn a shot, it will take at least that amount of time again to learn it so that you can produce it reliably when not under competitive stress. To perform as well under stress will need much longer. This is why we practise. Remember: amateurs practise until they get it right; professionals practise until they can't go wrong.

Experiment with techniques to control anxiety and if possible use it; channel it. You don't want to get rid of the butterflies but you want them to fly in formation.

Confidence Building

Your confidence is to a large extent under your own control. Be positive and think positively to build confidence. Below are some examples of practical steps to build-

ing confidence, which include positive thinking.

1 Squash confidence is based on hard work. A major difference between the top-class and the club player is that the former has worked far harder at his game. Not only does practice make perfect, but practice makes confident. The soccer player, Pele, for instance, acknowledges the importance of the thousands of hours of practice which underpinned his genius.

2 Good players are positive in that they work at their deficiencies. This is not as much fun as just playing a game, or practising shots that you are good at. Yet the benefits to confidence of extensively practising originally weak shots are great. If you don't think efforts are worthwhile, then why be filled with despair, or be ungracious to your opponent, when you lose?

3 For a match, begin as you mean to go on: success in squash depends on momentum. Thus, don't just use the knock-up to get the ball warm, as so many club players do. Practise a variety of shots, practise your

235

lengths, and look for points of vulnerability in your opponent's game.

4 Players often say to themselves things like 'Don't hit the tin', which has the effect of making it more likely that they will. Think of successful outcomes and express thoughts positively in terms of what you will do rather than what you won't do.

5 You have had the worst of a string of dubious refereeing decisions, and say to yourself, 'It's not my day . . . the referee's biased/useless . . . I'm wasting time here . . . what's the use of trying?' Although you might have little difficulty being positive when on top, you need to work on a mental strategy along the following lines: 'This is no problem . . . I'll just have to beat him twice . . . the decisions will even out in the end . . . win the next rally!'

6 You have negative memories of a particular court, lack confidence as a consequence, and face the prospect of 'going through the motions' when the match begins. A positive strategy might involve the following: 'Okay, I didn't like the court last time, but everyone has an off day. This is a different opponent, and it's the same for both of us. If I want to call myself a good player, I've got to be able to adapt to different conditions – concentrate on the tactics demanded by the conditions.'

7 In a long match, you're feeling very tired and the easiest thing to do is give up, using the following coping strategy: 'I'm tired. This guy's too fit for me, but I'm a better player. I won the first game when we were both fresh!' Positive thinking could make all the difference because often the other player is as tired as you. A strategy might be: 'I'm a bit tired, but so is he! Don't show you're breathless; look relaxed.'

8 If you set appropriate goals you will be able to achieve them. Success breeds confidence. Failure can lead to the slippery downward spiral of doom and despondency.

9 Self-confidence can be improved by imagining yourself performing successfully.

10 Use positive statements about yourself, such as 'I can do it'.

11 Use 'thought-stopping' to stop negative thoughts. Train yourself to stop negative thoughts. Once you start thinking negatively, paranoia can set in. 'I've got no chance,' you think or 'I can't play the drop.' If negative thoughts crowd in, say 'Stop' to yourself and substitute positive thoughts.

Concentration Training

Concentration, the ability to focus all your attention on one thing, here and now, can be trained. Players need to learn how to handle distractions and we can train this ability. Games in which one player deliberately tries to distract another, verbal abuse is used, bad refereeing decisions are given and hostile crowd noise and the like are used can help desentilize a player to events he finds offputting.

Take a player who is distracted by poor refereeing decisions and lapses into mistakes for a period thereafter. Create a game with several bad decisions and gradually build up the number he can handle. If he loses his temper, point out the purpose of the exercise. Eventually introduce these 'bad decisions' into matches.

It is dangerous to practise solely in per-

Fig 198 A frustrated Phil Kenyon in danger of losing concentration.

fect conditions on your favourite court, with perfect lighting and no noise or movement. Practise on different courts and environments, and practise your concentration.

Competition Training

The idea of gradually desensitizing performers to harmful stimuli in sport is the basis of what's called general competition training. Players prone to anxiety in important competitions need to practise competition.

In squash, elements of competition and competitions at various levels can easily be set up by introducing markers and referees, audiences, rewards and prizes. Challenge matches and exhibitions are relatively easy to set up. Lower-level competitions, team events and tournaments can all be used. After a period of basic training it's going to take time for a player to think his way into competition. Allow for this.

Progressive Muscular Relaxation

One of the simplest physical relaxation techniques, PMR helps reduce anxiety and also enables you to gain precise control over muscle tension, helping to develop a more flowing movement.

Lie on your back, preferably in a darkened room, with your eyes closed. Now work through each major muscle group in turn, first tensing and then relaxing them. Focus attention on the difference in sensation between tension and relaxation. The muscle groups are:

1. The shins and calves.
2. The thighs and buttocks.
3. The small of the back and the stomach.
4. The chest.
5. The shoulders and arms.
6. The face and neck.

After working through the muscle groups and gradually sinking into a deeper state of

Fig 199   Chris Dittmar displays concentration and determination as he waits to receive serve.

relaxation, start focusing your attention on deep, slow breathing. Wake gradually.

Mental Rehearsal

Mental rehearsal uses imagery, a mental practice in which you see yourself performing, to practise skills and play. The pictures you see may be the same as if you were actually performing (internal imagery) or how someone else would see you if they were watching you (external imagery).

It is a powerful tool that can be used to warm up, between games, to improve self-confidence (see yourself do it), to overcome previous disasters and to relax.

Goal Setting

Success is about achieving goals. The setting of appropriate goals is therefore important. The more goals achieved and the more success a player experiences, the greater his self-confidence. Confident players are higher achievers and also more persistent in the face of failure.

It is easier to get motivated and psyched up for a squash match than to find the motivation to endure the long hours of training and self-sacrifice necessary to move towards long-term objectives. Goal setting encompasses both the long-term and the short-term aspects of motivation and every player and coach should be aware of the benefits to performance of setting and achieving goals.

On one level, we all set goals and aim to achieve them (a player obviously aims to win a match), but the principles of goal setting are more subtle than that. In general, goals can enhance performance by focusing activity, mobilizing effort, increasing persistence and encouraging the use of optimum strategies. Research into goal setting suggests the following guidelines for players and coaches.

1 It is much more effective to give a player a specific goal than a general goal; telling a player 'Do your best' is too vague to be useful and doesn't specify what the player should actually do.

2 Goals should be challenging but not so severe as to be unrealistic. Theoretically, the player should be capable of meeting the challenge but goals should not be so easy as to excite little interest or effort.

As a rule of thumb in most sports, competition goals should be set at a level which the performer could expect to achieve at least 70 per cent of the time during normal training. Encouraging a performer to set goals which are beyond his ability may well improve his short-term performance, but a performer who consistently fails to achieve the goals he aims for is likely to become first of all frustrated and then self-critical, despite the improvements in actual performance that may have occurred.

3 Short-term goals should be used as an incremental means of achieving long-term goals. A talented junior's aspirations of being a world-class senior player will be less overwhelming if progress is made via a series of itemized shorter-term goals, such as national age-group honours, senior county honours, senior national honours, top-fifty world ranking, and so on.

4 Goals must be quantifiable so as to allow comparison between aspiration and achievements. In practice sessions goals are easily quantified but it is a little more difficult in matches. Coaches, however, can do more than provide subjective judgements by using match analysis techniques. This precise information can serve to focus a player's attention on the extent to which goals are being achieved and can lead to less possibility of faults being overlooked or ignored.

Detailed records over time of performance in training and competition against stated goals will reveal the level of progress and the extent to which goals need modification to remain challenging. Players should be encouraged to keep a daily log relating to performance.

5 Goal setting is an ongoing activity involving a constant evaluation of goals and the setting of new goals. For example, progress during a season might be different from what was expected at the outset, and goals must be modified accordingly in order to avoid complacency on the one hand and despondency on the other.

In match play it is best for goals to be framed in such a manner as to allow the player some flexibility in their implementation – for example, win with least possible points against, 'work' an opponent with known limitations in fitness, play to a good length, get back to the T between shots. These goals are, of course, basic tactical principles, but in the heat of competition one or more of them are frequently ignored. Highlighting them before a match and evaluating success during and between games will increase the likelihood of their being achieved.

6 Goals are most likely to be effective if they are accepted by the player rather than merely imposed by the coach. Ideally, goals for a particular player should emerge as a result of dialogue with the coach so that the player feels ownership.

PART 8
TRAINING

In squash the fittest survive and often win. It's the last point that counts. Fit players arrive at it while maintaining the consistency and accuracy of their shots, good movement and the ability to think tactically.

The fast bursts of movement involved – anticipating, taking off, running, skipping, lunging, twisting, turning, stretching, jumping, braking and bracing – are fatiguing, especially when a player is pushed repeatedly over the full length (9.75m (32ft)) or diagonal (11.67m (38ft 3in)) of the court. They are even more fatiguing when the average 1½ seconds between shots is cut down by an opponent taking the ball early and hitting hard.

The longer and more intense these fast bursts of movement are, the greater the fatigue and the more difficult the recovery. These bursts of movement vary in length. I counted the first rally of the 1988 World Championship final in Amsterdam between Jahangir Khan and Jansher Khan at 247 shots in 6 minutes 16 seconds. Geoff Hunt and Gamal Awad are reputed to have played a 400-shot rally of over 10 minutes.

At a top international level an average rally length of around 20 shots is quite common. In the 1987 World Open semifinal between Jahangir Khan and Jansher Khan in Birmingham the average rally lengths for the four games were 19, 22, 21 and 15 shots respectively. More generally, Dr Craig Sharp has found that rallies tend to be distributed into three groups; those lasting less than five strokes, those between 6 and 15 strokes, and those above 15 strokes, and that there is usually 7–10 seconds between rallies.

Squash players need to maintain their bursts of activity not just over average-length rallies but over long ones as well and they need to sustain these throughout the match. Players need to recover from their efforts in the short 7–10 seconds between rallies, in discussions on lets, in the 90 seconds (longer for pros, especially with TV) between games and by varying the pace during the match itself.

Jahangir Khan and Gamal Awad explored the upper limits of squash endurance in the final of the Chichester Festival in 1983 when they played for 2 hours 48 minutes with a 71-minute first game. International games often last 1½ hours and occasionally go over 2 hours. In club level games these bursts of movement are often kept up for 45 minutes or more.

The ability to perform squash movement, sustain it over time and recover calls on a wide variety of fitness attributes. These can be trained for so that you not only survive to the last point but get there in shape to apply and maintain pressure.

How fit you are and what your personal fitness needs are we discover in Chapter 37. Fitness training is explored in Chapter 38 and Chapter 39 provides a general endurance programme. Chapter 40, 'The Fitness Programme', outlines the general principles of a training programme.

37
Testing Fitness

In some sports such as running, jumping and throwing, performance is easily measured. In squash, on the other hand, performance is unmeasured and it is more difficult to assess the progress of off-court training. However, information on the wide variety of fitness qualities involved in the game can be useful in assessing progress, pinpointing relative weaknesses and modifying training schedules.

Ideally, fitness monitoring would be performed in an established physiology laboratory but this facility is not generally available so simple field tests are used. Here comparisons can be made with the fitness scores attained in previous tests. Tests should be used to check a player's level before a training programme and then again at the finish in order to provide a measure of the improvement gained.

Aerobic fitness

1 Harvard Step Test
This is fairly easy to perform. You will need a bench or box (a 50mm (20in) step for men, 45mm (18in) for women, 40mm (16in) for children), a metronome and a training clock or stop-watch. Each complete step cycle up and down comprises four movements, so a metronome setting of 120 will give a step rate of 30 per minute. Most keen players will manage this rate for the 5-minute duration of the test. However, if they fall behind the metronome rhythm for more than 15 seconds, stop their stepping and note how long they have managed to that point. Either way, allow 1 minute after stopping, then count the number of pulse beats at the wrist just below the base of the thumb for 30 seconds. (It is essential to stop the metronome before counting or you will count metronome beats, not heartbeats.) Then multiply the achieved stepping time in seconds (usually 300 for the 5 minutes) by 100, and divide this by 5·5 × the number of beats you counted in the 30 seconds. This will give you a number somewhere between 50 and 180.

This procedure gives the standard formula for the 'fitness index' (FI).

$$FI = \frac{(\text{time in seconds}) \times 100}{(\text{pulse count for 30 seconds}) \times 5 \cdot 5}$$

As an example, a pulse count of 42 after 5 minutes of stepping:

$$FI = \frac{300 \times 100}{42 \times 5 \cdot 5} = 130$$

gives a fitness index of 130.

The higher the fitness index the better. Very roughly, for the 5-minute test, an FI of 180 or above is superb; 160–179 excellent; 140–159 very good; 120–139 good; 100–119 creditable; and 80–99 is reasonable, and what we would expect many good club squash players to score.

2 The 1½-Mile Run
This is a more convenient alternative to the Cooper 12-minute run test. Subjects cover a 1½-mile course as fast as possible. Rate performance by the times (minutes and seconds) in the table.

3 Pulse-Rate Test
A very simple test of cardio-respiratory fitness is to record the pulse rate first thing in the morning. This is useful as a broad guide only but can show a pattern which is a valid indicator of progress.

241

Age (years)	Very poor	Poor	Fair	Good	Very good	Excellent	Superb
Women							
17–29	19·48+	17·24+	14·24+	12·18+	9·54+	9·00+	8·06+
30–34	20·24+	18·00+	15·00+	12·36+	10·12+	9·18+	8·24+
35–39	21·00+	18·36+	15·36+	12·54+	10·30+	9·36+	8·42+
40–44	21·36+	19·12+	16·12+	13·12+	10·48+	9·54+	9·00+
45–49	22·12+	19·48+	16·48+	13·30+	11·06+	10·30+	9·36+
over 50	22·48+	20·24+	17·24+	13·48+	11·24+	10·30+	9·36+
Men							
17–29	16·30+	14·30+	12·00+	10·15+	8·15+	7·30+	6·45+
30–34	17·00+	15·00+	12·30+	10·30+	8·30+	7·45+	7·00+
35–39	17·30+	15·30+	13·00+	10·45+	8·45+	8·00+	7·15+
40–44	18·00+	16·00+	13·30+	11·00+	9·00+	8·15+	7·30+
45–49	18·30+	16·30+	14·00+	11·15+	9·15+	8·30+	7·45+
over 50	19·00+	17·00+	14·30+	11·30+	9·30+	8·45+	8·00+

Recoverability

Shuttles using court lengths (and quarters) or runs from the T to the corners reached in a set time of 40–50 seconds with a rest period of 10–20 seconds repeated 6–12 times can be recorded. Times and repetitions can be varied, depending on the player's level.

Local Muscle Endurance

1 Legs

The number of squat thrusts on either side of a line achieved in 1 minute is a good test. Alternatively, the number of burpees or star-jumps achieved in 1 minute is a useful measure.

Squat Thrusts in 1 Minute		
Poor	Average	Excellent
15	35	65

2 Arms

The number of press-ups completed in 30 seconds or 1 minute. Women may prefer adopting a position with the knees bent and in contact with the floor instead of the legs being straight and the feet in contact with the floor.

Press-Ups in 1 Minute		
Poor	Average	Excellent
5	20	50

Speed

1 Shuttle Speed Test

The player starts from the back wall, runs to touch the back line of the service box and returns to touch the back wall nick; then to the short line and back; front and back; short line and back; service box and back. Conditions should be standardized and the results be a best of three. An alternative is to time runs of five or ten straight lengths of the court.

2 Flying 25-Metre Sprint

Strength

1 Vertical Jump Test

The vertical jump test, or Sargent jump test, is a simple measure of leg power and provides a useful approximation to off-the-mark speed.

The player stands against a wall and makes a mark with chalked fingers as high on the wall as possible while standing flat on the ground. Then the player crouches and springs as high as possible, making a second mark. The best of three trials is accepted. The difference between the marks may be anything from 20mm (8in) to over 100mm (40in). This test should not be used as a comparison between players but as a measure of improvement in one player over a period of time.

Poor	Average	Excellent
12	16–20	20–30

2 Standing Broad Jump

Measure the best of three attempts. Toes to a line, knees bent, swing arms and spring forward from both feet. Measure the distance reached at right angles to the take-off line. Evaluate performances in terms of inches jumped *in excess of the jumper's height*.

Poor	Average	Excellent
0	9–16	20–30

3 Grip Dynamometer

This provides a measure of grip strength. Craig Sharp states that if this is much below 45kg for men and 25kg for women then, towards the end of long matches, forearm muscle fatigue may well loosen the grip just enough to induce inaccuracies if the ball is stuck hard but off centre.

4 Multi-Station Tests

Working progressively through a strength training programme provides its own intrinsic form of assessment. The known resistances and the increases in resistances being used provide regular feedback on improvement.

Flexibility

Sit and Reach

Flexibility in the hamstrings – the most useful to a squash player – can be measured by the 'sit and reach' method. The legs are kept straight, toes pointing vertically up-wards, head held up and fingers reaching for and past the toes. Measure the distance from fingertips to the toes. Scores may be plus or minus. If the fingertips extend beyond the toes, the score is plus; if they cannot, it is minus.

A box which the feet rest against, with an overlap projecting towards the subject so that the hands can slide along it, allowing the distance reached to be noted on a ruler, can be useful.

Percentage Body Fat

The usefulness of a body-fat measure derives from the fact that a player's weight may remain the same, although the body composition may alter. For example, a player training hard in the off season may lose fat and gain muscle – and his weight may not change. A player may put on weight, having gained more in extra muscle than he has lost in fat. Or vice versa! In all the racket sports, extra fat has to be carried everywhere about the court.

The simplest way to measure body fat is by the use of skinfold callipers. Men players will range from below 10 to above 20 per cent and women between 20 and 30 per cent. Top-class players tend to have percentages 7 and 12 per cent, with their female counterparts having a range of 16–24 per cent.

Conclusion

Players respond well to a battery of a few simple but consistent and carefully performed tests. It gives them both a guideline and a means of motivation – and may well be a source of satisfaction when hard training is seen demonstrably to pay off. The runner, swimmer, jumper and thrower – because their sports are all measured – have their performance as a calibration of their training. Racket players have no such objective evaluation and find the reassurance of testing welcome.

Retest after a training programme.

38
Fitness Training

The Training Session

Your training sessions should be planned and fit into an overall programme. It's one small step on the path towards your goals. What you do within a session needs to be thought through, planned and organized. This may involve a written plan and written records on targets and results. There are four parts to your training session.

1 Organization
Arrive early for your session so you can be prepared and think through what you will be doing and organize any equipment.
2 Warm-Up and Stretch
3 Main Session
4 Warm-Down and Stretch
This is a period when the body is fully warmed and is suitable for 'development' stretching.

If you incorporate different activities in the same session (or on the same day) speed training should be first and any anaerobic training last.

Warm-Up

The warm-up prepares you mentally and physically for exercise and is important in preventing injury. Always warm up before you practise, play or train. Develop this as a good training habit and give yourself the best chance of performing well in competition.

A warm-up should raise your body temperature (you are warm when you begin to sweat slightly), raise your breathing rate (until you are slightly puffing), raise your heart rate, loosen your joints and stretch your muscles. Psychologically, the warm-up allows you to focus your mind on the competition to come or on the subsequent training. It allows for physical and mental rehearsal of techniques and tactics.

There are three main parts to your warm-up session. The first is to raise your temperature, and your heart and breathing rates. You can do this by jogging, starting slowly and gently and then involving swinging of the arms. This can be performed for several minutes until you are sweating slightly. The exercises used can be varied and it can be useful to use some that involve squash-type movements. Wearing loose-fitting layers of clothing which can trap heat next to your body helps the heat-generating process.

After warming you need to loosen and mobilize your joints. This should involve wide-ranging movements for all major joints and muscle groups. One method of achieving this is to work your way down through the body – top to toe.

You are now warm and loose and you need to prepare your muscles for play by stretching. Stretch so that you are ready to use a full range of movement, so that you are not stiff, and to help prevent minor muscle, tendon and joint injuries. This is preparatory stretching and is not designed to significantly improve the range of movement. That can be done later. Hold each stretch for a count of 10 or more in the position in which you feel a passive pull, but make sure that it feels comfortable.

Warm-Up Exercises

Start with the warming exercises to raise body temperature, then move on to the mobilizing exercises before stretching. Warming exercises may be interspersed throughout the sequence. Spend at least 10 minutes on the warm-up – like the pros, you could usefully spend much longer. You will need to spend longer in cold weather. You know that you are sufficiently warm when you feel generally mobile and are perspiring lightly.

Warming Exercises

Perform one or more of these running-on-the-spot-type exercises for several minutes until you are sweating lightly, or in 30-second or 1-minute work intervals with 15-second or 30-second rest intervals. (Avoid exercises which result in heavy leg fatigue.) Wear training or squash shoes and use sprung floors or carpet for any prolonged spot running or skipping sequences.

1   Running on the spot: gradually build up pace.
2   Running high knee raises: use the arms as well as the legs.
3   Side astrides: bounce astride and swing the arms high overhead.
4   Astrides alternating front and side arm movements: bounce astride and swing the arms overhead; bounce together, arms to side; bounce astride and swing the arms in front of the body overhead; bounce together, arms to side.
5   Front astrides: swing the arms overhead.
6   Punch-ups: run on the spot, lifting the knees high. Point the fists up and punch the arms out straight overhead. Alternate punches. Punch and lift on the same side.
7   Skipping: continuous and rhythmic.
8   Other: many exercises can be used for a whole body warm-up, including squash movement exercises such as the stroking sequence on page 58.

Experiment and develop your own routine.

Stretching Exercises

Lunge Stretch (Hip Flexer Stretch)
Bend to the lunge position with the front knee directly above the ankle, your weight on the ball of the foot and the back leg mainly straight. Use your hands for balance and lower the front of your hips to create a stretch. This stretches the groin, hamstring, hips and back of the knee.

Hamstring Stretch (Seated)
Sit with your legs straight and feet upright and bend forwards from the hips. Feel the stretch behind the knee, in the back of the upper legs, and, if it is tight, in the lower back. Push forwards from your hips without lowering your head or rounding your back.

From this position it is easy to move into a seated calf stretch. Reach down and pull your toes towards you with your hands.

One-Leg Standing Stretch
Place the back of your heel on a support about waist-high and keep this leg straight.

Fig 200   'Another little stretch while I'm waiting.' Del Harris performs the Standing Quadriceps Stretch.

Fig 201   Sarah Fitzgerald in a crouching stretch warms up before her match.

Look straight ahead and bend forwards from the hips, keeping your back straight.

Seated Groin Stretch
Sit tall, bend your legs up towards you and place the soles of your feet together. Hold on to your feet, let your knees fall easily to the floor and gently pull yourself forwards, bending from the hips.

Calf Stretch
Lean forwards and rest your hands on a wall, bending the forward leg with the back leg away from the wall straight, heel on the ground and toe pointing forward. Slowly move your hips forward, but keep your back straight. To stretch the Achilles tendon, lower your hips and bend your knees.

Standing Quadriceps Stretch
Standing on one leg, clasp the ankle of the free leg and raise it gently backwards with the knee bent, arching back. Feel the stretch in the front of the thigh.

Avoid a time-lag between your warm-up and competition. Stretch only when you are warm and if you cool down during stretching warm up again before play. Start your stretching easily and don't bounce. There are many different warm-up exercises you can use. Develop your own routine, become familiar with it, allow time to use it and get into the habit of using it regularly.

Cool-Down and Stretching
Cool-Down

The body takes time and makes adaptations in returning to normal from a period of exertion. Where strenuous exercise suddenly ceases the muscles can fail to clear waste products and their build-up results in stiffness or soreness. Recovery can be aided by mild rhythmic-type muscular activity, gradually decreasing in intensity,

Fig 202 Jahangir Khan's preparations for a match include stretching. Here he stretches both his hamstrings and calves.

and by some stretching. Use the warm-up exercises above to produce a gradual cool-down, but don't stop suddenly. Use extra clothing if you become cold. A hot shower, bath or massage will also aid recovery.

Stretching

After exercise when the body is warm is the best time to stretch to improve your range of movement. Stretches at this time can be held for up to 30 seconds (or counts), moving further into the stretch if the feeling of stretch subsides. Stretching should be static: ease smoothly into position and avoid bouncing.

1 Warm up thoroughly before stretching. Warm muscles are more pliable and cold muscles resist stretching.
2 Use a preliminary stretch causing mild tension for 10 seconds then relax it before the main stretch. This reduces tightness.

3 Don't strain. Ease into a stretch position where tension, even mild discomfort, is felt, but nothing more.
4 Hold the main stretch for 10–30 seconds. If the tension decreases, stretch a little further. Stretch so that the pull is in the central part of the muscle.
5 Breath calmly and rhythmically.
6 A routine carried out three times a week should give good gains in flexibility.

Upper-Body Stretches
1 *Forward stretch* Sit with legs straight and bend forwards, trying to place your head between your knees.
2 *Twisting stretch* Sit with one leg straight, bend the other leg and put the foot across on the outside of the straight leg. Turn towards the bent knee so that the opposite elbow rests on it, helping to hold the twist position. This spiral twist is good for the upper back, the lower back, the side of the hips and the rib cage. Good flexibility here will aid looking behind you from the

247

T, without having to turn your entire body.

3 *Side-bend stretch* Stand with feet apart and reach down one side, letting the opposite arm bend up and over your head. Bend and hold.

Abdominal Stretch

Front of Trunk Stretch Lie on your stomach with your hands under your shoulders. Straighten your elbows to arch back as far as you comfortably can.

Shoulder Stretches

1 *Overhead stretch* Interlace your fingers above your head, palms up. Push your arms slightly back and up. Feel the stretch in your arms, shoulders and upper back.

2 *Shoulder stretch* Reach behind your head and down your back to grasp your other hand palm out. Grab hold if possible, have someone pull your hands slowly together, or use a towel between your hands and gradually move them together.

3 *Clasp stretch* Clasp your hands behind your back and lift the arms straight.

Adductor Stretches

1 *Straight-leg sitting stretch* Sit with the legs straight and as far apart as possible. Lean forwards slowly from your hips. Keep your back straight and your head up and relax your quads.

2 *Crouching stretch* Crouch on one knee with the other leg out straight sideways. Keep your feet parallel with the ground, your toes on the ground, and lean gently towards the straight leg.

Hamstring Stretches

1 *Hurdle stretch* Sit with one leg straight and forward, the other tucked out of the way sideways. Lean forwards from the hips over the straight leg, with the back straight and the head up.

2 *Crouching stretch* Crouch with one leg straight out sideways and the foot pointing up. Use your hands for support. Gently lean over the straight leg from the hips.

3 *Inner hamstring stretch* Crouch as above but turn your foot so toes are at 45 degrees.

Lean over the straight leg. Feel the 'pull' over the inner hamstring.

4 *Standing stretch* Stand with your legs together and straight. Lean forwards from the hips, keeping your back straight. Hold your ankle or leave your hands free.

Alternatively, cross your feet, keeping the back knee pressed straight with the forward knee. Bend from the hips.

5 *Hamstring and groin stretch* Sit tall with one leg outstretched and the other bent with the foot resting on the inner thigh, and the knee as close to the floor as possible. Hinge forwards from the hips, reaching for the flexed left foot.

Quadriceps Stretch

Kneeling stretch Kneeling with the knees and feet together, lean backwards, pressing the hips forwards.

Calf Stretch

Two-legged calf stretch While leaning on a wall, move your legs backwards as far as you can while still keeping your heels flat on the ground.

Soleus Stretch

Stand with your heels flat on the ground. Bend both knees so that your legs move down and over your ankles as far as you can.

Running

Long continuous running is ideal for building a base of aerobic fitness. Start slowly and gradually build up to 20–30 minutes. Progress to a hard pace at about 90 per cent effort. Run over an established course, keep times and gradually try to reduce them. A competitive player should aim at a pace of 6–7 minutes per mile and to cover 3–3½ miles in 20 minutes. A basic aerobic endurance programme is set out in the next chapter. The club player will need to start at more comfortable levels and need a longer programme cycle. When building up aerobic fitness, aim to run at least three times a week. Build up gradually.

Fig 203 Chris Dittmar hill-running with Danny Meddings. Interval training can build both aerobic and anaerobic fitness.

If you are just a beginner to training, start on alternate days with jogging or jogging and walking (for 5 minutes) and gradually build up times.

Use trainers with well cushioned soles for running. Sorbothane can be used for extra shock-absorption. Thin-soled squash shoes are not designed for running.

Varied Pace Running

Varied pace running – or fartlek (speed play) training, as the Swedish call it – uses steady continuous running with occasional faster running and short sprints. Periods of anaerobic work are followed by easy running. Fartlek training is designed to improve endurance and recovery.

Interval Running

Geoff Hunt, eight times British Open champion, built up a fearful reputation for his successive 400-metre sprints. This type of running is based on bouts of heavy work interspersed with short rest periods, allowing the work load to exceed that achieved in a single burst. Interval training can improve both aerobic and anaerobic fitness and is most effective after aerobic fitness has been built up with the basic continuous programme. An interval programme is set out in the next chapter. Club players attempting interval running or a shuttle programme should do so two or three times a week.

Other Aerobic Training

Skipping

Start with 100 skips and gradually build up at a rate of 130 per minute for 20 minutes. Use different steps to practise co-ordination and footwork. Skipping is an ideal sharpening and footwork exercise. Skip in trainers and on a piece of carpet if on an unsprung floor.

Cycling

On a static bike, start with 5 minutes and build up to 20 minutes. Your pulse rate should be 75 per cent of maximum.

Swimming

This can be a good substitute for running if you are injured or have muscle soreness. Build up to 30 minutes at a good pace.

Interval Training

This involves periods of high-intensity training followed by rest, during which time the waste products from the anaerobic energy system are removed, allowing a further burst of activity. Any very hard exercise can be used. Often this is sprinting or shuttle running when on court, but you should also consider skipping, cycling or a series of conditioning exercises.

A simple formula to use is to start at 30-second intervals and gradually build up, adding one set each session until twelve sets. You can then increase the length of the work and rest intervals and build up again.

Sets	Work interval (in seconds)	Rest interval (in seconds)
6–12	30	30
6–12	35	35
6–12	40	40
6–12	45	45
6–12	50	50
6–12	55	55
6–12	60	60

Table 1 (opposite) sets out a number of different exercises that can be used for shuttle runs. It's a sensible idea to incorporate some squash movements as well as running. The programme outlined allows a simple progression from 6 to 12 shuttles and through the various levels. Each shuttle can be timed. Total times can be a relative measure of fitness.

Adapt this programme and these exercises as you wish, but remember – it must be progressive. Anaerobic interval training of this sort is best scheduled after the aerobic build-up, should be attempted 2 or 3 times a week and is best built up over 4 to 8 weeks.

Shuttle Sequence (Table 1)

1 *Lengths* Run lengths of the court, bending and touching at tin height on turning. Count each length.
2 *Forwards, backwards and changing* From the short line run to the front and touch (count one), run backwards to the short line (count two), change direction and run forwards again.
3 *Lunging* On the front foot, lunge to the left and touch in front of your toe. Push back and lunge on the other side. Count each lunge.

Fig 204   Chris Dittmar running lengths of the court in a shuttle sequence.

4 *Forwards, backwards and turning* From the short line, run forwards to the front (count one), run backwards to the short line, turn with one step and run forwards to the back (count two). Run forwards to the front again, and so on.
5 *Sidesteps and lunge* From the ready position, sidestep across court and lunge on the front foot and touch the side (count one) push back and sidestep across court and lunge on the other side (count two), and so on.
6 *Four touches* From the back, run to the back of the service box touch the line (count one) and return to the back, repeat to the short line (count two), repeat at the ¾ mark (count three) and the front (count four).
7 *Lengths*   Count each touch.
8 *Forwards, backwards and changing*
9 *Lunging*
10 *Forwards, backwards and turning*
11 *Sidesteps and lunge*
12 *Four touches*

Exercise	Level (and rest time in seconds)				
	1 (30)	2 (40)	3 (45)	4 (50)	5 (60)
1 Lengths	12	14	16	18	20
2 Forwards, backwards and changing	16	20	24	28	32
3 Lunging	20	26	32	38	42
4 Forwards, backwards and turning	10	13	16	18	20
5 Sidesteps and lunge	12	16	19	22	24
6 Four touches	8	10	12	14	16
7 Lengths	12	14	16	18	20
8 Forwards, backwards and changing	16	20	24	28	32
9 Lunging	20	26	32	38	42
10 Forwards, backwards and turning	10	13	16	18	20
11 Sidesteps and lunge	12	16	19	22	24
12 Four touches	8	10	12	14	16
No. of sets completed Average time taken					
Date					

Table 1

Programme

Start at level 1, shuttles 1–6. Add one more shuttle at each session up to 12 and then progress to level 2, and so on.

Times

Each shuttle can be timed. Total time can be a relative measure of fitness.

Shadow Training

Shadow training with the racket in hand seeks to utilize the exact stroking sequence used in hitting the ball to practise movement and build fitness. To get the best from this training take time to work out the path, position and movement you will use for a particular shot before you put it under pressure.

Shadow Sequence (with Racket) (Table 2)

1 *Front corners* From a ready position behind the short line, run to the front corner and play a forehand straight drive. Return backwards to behind the line, run to the opposite front corner and play a backhand straight drive. Count each stroke.
2 *Back corners* From a ready position in front of the 'line' joining the back of the service boxes, step back and turn on the foot nearest the corner. Move to the corner into a back-corner stance to play a straight drive. Return to the T and repeat on the other side. Count each stroke.
3 *Turning* From a ready position step and play a forehand stroke, step back, turn and play a backhand stroke. Count each stroke.
4 *Four corners* From a ready position move to and recover from the four corners in turn.
5 *Lunging* As for 3, except lunging for each stroke. Count each stroke.
6 *Sidesteps and lunge* Count each stroke. Sidestep across court and lunge to the side wall.

Programme
As for the shuttle sequence above.

Exercise	Level (and rest time in seconds)					
	45	1 (30)	2 (40)	3 (45)	4 (50)	5 (60)
1 Front corners	4	7	9	11	13	15
2 Back corners	4	9	11	13	15	17
3 Turning	20	28	36	44	52	58
4 Four corners	4	9	11	13	15	17
5 Lunging	10	20	26	32	38	42
6 Sidesteps and lunge	6	12	16	19	22	24
No. of sets completed Average time taken						
Date						

Table 2   Shadow Sequence

251

Ghosting

Random ghosting, using stations or numbers and signs, can all be used as interval training using the above times.

Speed

Speed work is performed at maximum for about 10–15 seconds, with 50 seconds recovery. Straight sprint repetitions of 30–50 metres can be used but it may be more economical and useful (in terms of helping squash movement) to use on-court shuttle running and bursts of fast skipping.

Speed Shuttle Sequence

Warm up fully before attempting this routine. Complete each exercise as fast as possible. Stretching or movement exercises can employ the rest period time. The approximate work period is 15 seconds, and the rest period 45 seconds. Build up the numbers of sets (not repetitions) and alter the routine as you wish. Eventually you may build up to twenty sets. Do not decrease the rest period.

Sets	Repetitions
1 Lengths	× 6
2 Forwards, backwards and changing (front half-court)	× 6
3 Turning	× 20
4 Lengths	× 6
5 Forwards, backwards and turning (whole court)	× 6
6 Lunging	× 10
7 Lengths	× 6
8 Turning jumps	× 20
9 Sidesteps and lunge	× 6
10 Lengths	× 6

Skipping

1 *Skipping*   Rate 180; 30 seconds; 5 sets; rest 1 minute.
2 *Double Skipping*   20 jumps; 10 sets; rest 45 seconds.

Plyometrics

1 *Depth jumping*   Place two boxes a metre apart with a mat between. Jump from one box to the ground and up onto the other repeatedly. Keep the feet together and emphasize knee flexing.
    20 repetitions; 3 sets; rest 5 minutes.
2 *Hurdle spring*   Jump repeatedly over a single hurdle, keeping the feet together and flexing the knees through as large an angle as possible.

Movement Training

In Part 2 of *The Squash Workshop* we looked at court movement and recommended solo and pairs practice, shadow practice and ghosting to help develop movement round the court. Movement exercises can also be usefully incorporated into shuttle, speed and shadow sequences.

Here we introduce a number of footwork and co-ordination exercises that can be incorporated in warm-ups and circuits. They will help develop your basic movement abilities as well as your court movement.

Your movement can also be improved by dancing, aerobics and stretching. All types of skipping are particularly useful – jumping, slow jumping, alternate leg jumping, two jumps on each leg then alternating legs, hurdle skipping, sideways jumping, astrides, running, knees up, double skips, toes forward and cancan.

When working with a partner or a coach, a call of 'Change' in a shadow sequence can provide you with a useful change-of-direction practice.

Movement Exercises (A) (Table 3)

The following exercises can be used as warming exercises or incorporated into circuits to add an aerobic element.

1 *Run* On the spot at sprint speed, lifting the knees high. Count one side.
2 *Side astrides* Jump to feet astride and clap hands overhead. Jump to feet together again and arms at side. This is one count.
3 *Front astrides* Jump to feet astride (front to back) and swing the arms high from the shoulders. Count one side.
4 *Punch-ups* Run on the spot, lifting the knees high. Point the fists up and punch the arms out straight overhead. Alternate punches. Punch and lift on the same side. Count one side.
5 *Springing* Bounce from the ball of one foot to the ball of the other with a slow-motion running-on-the-spot action, lifting the knees above waist. Count one side.

Aerobic Movement Circuit (B) (Table 3)

This circuit is designed as an aerobic workout in the same way as 15–20 minutes of skipping but utilizing a variety of movement and footwork exercises.

1 *Astrides* Feet together, feet astride, feet together, left foot forward, right back (front astride), feet together, right forward (front astride), feet together. Astride together is one count. Repeat on the other side. Repeat A.
2 *Front bouncing* (a) In a long stride bounce from the ball of the front foot to the ball of the back foot and return. (b) Repeat on the other side. Once forward, back and forward is one count. Repeat A.
3 *Fast feet* Running on the spot. Short fast steps. Count one side. Repeat A.
4 *Turning jump* Stand astride in a ready position facing the front. Jump and turn 90 degrees to land in the same position facing the side. Count one. Jump to the front. Count two. Repeat on other side. Repeat A.

Exercise		Level		
		1	2	3
A	1 Run	1	2	3
	2 Side astrides	1	2	3
	3 Front astrides	1	2	3
	4 Punch-ups	1	2	3
	5 Springing	1	2	3
B	1 Astrides	20	30	40
	2 Front bouncing	20	30	40
	3 Fast feet	30	40	50
	4 Turning jump	20	30	40
	5 Overline stepping	30	40	50
	6 Side jumps	30	40	50
	7 Reverse jumps and twists	10	15	20
	8 Side kicks	30	40	50
	9 Cross-overs	30	40	50
	10 Side bouncing	30	40	50

Table 3   Aerobic movement circuit

5 *Overline stepping* Sidestep over a line and bring the inside foot to the together position. This is one count. Repeat A.
6 *Side jumps* Side jump over a line to land both feet together. This is one count. Repeat back and forth. Repeat A.
7 *Reverse jumps and twists* Point the feet at the side and the body to the front. Jump and turn 180 degrees and twist the body to the front. This is one count. Repeat A.
8 *Side kicks* Stand on your left leg and hold your right out to the side. Swing it in and hop to your right and lift left. This is one count. Repeat A.
9 *Cross-overs* Feet astride. Jump to cross the legs left over right, astride, then right over left, and so on. Count each cross-over. Repeat A.
10 *Side bouncing* With feet in a long astride, bounce on the balls of the feet side to side. Count each movement. Repeat A.

Weight Training

A strength-training programme uses repetitions, sets and resistance. Repetitions are the number of times an exercise can be performed (say, 10). A set is a specific number of repetitions (for example, 2 sets of 20). Resistance is the load which the muscle group moves.

Exercises involving high repetitions and low resistance will improve the endurance qualities of the muscle. Low repetitions with high resistances will develop pure strength. Faster repetitions produce a more dynamic kind of strength through nerve adaptations. Between repetitions rest should be less than a second with, 1½–2 minutes between sets.

Two or three sessions a week will produce significant gains in strength and allow plenty of recovery time.

For squash use explosive repetitions with relatively light resistances. Work until some muscle fatigue appears (about 20–25 repetitions) but stop before quality deteriorates.

Select from the following exercises to make a circuit using either free weights or the multigym.

Upper body	Legs
Arm curls	Half-squats
Shoulder press	Hamstring pulls
Bench press	Quadriceps pulls
Pull-overs	Two-leg leg press
Flies	Alternate-leg leg press
Pectoral pulls	Step-ups
Latissimus pulls	Squat jumps
Inclined sit-ups	Calf raises

Alternatively, body-resistance exercises allow you to do some strength work during or after any other form of training or practice (for example, on-court practice) and can also be used in circuits. There are many varieties of these exercises and some examples are sit-ups, press-ups and leg exercises.

39
A General Endurance Programme

Dr Craig Sharp, director of the British Olympic Medical Centre, devised the following programme in conjunction with Mike Fitchett, of the Department of Physical Education, Heriot-Watt University, Edinburgh. It is a programme for national-standard men squash players and will need to be adapted and modified to individual requirements. It was first published by the National Coaching Foundation under the title 'Example of a General (Aerobic and Anaerobic) Endurance Programme'.

For training purposes, the squash year can be divided into two periods, the pre-season (June–August) and the playing season (September–May).

The pre-season can be further divided into three 4-week cycles, as detailed below. The emphasis during the first period is mainly on aerobic work, with the introduction of the anaerobic work in the second cycle. This leads to more specific court-related exercises in the third cycle.

In the playing season, the emphasis is very much on tournament and match play, so the amount of specific training depends on the number of competition and practice matches being played. Nevertheless, the player should decide which tournaments he is going to peak for (such as nominated selection tournaments) and programme training and practice accordingly.

General Principles
FUNDAMENTALS OF THE PROGRAMME

Before detailing any specific items in a training programme, it is important to note the following general principles:

Specificity The effect of training is specific to the type of training undertaken. This means that training must be geared to the relevant energy systems (aerobic, phosphagen, lactic), muscle groups (for example, overhand forearm curls for canoeists and rowers, not underhand curls), and range of movement (that is to say, don't train on the inner range only if the sport action involves mainly outer range movement).

Reversibility The effects of training are reversible: if training is infrequent or not sufficiently intensive, the training effects will diminish. However, a competition 'edge' lost by a week's injury or bed-rest illness will usually be recovered in two or three weeks.

Overload Training adaptation is dependent on overload; exercises are progressive to higher successive levels, meaning higher levels than usual.

Progression The intensity and/or duration of training sessions should be increased in logical and reasonable progression. As the competitor improves his fitness, it will take a higher level of exercise stress to create an overload.

Monitoring Training effects should if possible be monitored periodically, even by quite simple means, to ascertain if the programme is working.

Adaptability Programmes must be flexible, and allow for adjustments to be made for individual differences, and for illness or injury.

ELEMENTS OF THE PROGRAMME

All programmes designed for training endurance should include the following elements.

Intensity The speed at which the exercise is undertaken.

Duration The length of time of the exercise (excluding rests).

Volume The total time of the exercise session. If the session consists of one continuous effort, then the duration and volume are identical. If the session is split into periods of work and rest, the volume is the total time.

Rest The time allowed for recovery between exercise periods. Note that rests may often be 'active'.

Repetitions The number of times a specific exercise is repeated during a fixed part of the session.

Sets The number of groups of repetitions, for example 3 sets of 10 repetitions.

Mode of training The various activities which can be employed to fulfil a training function.

Type of training Continuous and interval, as two main forms.

AEROBIC ENDURANCE

Intensity Unlike anaerobic training, aerobic exercise does not have to be at maximum in order to have a maximum training effect. A rough guide to training intensity is found by adding 25 to the athlete's age, and subtracting that from 220, to give an approximate training pulse rate. In general, for younger age groups, between puberty and adulthood, one can say that an aerobic training effect occurs at heart rates above 150.

NB Aerobic training does not need to become anaerobic over the final stages; the pace should be maintained equally over the work period without necessarily ending in a sprint.

Duration/volume Aerobic training implies that the oxygen that is taken in is sufficient to supply the energy needs of the activity. Being more fatigue-resistant, the aerobic system takes longer to fatigue than the anaerobic system. The minimal duration/volume is 20 minutes for continuous training, with a volume of 15 minutes for equivalent effect in interval training. The aerobic system is a function of both cardio-respiratory and muscle systems. Overloading it may require first an increase in duration to improve aerobic efficiency of muscle, then an increase in intensity to improve cardio-respiratory function. An increase in intensity may be matched by a fall in duration.

Rest For interval training it should be sufficient to allow the heart-rate to fall to approximately 110–120 bpm, which usually comes out at about a 1:1 ratio of work:rest.

Mode of training Running.

Type of training Continuous and interval training.

Example: Aerobic endurance programme.

Exercise mode	Repetitions	Sets	Intensity	Rest (recovery)
3 miles	1	1	20 minutes	6 minutes jog/walk
4 miles	1	1	28 minutes	8 minutes jog/walk
800 metres	6	1	3 minutes	3 minutes jog
600 metres	8	1	2 minutes	2 minutes jog

ANAEROBIC ENDURANCE – PHOSPHAGEN ENERGY SYSTEM

Intensity In order to improve anaerobic phosphagen endurance and power the exercise must be performed at maximum.

Duration The work periods should last for not less than 5 nor more than 20 seconds.

Volume Set volumes should not exceed one minute. A target total volume of 6–8 minutes is recommended.

Rest Since this area of training must be maximal or very near it, it is essential to maintain the quality of the work, which implies adequate rests. A 5:1 or 6:1 ratio of rest to work should therefore be allowed between repetitions. A more complete recovery period of approximately 5–10 minutes is required between sets. The rests should not be passive rests, but be gently active.

Mode of training Running (40–50 metres), on-court shadow running, shuttle running.

Type of training Interval training.

ANAEROBIC ENDURANCE – LACTIC ENERGY SYSTEM

Intensity Generally, this system begins to be taxed at around 80 per cent of maximum effort for a given duration of exercise. In order to ensure maximum recruitment of type 2B glycolytic fast fibres (the most anaerobic), exercise should be performed at no less than 90 per cent of maximum effort.

Duration Work intervals should often not last longer than 40 seconds, seldom longer than 60 seconds, and but rarely up to 2

Example: Anaerobic endurance programme – phosphagen energy system.

Exercise mode	Repetitions	Sets	Intensity	Rest (recovery)
50 metres	6	3	7 seconds	45 seconds walk between repetitions 5 minutes jog between sets

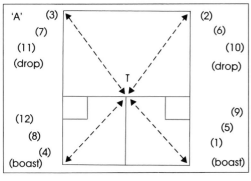

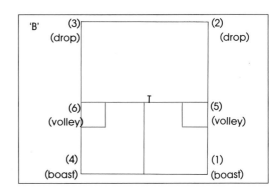

Fig 205   Court shuttles.
(a)   Court shuttles: stand on the T with racket. Move to first corner and play appropriate shot – back to T – to second corner, back to T etc. until twelve corners have been touched. N.B. Alternate the direction you travel i.e. 12, 11, 10, 9 . . .
2. Ensure that your court movements are the same as in a game.

(b)   Stand on the T with the racket. Run the court pattern as indicated playing the appropriate shot. Run alternate court patterns.   1.   T–1–2–T–3–4–T.
2.   T–5–4–T–6–2–T.

minutes. Any longer duration will not increase the load on anaerobic lactic acid capacity, but instead will begin to depend more on aerobic energy supply.

Volume Set volume should not exceed 2 minutes, and usually not more than 1. A total target volume of between 10 and 20 minutes is recommended.

Rest A 1:2 ratio of work:rest should be followed between repetitions at the start of the programme, with approximately 10 minutes of active rest (for example jogging)

between the sets. The ratio of work:rest should gradually change to 1:1 and then to 2:1 as the player gets through the schedule. For example, this would give a timing for on-court shadow training of 30 seconds work, 60 rest; going through 30 work, 30 rest; to 60 work, 30 rest, and gradually increasing from 10 repetitions up to 20.

Mode of training Running, skipping, step-ups, on-court shadow running, shuttle running.

Type of training Interval training.

Examples: Anaerobic endurance programme – latix energy systems.

Exercise mode	Repetitions	Sets	Intensity	Rest (recovery)
200 metres	6	2	35 seconds	2 minutes jog between repetition 10 minutes jog between sets
Skipping	10×30 seconds	1	180 skips/minute	2 minutes jog between repetitions
Step-ups	5×1 minute	2	60 steps/minute	2 minutes jog between repetitions 10 minutes jog between sets
On-court shadows	10	1	95 per cent effort for 30 seconds	30 seconds jog on spot

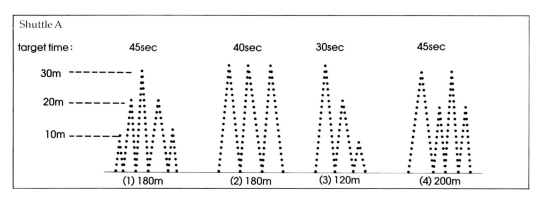

Fig 206 Shuttle A: In a suitable area mark out the recommended distances from a start line. Sprint to each mark and back to the start line in turn as represented in the diagram. Shuttle B: From a start point, sprint at maximum in the directions indicated, to and from the distances shown.

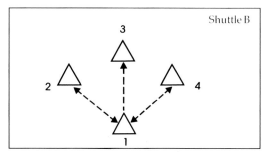

General points

1 Training and playing should be preceded by a 5–10 minute warm-up consisting of a balanced section of dynamic flexibility exercises.

2 Where training is scheduled for four or five sessions per week, make the rest days flexible. If one session was particularly exhausting then you should make the next day a rest day.

3 All interval and continuous training together with shuttle runs should take place on grass or on a sprung wooden floor. All interval times are from a rolling start.

4 Since it is generally recognized that mild activity increases the speed of recovery from exhaustive work, the rest periods should consist of either walking or jogging.

5 In a multiple session speed work should always be done first.

Sample of actual pre-season endurance training programme for a 12-week period divided into three 4-week cycles, for a national-standard male squash player.

First cycle   The first cycle is a basic aerobic endurance programme, getting faster in the last week. The player will also be on court six days a week.

Session	Exercise (mode)	Repetitions	Sets	Intensity (target times)	Rest (recovery)
Week 1					
1	3 miles	1	—	22·00 minutes	
2	4 miles	1	—	30·00 minutes	
3	5 miles	1	—	38·00 minutes	
4	6 miles	1	—	45·00 minutes	
Week 2					
1	5 miles	1	—	38·00 minutes	
2	7 miles	1	—	52·00 minutes	
3	8 miles	1	—	60·00 minutes	
4	5 miles	1	—	35·00 minutes	
5	6 miles	1	—	42·00 minutes	
Week 3					
1	4 miles	1	—	26·00 minutes	
2	7 miles	1	—	47·00 minutes	
3	5 miles	1	—	33·00 minutes	
4	8 miles	1	—	54·00 minutes	
5	5 miles	1	—	32·00 minutes	
Week 4					
1	600 metres	6	1	2·05 minutes	2½ minutes walk
2	4 miles	1	—	25·30 minutes	
3	1 mile	4	1	6·00 minutes	6 minutes walk/jog
4	5 miles	1	—	31·00 minutes	
5	800 metres	6	1	2·50 minutes	3 minutes walk

NB   The above training programme is designed for a member of the Senior Men's National Team and is included as an example only.

Second cycle   The second cycle continues the aerobic theme twice a week, but the emphasis is very much on anaerobic (lactacid) endurance, as exemplified by the 400-, 600- and 800-metre interval runs and the skipping and shuttles.

Anaerobic (phosphagen) training is also introduced with the 50-metre intervals.

Session	Exercise (mode)	Repetitions	Sets	Intensity (target times)	Rest (recovery)
Week 1					
1	400 metres	4	1	70 seconds	90 seconds walk between reps (8 minutes jog)
2	100 metres	6	1	14 seconds	60 seconds walk between reps
	4 miles	1	—	24·00 minutes	(10 minutes walk/jog)
	skipping	8 × 30 seconds	1	180 skips/minute	1 minute walk between reps
3	shuttle runs A	4	3	(see Fig 206)	2 minutes walk between reps / 6 minutes walk between sets
4	600 metres	6	1	2·00 minutes	2 minutes walk between reps (10 minutes walk/jog)
5	50 metres	6	6	6 seconds	30 seconds jog between reps
	1 mile	4	1	5·45 minutes	6 minutes walk/jog between reps
	skipping	8 × 30 seconds	1	180 skips/minute	45 seconds walk between reps
Week 2					
1	3 miles	1	—	18·00 minutes	(10 minutes walk/jog)
	50 metres	7	1	6 seconds	30 seconds walk between reps
2	shuttle runs B	5	3	12 seconds (see Fig 206)	60 seconds walk between reps / 5 minutes jog between sets
3	4 miles	1	—	24·00 minutes	(10 minutes walk/jog)
	skipping	8 × 30 seconds	1	180 skips/minute	30 seconds walk between reps
4	600 metres	6	1	1·50 minutes	2·00 minutes walk between reps (10 minutes walk/jog)
5	100 metres	6	1	14 seconds	60 seconds walk between reps
	shuttle runs A	4	3	(see Fig 206)	1 minute walk between reps / 6 minutes walk between sets
Week 3					
1	400 metres	6	1	65 seconds	90 seconds walk between reps (8 minutes walk/jog)
2	100 metres	6	1	14 seconds	60 seconds walk between reps
	800 metres	4	1	2·45 minutes	3 minutes walk between reps (10 minutes walk/jog)
	shuttle runs B	5	4	12 seconds	60 seconds walk between reps / 5 minutes jog between sets
3	600 metres	6	1	1·45 minutes	2·00 minutes walk between reps (10 minutes walk/jog)
4	50 metres	8	1	6 seconds	30 seconds walk between reps
	3 miles	1	—	18·00 minutes	(8 minutes walk/jog)
	shuttle runs A	4	3	As per sheet	45 seconds rest between reps / 5 minutes walk between sets
5	4 miles	1	—	24·00 minutes	(10 minutes walk/jog)
	skipping	10×30 seconds	1	180 skips/minute	30 seconds walk between reps
Week 4					
1	300 metres	6	1	45 seconds	90 seconds walk between reps (6 minutes walk/jog)
2	50 metres	8	1	6 seconds	30 seconds walk between reps
	3 miles	1	—	18·00 minutes	(10 minutes walk/jog)
	shuttle runs A	4	4	(see Fig 206)	45 seconds rest between reps / 5 minutes walk between sets
3	800 metres	5	1	2·45 minutes	3 minutes walk between reps (10 minutes walk/jog)
4	100 metres	6	1	14 seconds	60 seconds walk between reps
	5 miles	1	—	30·00 minutes	(10 minutes walk/jog)
	skipping	10×30 seconds	1	180 skips/minute	15 seconds walk between reps
5	600 metres	6	1	1·50 minutes	2·00 minutes walk between reps (10 minutes walk/jog)
	shuttle runs B	5	4	12 seconds	60 seconds walk between reps / 5 minutes jog between sets

Third cycle This is still loaded on the anaerobic (lactacid) side, but with a greater emphasis on anaerobic (phosphagen) training – which is virtually the same as speed training. A small aerobic endurance thread is maintained in the 3-, 4- and repetition 1-mile elements.

Session	Exercise (mode)	Repetitions	Sets	Intensity (target times)	Rest (recovery)
Week 1					
1	court shuttles A	4	3	45 seconds (*see* Fig 206)	45 seconds walk between reps / 5 minutes between sets
2	200 metres	4	1	30 seconds	45 seconds walk between reps
	100 metres	6	1	14 seconds	5 minutes jog between sets
	50 metres	8	1	6 seconds	
3	shuttle runs A	4	5	(*see* Fig 206)	45 seconds walk between reps / 5 minutes walk between sets
4	4 miles	1	—	24·00 minutes	(10 minutes walk/jog)
	skipping	10×30 seconds	1	180 skips/minute	10 seconds walk between reps
5	court shuttles B	6	3	As per sheet (*see* Fig 206)	60 seconds walk between reps / 5 minutes walk between sets
Week 2					
1	court shuttles A	4	3	45 seconds	30 seconds walk between reps / 5 minutes walk between sets
2	court shuttles B	6	4	(*see* Fig 206)	60 seconds walk between reps / 5 minutes walk between sets
3	shuttle runs A	4	5	(*see* Fig 206)	30 seconds walk between reps / 5 minutes walk between sets
4	1 mile	4	1	5·30 minutes	8 minutes walk/jog between reps/sets
	skipping	12×30 seconds	1	180 skips/minute	10 seconds walk between reps
5	court shuttles A	4	3	45 seconds	15 seconds walk between reps / 5 minutes walk between sets
Week 3					
1	court shuttles B	6	5	(*see* Fig 206)	60 seconds walk between reps / 5 minutes walk between sets
2	4 miles	1	—	24·00 minutes	(10 minutes walk/jog)
	skipping	12×30 seconds	1	180 skips/minute	10 seconds walk between reps
3	court shuttles A	5	3	45 seconds	15 seconds walk between reps / 5 minutes walk between sets
4	shuttle runs B	5	5	12 seconds	60 seconds walk between reps / 4 minutes jog between sets
5	1 mile	4	1	5·30 minutes	8 minutes walk/jog between reps/sets
	skipping	14×30 seconds	1	180 skips/minute	10 seconds walk between reps
Week 4					
1	court shuttles A	6	3	45 seconds	15 seconds walk between reps / 5 minutes walk between sets
2	800 metres	6	1	2·45 minutes	3 minutes walk between reps (10 minutes walk/jog)
	skipping	14×30 seconds	1	180 skips/minute	10 seconds walk between reps
3	court shuttles B	6	6	(*see* Fig 206)	60 seconds walk between reps / 5 minutes walk between sets
4	3 miles	1	—	18·00 minutes	(6 minutes walk/jog)
	skipping	14×30 seconds	1	180 skips/minute	10 seconds walk between reps
5	court shuttles A	6	3	45 seconds	15 seconds walk between reps / 5 minutes walk between sets

40
Your Training Programme

The programme given in the previous chapter was an example of a pre-season endurance programme for national-standard men. It is not something you should necessarily try to follow yourself but it is a highly professional example of how to set out a programme.

Your fitness programme will be part of your overall squash training programme. It's significance will depend on your individual strengths and weaknesses and on what is a suitable level of fitness for your standard. Fitness training must be balanced with the other areas of your game. It is easy enough to assume that all your problems in squash arise because you're not fit enough and that just getting that little bit fitter will make all the difference. However, there may be real inadequacies or limitations in your technique, shots, tactics and the temperamental area which could be more profitable to work on. You need to be realistic (and to take advice) about your level of fitness and how it is affecting your performance.

That said, fitness is a key element in your success and the higher your standard the more important it becomes. The previous chapters have set out the tests and exercises you can use at your level to develop your fitness. Your programme should follow the basic format given below.

Programme Format

1 *Foundation (4–8 weeks)* Fitness training concentrates on building aerobic fitness and strength.
2 *Preparation (4–8 weeks)* Fitness training moves to anaerobic training (possibly shuttles, shadow practice and ghosting), some speed and agility work and circuits for muscular endurance.
3 *Competition* Fitness training is on a maintenance programme but with the emphasis on speed, agility and movement. Make sure that you are fresh for competition – that is, no hard training before competition.

4 *Rest* Off-court and recreational activities to maintain fitness during the break, moving into a build-up (running) and foundation phase again.

It is easier to maintain fitness than to attain it. Once fitness is built up a maintenance programme of approximately a third will help maintain it. Often we concentrate on one aspect of fitness at a time, build it up and then maintain it while developing another area.

To get results at building fitness, aerobic training for stamina should be carried out three or more times a week, anaerobic two or three times, speed two or three times, and muscle endurance circuits two or three times. Stretching should be a daily exercise.

Use the tests and keep records on the results of your training. This will allow you to check the effectiveness of your programme and develop progressions by gradually increasing the loads.

Your Programme

Fitness is just one of the ingredients in your overall squash performance. Your total performance is the summation of your physical, mental, tactical and technical performances. *The Squash Workshop* provides the activities you can use to improve performances in each of these areas. How you go about selecting them and how often you use them depends on your individual needs and on where you want to go in your game.

Your programme should satisfy your needs. Think through realistically what your goals are and how you are going to go about achieving them.

Planning

Successful training is planned and thought through thoroughly. Here are some questions to help you (and perhaps your coach) think through how you can go about planning effectively.

Where are you at?
This includes an analysis of your standard, potential, weaknesses, limitations and problems.
Where do you want to go?
This includes analysis of your goals (not dreams), motivation, attitudes and lifestyle.
What can you realistically achieve?
What is a sensible goal or level to aim for, within the time you have to put in and your potential, ability, determination (stickability) and opportunities.
What are the steps you have to take?
These should be as clear and specific as you can make them.
How will you divide these steps up over time?
Plan blocks of time for your main goals.
How will you organize the activities you have planned?
Plan, organize and timetable your programme.
How will you record your activities and results?
How will you evaluate your programme?

From the results of your programme you can evaluate each step in the planning process. Use feedback on goals, steps, timetable, and so on to adjust your programme and to help develop your next one. This experience of having a programme will then allow you to plan more effectively and develop a programme more suited to your needs and one that will be successful.

Programming

Your programme is a plan of the activities you have selected to use to reach your goals. Planning is important so that you can think ahead and work out where you are going in the long term and not get excited, depressed or bogged down in day-to-day activities. Select activities that will work on your particular needs. Work on weaknesses. This needs discipline and advice.

Think long-term. Take time out from competition and from seeking immediate results. If you seek only immediate results you will be continually doing the same thing. Trying something once or twice may not have any impact on your skills or game. You may get worse. Practise it twenty times and you could well make considerable or dramatic improvement. Twenty times would be twice a week for ten weeks. If you lack stamina, start running daily. In one week you will be tired; in six weeks you will be fitter.

Progress your training. Start with something you can be successful at and then progress it.

Balance your training. In the end it must provide the correct balance between practice and play, between squash and fitness training and between work and rest.

Motivate yourself by providing achievable targets and also rewards when you have done well. Don't overtrain. It will lead to boredom and less intense effort. Don't just go through the motions.

Peaking

With experience you will know what works for you. What are the conditions and what training precedes playing your best squash? How can you get everything together so that you have your best performance in all areas? It is unlikely that you will walk on court after a summer's fitness training and play your best squash. How much practice do you need in order to get all your shots grooved? Does speed training sharpen you up? How much competition will you need?

Learn from your experiences. Keep records which will help you take control and plan for peak performance rather than have it occur as a random event.

A Squash Programme

The whole structure and content of this book is designed so that you can improve your game by using appropriate practices and training exercises. Your squash programme should move through a similar progression to your fitness programme. Foundation work should be on technique and skills; preparation, on shots and movement; and match play, on tactics, match preparation and grooving strokes.

Squash is a game to work at, a game you will get better at by working on. *The Squash Workshop* will help you. Think through what you want to achieve. Select practices and sequences and build on them. You will then be building on your game.

Rest

Rest is important after major competitions to replenish energy reserves, provide a mental break (so that you will be mentally fresh later for playing and training) and to reassess your programme. Use an active rest, indulging in non-squash activities that will help maintain fitness. The professional in training should have one rest day a week, a three-day break once a month, and perhaps one week off every three months.

The Season

It is unlikely (and not necessarily desirable) that the squash year or squash season will be a build-up to just one major competition (as it is for an athlete) or competition period. Your season will be divided into segments, covering periods of competition, the build-up to these and short rests. Careful selection of competitions to provide peaking targets as well as time for basic training towards long-term goals is the professional player's problem.

Adapt the training cycle to your needs

Levels

Beginner It is hard to improve at squash playing once a week. A club player should be on court a minimum of three times a week and this is what a beginner should build up to. Initially try to practise at least once a week. Try to obtain coaching and use it in conjunction with this book.

Club Player You must play at least three times a week. Put some time aside for solo practice and if possible get a regular practice partner or do a squad practice session.

Competitive Player You need to set out your goals, organization and programme. Plan your season, foundation, preparation and competition.

Professional With your coach, work out the areas in your game that you need to develop. Work out a long-term programme for them. Fit this in with your medium-term competitive targets.

---

but be prepared to make short-term sacrifices (in terms of forgoing events) in an endeavour to reach long-term goals. The in-season training programme is an example of adapting to some of the many considerations involved in competition play.

Sample Programme

The following is an example of an in-season training programme developed by Dr Craig Sharp and the Scottish team manager, Dorothy Sharp. It shows how training has to be adapted to a competitive timetable.

The programme has been worked out well in advance and divided into phases.

When you are planning your training, set down the competitions you will be entering and work backwards. The more complex your competitive schedule, the more important it is to plan the activities that will put you in the best form. Planning should be flexible enough to take account of day-to-day eventualities.

The sooner you plan a programme for yourself the better. The experience will be important in planning future programmes.

Sample of actual in-season training programme for a 24-week period divided into four phases. It extended from the difficult time of adjustment following the World Championships in Perth, Australia, leading through the Home Internationals and major tournaments to the European Championships.

Scottish Women's Squash Team 'Post-Worlds' training schedule leading to Home Internationals and European Championships.

Four phases totalling 24 weeks

1   Period 7 November to 25 November, leading up to Scottish Closed;
2   Period 28 November to 6 January, leading up to Home Internationals;
3   Period 9 January to 2 March, leading up to Scottish Open;
4   Period 5 March to 20 April, leading up to European Championships.

Phase 1   Week 1   (ending 13 November) will be spent recovering from jet-lag effects of time-zone travel. Suggest jogging or swimming gently for first two days post travel, then going on court for 30–40 minutes on some or all of next 4–5 days (just to knock a ball about – no matches).

Week 2   (ending 20 November). Purpose of this is to re-acquire lost fitness edge, so:
a)   daily programme of endurance shuttles – 40 seconds on, 20 off shadowing, starting with 8 and increasing one daily to 12.
b)   on court for at least an hour a day. The volume of work is important at this stage.

Week 3   (ending 27 November). Monday–Wednesday of this week should be spent on:
a)   speed shuttles – 10 seconds on and moving fast, 50 off; 10, 12 and 14.
b)   try for two separate 30-minute sessions on court with emphasis on practising shots – including high and low tight sidewall, daily.
Practise, but don't play on Thursday; same on Friday morning for 20 minutes – then into Scottish Closed 25–27 November.

Phase 2   Weeks 4 and 5   (ending 4 December). This week should be same as previous one for those playing in British Closed Qualifying, 2–4 December. Otherwise, this week and Week 5 should be spent playing steadily, with preferably two of the games in each week against a reasonable man who moves you around.

Week 6   (ending 18 December). This week will end with a fairly heavy training weekend, 16–18 December, so work accordingly; i.e. play harder games in the first half of week, and do speed shuttles (×16) Wednesday and Thursday.

Weeks 7 and 8   (ending 25 December). This will have to be a fortnight of fairly hard work, in view of Home Internationals. Try to play 6 good hard games within this 14-day period, and try also to fit in 4 endurance shuttles (×12) and 4 speed shuttles (×20).

Week 9   (ending 8 January). Difficult though it may be, try for a couple of fairly fast games on Monday and Tuesday, steadier game and/or practise on Wednesday. Just practise, pair or solo, for 30 minutes on Thursday. Stoke up on carbohydrates from Wednesday onwards – no extra calories, just switch over more to starches, and pastas.

Home Internationals begin on the Friday.

Phase 3 Week 10 (ending 15 January). Take a bit of a break here if you can. For those formerly in the World team, this is the break you should have had on return! For other contenders, ease off a bit.

Week 11 (ending 22 January). For both groups, do the same as the previous week. This is the time for any dental treatment, for example.

Weeks 12 13 and 14 (ending 29 January, 5 February, 12 February) should consist of normal mid-season play, matches, and so on.

Week 15 (ending 19 February). Play the normal 4–5 games; and try to get an extra one in in which your opponent is a player who moves you around a lot, and keeps the pressure on by being a good retriever.
Also do 4 sessions of endurance shuttles (×12).

Week 16 (ending 26 February). Play the normal 4–5 games; try to get an extra game in in which you play a player who cuts the ball off and plays it early – thus putting you under pressure.
Also do 4 sessions of speed shuttles (×20).

Week 17 (ending 4 March). This week culminates in the Scottish Open. Fast games, together with speed shuttles (×15) on Monday and Tuesday.
Have a practice game on Wednesday and do some solo practice on Thursday.
Carbohydrate feeding.

Phase 4 Week 18 (ending 11 March). Have an easy week, unless entered for the British Open, in which case try to have four quality games against opponents who take the ball early and put pressure on. Try to resist this pressure by playing tight, and only going for the winner when the opening is really there.
Also, do 4 sessions of speed shuttles (×20) – all the squad.

Week 19 (ending 18 March). Those entered for British Open should repeat week 18. Those not entered should go for normal steady games most days, with four sets (×20) of speed shuttles.

Week 20 (ending 25 March). British Open entrants should have fast games and speed shuttles (×15) for the first three days of this week. The others should play their normal schedule, plus 4 sets (×15) of speed shuttles.

Week 21 (ending 1 April). Returning Open players should have two days off except for speed shuttles (×15) or ten minutes of fast skipping on each day (1 minute on, 1 minute off). Others should put in a good week of time on court, with 4 sets (×12) of endurance shuttles.

Week 22 (ending 8 April). Arrange your harder games for Monday–Wednesday, with easier ones Thursday and Friday together with 2 sets (×20) of speed shuttles. This week will end with a training weekend (Saturday–Sunday), so you want to come in fairly fresh.

Week 23 (ending 15 April). This week should be arranged some time in advance, so that you have 5 quality opponents to play – those who take the ball early and cut it off – and request they do this!
Also, before these games, do 4 sets of speed shuttles (×25) Monday–Thursday.

Week 24 (ending 22 April). The European Championships start on Friday, so you'll probably travel Thursday, leaving Monday–Wednesday for training. Speed shuttles (×25) Monday and Tuesday. 30-minute quality games Monday and Tuesday. Practise, solo or pair, on Wednesday. Rest from play on Thursday except possible knock-up on court when you get there, just to get the feel of it.
From Wednesday breakfast on, stoke up on carbohydrates; no extra calories, just switch your normal intake over to pastas, potatoes, porridge and other starchy foods.

Appendix

An At-a-Glance Guide to Shot Practices

Straight Drive (Chapter 11)

Solo (page 71)
11.1   Drives: service box
    1   above
    2   above and below
    3   below
11.2   Drives: moving
11.3   Length:
    1   rhythm
    2   tight
11.4   Length: 3 and 1; 1 and 1
11.5   Length: vary pace
    1   soft
    2   soft; medium; hard ᷍
    3   hard

Pairs (page 71)
11.6   Drives and feeds
11.7   Boast and drive
11.8   Drive and boast or drop
11.9   Circling

Condition Games (page 71)
11.10   Straight to the half, corner, side
11.11   Boast and drive

Practical Games (page 71)
11.12   Straight

Crosscourt Drives (Chapter 12)

Solo (page 76)
12.1   Solo crosscourts
12.2   Length and crosscourts

Pairs (page 77)
12.3   Pairs crosscourt
12.4   Crosscourts and boast
12.5   Drop and crosscourt: straight and boast
12.6   Boast and alternate drives

12.7   Crosscourt, volley, boast
12.8   Crosscourt, drive, boast
12.9   Crosscourt and drops
12.10   Crosscourt and alternate, boasts and drops

Condition Games (page 77)
12.11   Normal with crosscourt rule
12.12   Back-court
12.13   Back court plus crosscourt rule
12.14   Back corner

Practice Game (page 77)
12.15   Emphasizing crosscourt drive

Lob (Chapter 13)

Solo (page 82)
13.1   Lob and feed
13.2   Lob straight and feed
13.3   Length and lob

Pairs (page 82)
13.4   Boast and lob
13.5   Drop and straight lob
    1   drops
    2   volley drops
13.6   Boast and alternate lobs
13.7   Lobs and alternate drop and boasts
13.8   Lob, volley, boast

Condition Games (page 82)
13.9   High game
13.10   Lob short ball rule
13.11   Front and back
13.12   Soft game
13.13   Hard and soft game

Service (Chapter 14)

Solo (page 89)
14.1   Serving

Pairs (page 89)
14.2   Serving and receiving
14.3   Three-shot rally

Fig 207   Chris Dittmar appeals to the referee.

Back Corners (Chapter 19)

Fig 208   When interference occurs stop and ask for a let. The referee may award a stroke if a player does not make every effort to get out of his opponent's way.

Index